GARDEN STYLES

AN ILLUSTRATED HISTORY OF DESIGN AND TRADITION

GARDEN STYLES

AN ILLUSTRATED HISTORY OF DESIGN AND TRADITION

GENERAL EDITOR · DAVID JOYCE

SPECIAL ADVISERS · PATRICK GOODE AND MICHAEL LANCASTER

PYRAMID BOOKS

CONTRIBUTORS

Baron Gösta Adelswärd, Mavis Batey, Dr W.A. Brogden, Associate Professor Magne Bruun, Dr Stephanie Dalley, Ray Desmond, Ursula, Gräfin zu Dohna, William Lake Douglas, Paul Edwards, Dr Brent Elliott, Patrick Goode, Dr Harri Günther, Dr John H. Harvey, Peter Hayden, Sheila Haywood, Robert Holden, Keith A. Honess, Dr Florence Hopper, David Jacques, Sir Geoffrey Jellicoe, Denis Lambin, Michael Lancaster, Professor Jonas Lehrman, Barbara Levinge, Professor Diane Kostial McGuire, Paul Miles, Professor Hubert B. Owens, Sir John Pilcher, Sandra Raphael, John Sales, Shigemaru Shimoyama MLACP, Miss Dorothy Stroud, Michael Symes, Christopher Thacker, J.M. Turfa, Peter Willis and Denis Wood.

This work, based on *The Oxford Companion to Gardens*, is published by Pyramid Books, an imprint of the Octopus Publishing Group, Michelin House, 81 Fulham Road, London SW3 6RB, by arrangement with Oxford University Press

Text © Oxford University Press, 1986
Design © the Octopus Group Limited, 1989

ISBN 1–871307–78–3

Senior editor **Tessa Rose**
Art editor **Lisa Tai**
Copy editor **Diana Vowles**
Picture researcher **Julia Pashley**
Production **Garry Lewis**

Half-title illustration: An Elizabethan garden, depicted in the late 18th-century Stoke Edith Tapestry, Montacute.
Title-page illustration: The Fountain of Neptune, Villa d'Este, Tivoli; see page 25.

Colour origination by Mandarin Offset, Hong Kong
Typeset by Bookworm Typesetting, Manchester, England
Printed and bound in Hong Kong

CONTENTS

PREFACE

The making of gardens is one of man's oldest occupations and even in very early times was transformed from a purely utilitarian activity into one in which art and science were united. However, despite the major contribution made by garden design to the visual arts, the history of its development is a relatively recent subject of study.

The publication in 1986 of *The Oxford Companion to Gardens* marked an important development in this field, for the *Companion* provided the first comprehensive reference work on the history of garden design from the earliest records of civilization to the present day.

The lack of authoritative general works on the subject prompted the decision to recast information in the *Companion* in the form of an illustrated history of garden design. Although awed by the scale of the task – and by the distinction of the *Companion*'s editors and contributors – I was delighted to be asked to prepare a text for publication presenting developments in garden design on a national basis.

My brief and my intention throughout has been to reflect as accurately as possible within the limits imposed on the project the content and thinking behind the *Companion*, even when I have chosen to use my own wording. Those who know it well will be disappointed that so much has been left out and, in particular, that a number of significant gardens that do not fit into the main national categories receive no mention. My hope is that a clear statement of the main developments balances the loss of detail.

From the outset it was recognized that the 20th century posed special problems and that in the present state of studies it would not be possible to treat this period country by country. Michael Lancaster has played a major role in selecting information and drafting new text for the relevant section in this volume and his special contribution is gratefully acknowledged.

This book would not have been possible without the willing co-operation of those who played a part in the making of the *Companion* and the publishers join me in recording our thanks to all of them. Sir Geoffrey Jellicoe, the executive editors Patrick Goode and Michael Lancaster, and Pam Coote of Oxford University Press deserve special mention, as do the following contributors: Baron Gösta Adelswärd, Mavis Batey, Associate Professor Magne Bruun, Ray Desmond, Ursula, Gräfin zu Dohna, William Lake Douglas, Paul Edwards, Dr Harri Günther, Dr John H. Harvey, Peter Hayden, Sheila Haywood, Robert Holden, Keith A. Honess, Dr Florence Hopper, David Jacques, Denis Lambin, Professor Jonas Lehrman, Barbara Levinge, Paul Miles, Sandra Raphael, John Sales, Michael Symes, Christopher Thacker, Peter Willis and Denis Wood.

I would like to add my personal thanks to Julia Pashley, Lisa Tai and especially Tessa Rose, all of Octopus Books, who have done so much to make my own work easier.

David Joyce
General Editor

THE ANCIENT WORLD

A 1st-century fresco from the Casa di Livia, Rome, gives a glimpse of a Roman garden at the same time ordered and luxuriant.

All the ancient civilizations of the world, including those of China, Egypt and Mesopotamia, provide evidence that at a very early stage in their development gardens were being made that were more than simply utilitarian. We should not, of course, assume that the same priorities dictated the layout of the earliest gardens as influence the design of the modern suburban plot. Their prime function might have been to mark a sacred place, to provide food for gods that must be placated, to delineate a civic or court space such as a processional route, to provide shade in a cruelly hot climate or to embellish an irrigation pond. It is clear, however, that from very early times plants have been grown for their beauty and rarity as well as their usefulness and that the ordering of nature to please the senses and to provide a setting for the conduct of private and public life has been a mark of all developed cultures.

Egypt

Egypt, which is the source of the world's oldest pictures of gardens, has an exceptionally long and seminal tradition of garden-making. In the fertile zone of the Nile's floodplain, contrasting sharply with the desert plateaux and mountains, irrigation made it possible to cultivate vegetables all year round and to grow palms and fruit trees, sources of food and also providers of welcome shade. The general importance of gardens emerges in short 'biographies' of Old Kingdom high officials in the period from about 2350 to 2150 BC. Although these describe an idealized life in stereotyped form, it is clear that men of rank took pleasure in their estates, observing or participating in agricultural work, and that for them the laying out of gardens, with house, trees and pool, was an integral part of a full life. It is likely that no gardens from this period were exclusively ornamental, all producing at least fruit from trees and vines as well as flowers for cutting. A few reliefs show vegetable plots, some fruit trees and pools. The general design of a garden is implied in one relief where beds flank a central pool. This arrangement suggests that real gardens were already arranged symmetrically and were visually satisfying.

From the New Kingdom (c. 1500–1250 BC) there are paintings of estate gardens. The grandest of all these paintings belonged to the 'overseer of the plantation of the god Amun' of c. 1400 BC, from which 'all sorts of plants' were presented to the king. The picture probably shows this 'plantation', which is approached from a quay, beside which is a row of trees in front of a large temple-like entrance in the enclosure wall. Inside are four pools, many stands of trees, a large area of grape vines, inner groups of trees surrounded by their own walls, two pavilions, a small temple with another pool with marsh plants beside it, and a house. The layout, centred on the pools, which are distributed for ease of irrigation, is strictly symmetrical. Since this was the garden of a god, one is left wondering who was privileged to sit in its pavilions.

Large gardens of this kind would have contained flowerbeds but the beds are seldom shown, perhaps because of problems of scale. Many of the plants cultivated in Ancient Egypt were valued for their flowers, among them species of lotus, cornflower, poppy, *Chrysanthemum coronarium,* mandrake and, for its umbels, papyrus.

In the layout of temples there is evidence of landscaping from before 2000 BC, with groves of trees in public spaces acting also as a transition to the inner areas, where many of the architectural elements were derived from plant forms. In the 14th century BC the ceremonial capital, Thebes, was laid out on a grand scale, with alleys of sphinxes 3 km (2 miles) long linking temples; these were probably planted with trees, as later renewal programmes certainly were. An enormous temple was built on the opposite, west bank of the Nile near a vast palace with an artificial harbour excavated between the two. The outer parts of the temple contained plants, as surely did the palace, and the entire project was probably landscaped, the most colossal marriage of architecture and plants known from Egypt.

In about 1350 BC a spacious capital city was laid out at El Amarna, 300 km (186 miles) south of Cairo, on the low desert. Here the grander houses were arranged suburban-fashion on large plots with surrounding walls, and had gardens whose construction and maintenance, in which soil and water had to be brought from a distance, was extremely laborious. Preserved remains and paintings reveal several significant innovations, including the first representation of the *shaduf,* a water-lifting device of great value in horticulture. Some gardens abandon strictly formal layouts in favour of looser schemes. The decoration of palace rooms with paintings of plants, birds and swamp life brought the garden indoors, the distinction between interior and exterior being minimized in rooms looking on to courtyards with pools and plants.

During the Ramassid period in particular, from about 1300 to 1070 BC, the symbolism of the garden was important, especially in relation to the afterlife. Tomb paintings depicting pools and luxuriant vegetation present images that are in marked contrast to the plantless deserts of tomb sites. Gardens also feature in love poetry, lovers meeting in gardens. A character is sometimes identified with a tree, or a tree can speak on behalf of the lovers, who met in its shade or in a reed hut while it promises, if watered, to keep their secret.

In the Graeco-Roman period, from 332 BC to AD 641, though the pattern of gardening remained substantially unaltered, Ptolemaic rule brought in a number of innovations. New crops and varieties were introduced and the area under cultivation was increased, with many new settlements like Philadelphia being created by reclamation of land in the Faiyum. In Alexandria itself, gardens formed part of the great public and royal building complexes, like the palaces of the Ptolemies. The larger private houses also had gardens at all periods. The Byzantine writer John Moschus, describing the city shortly before the Arab conquest, remarked on the 'parks' belonging to the houses of the great in the centre. Centuries earlier Strabo had noted 'the many gardens and tombs' of the western Necropolis suburb but these were probably exploited commercially. Throughout the country the emphasis was almost certainly on the productivity of gardens, exceptions being the sacred temple groves, like those of acacia trees at Abydos and the grove of Osiris on Biga island, or occasional large estates with space for pleasure-gardens. Most settlements would have consisted of a dense mass of housing and an adjacent area of cultivation, with sporadic trees and vegetation marking the course of the river or canal, and gardens confined to potted greenery beside doors or on roofs.

In all periods, all types of cultivation – market-gardening in the city, crop raising in the fertile delta and Faiyum, specialized industries such as papyrus growing, and ornamental gardens – ultimately depended on the efficient working of the irrigation system. The mechanics of this were gradually improved by the introduction of two water-lifting devices in addition to the *shaduf*: the Archimedes screw and the water-wheel drawn by oxen, which came into prominence during the Roman period.

The best pictorial source for the appearance of late Egyptian gardens is Roman mosaics and paintings, created to satisfy a foreign demand for pictures of the 'land of wonders'. The Roman creation of Egyptianized gardens such as the 2nd century AD Egyptian garden in the grounds of Hadrian's Villa at Tivoli implies the existence of prototypes in Egypt itself but is also related to an idealized concept of the country. Its temperate climate and extraordinary fertility and the mysterious phenomenon of the Nile flood always attracted admiration in the ancient world. To some extent the country offered the ideal garden landscape, in which the hand of man apparently produced the maximum effect with the minimum of effort. In due course the Roman iconography of the Nile, its canals and gardens, was adapted to Christian needs and came to depict the riverine Paradise.

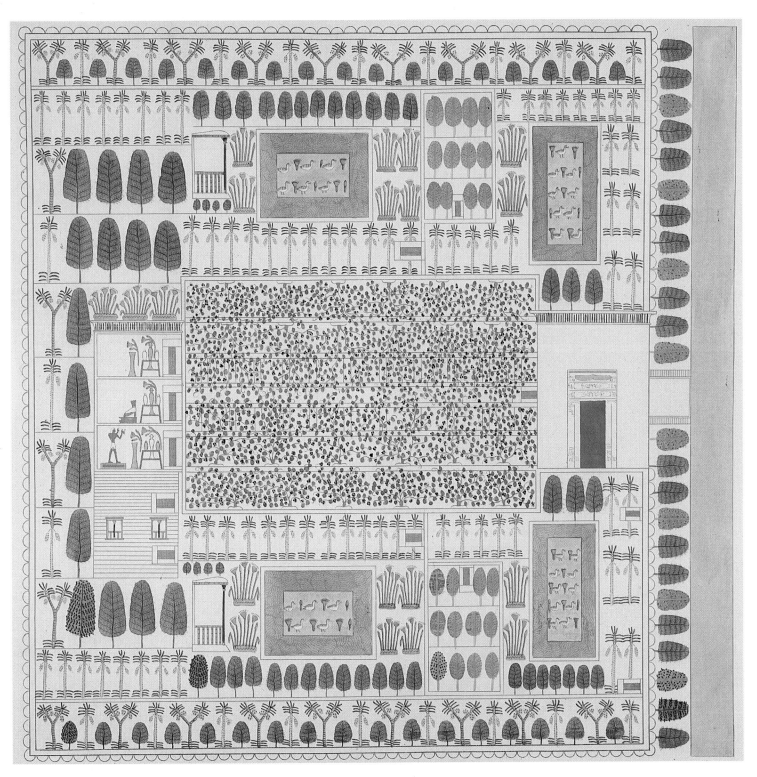

Water-tanks and useful plants such as dates and vines are recurrent features in surviving representations of Ancient Egyptian gardens.

*Groves charged with mystical significance are among the oldest of all garden features
and have been found at sacred sites of the Ancient World such as Delphi.*

Mesopotamia

In Ancient Mesopotamia, as in Egypt, there is evidence of gardens from a very early date. Perhaps because the early Sumerians developed their gardening skills under irrigation in a hot and dusty land, the pleasure of gardens, light hearted and joyful, was associated with shade, running water, fragrance and fresh produce. In the mythical days of Gilgamesh in the early third millenium BC, civic pride boasted a city of which one-third consisted of gardens or orchards. By the second millenium BC there is firmer evidence of royal gardens, the setting for festivals and banquets. The huge internal courtyards of palaces were planted with trees and perhaps also flowers, and some of these at least contained ponds. At this period some temples certainly had gardens, though their arrangement is unknown. One of their purposes was to provide fresh edible offerings for the deities. 'I planted a pure orchard for the goddess and established fruit deliveries as regular offerings,' proclaims an early Babylonian text.

By the first millenium BC there were large public parks in Assyria. The garden of Ashurnasirpal II (883–859 BC) was fed with water from the Upper Zab river diverted to Nimrud through a rock-cut channel. The orchards that it watered contained vines, cedar, cypress, juniper, almond, date, ebony, olive, oak, tamarisk, terebinth, ash, kamish, oak, pomegranate, fir, pear, quince, fig and apples, as well as other unidentified plants. Many had been collected abroad on campaign as young plants or seed. Like an earlier king of Assyria, Tiglath-Pileser I, Ashurnasirpal had herds of wild animals, which were probably enclosed in a zoological park. In the 8th century BC Sargon II laid out parks around his new capital, Khorsabad, as did his successor, Sennacherib, at Nineveh. In one place Sennacherib tried to re-create the marsh environment of southern Babylonia which had captivated his interest on campaigns. He made a swamp and filled it with cane-brakes and wild boar, and relates with satisfaction how herons came to nest there. In the 7th century his successor Esarhaddon created another great garden and tried to capture the character of the Amanus mountains in Syria, planting fruit and resinous trees.

Later in the same century Ashurbanipal continued in the same tradition. His stone sculptured reliefs show that he hunted lions and feasted with his queen to music in the gardens.

Nothing is known of palace courtyard gardens at this period but among evidence for temple gardens is one of Esarhaddon's inscriptions concerning a temple garden in Babylon: it was a garden of fruit trees with channels of water and burgeoning vegetable beds and so presumably its main purpose was still to provide fresh offerings to the gods. Real-estate records of the same period relating to the north of Mesopotamia mention gardens or, in some instances, rather parts of the estates of wealthy men.

A clay tablet names the plants in the garden of the Babylonian king Merodach-Baladan II, who reigned in the late 8th century BC, and subsequent copying of the text by scribes reflects perhaps the fame of a garden that was the forerunner of the Hanging Gardens of Babylon. The plants are listed in sections, possibly corresponding to the beds in which they were grown and, so far as they can be positively identified, all are edible vegetables and herbs.

It is not known whether Merodach-Baladan's garden was laid out on an architectural base but the gardens that were the seventh wonder of the ancient world were suspended upon vaults overlooking the Euphrates and watered straight from the river. The Hanging Gardens of Babylon are not mentioned in cuneiform sources and in classical Greek writings there are two different accounts of their history. The original gardens may date to Nebuchadnezzar II (605–562 BC) and after the Euphrates changed course in Babylon a new relocated garden may have been reconstructed by an Achaemenid king which was still flourishing in the time of Alexander the Great. Excavations in the palace of Nebuchadnezzar revealed an area with strong brick vaults and machinery for lifting water but the construction was too far from the river and lacked the stonework and the dimensions of the Greek sources so its identification as the site is probably wrong.

Babylonian temple garden contracts show that dates above all, but also figs and pomegranates, were cultivated in plots of land that flanked the processional routes to sacred buildings and each plot provided offerings for one month of the year. Gardens within temple precincts included cypress and juniper trees. Nebuchadnezzar mentions in his descriptions that he grew fruit and vegetables as offerings for Marduk but he had to import wine and raisins, for vines did not flourish in Babylonia.

There is no evidence for public parks in southern Mesopotamia but the lion hunt and falconry as royal sports almost certainly took place in a controlled environment, perhaps like the great estates with large enclosures filled with wild animals that 5th-century Greek travellers described as the parks or *paradeisoi* of the kings and nobles of Persia. However, there is no firm evidence of Persian influence on Mesopotamian gardens before the 6th century BC.

Greece

In 408 BC the Spartan king Lysander, visiting Cyrus the younger at Sardis, was shocked to learn that his Persian host worked in the ornamental palace garden himself. No Greek gentleman performed manual labour, certainly not in the pastime of gardening, since except in war or athletics physical work was considered degrading. This attitude did not preclude a delight in gardens but little is known of the nature of Greek gardens before the 4th century BC. However, early writings contain information about the cultivation of crops and we know that from archaic times roses and other scented plants were used to produce perfume, medicine or wreaths for sale.

From the earliest times, too, there were sacred groves associated with sanctuaries and these contained shade or fruit trees, often species symbolic of the appropriate god, so that at Daphni, for example, there were bays for Apollo. Typically, the grove included meadows, stands of timber, fields for commercial cultivation and hills for picnicking and hunting. Shrines to certain gods were set in gardens, one of the most famous being the sanctuary of Aphrodite in the gardens outside Athens. Adonis, associated with fertility and rebirth, was worshipped in special gardens, and Athenian women planted little 'gardens of Adonis' consisting of lettuce and fennel grown in broken jars to be offered at springs in honour of his harvest and death.

The only formal gardens so far excavated belonged to the so-called Temple of Hephaistos in the Athenian Agora. The garden, installed in about 300 BC, surrounded the 5th-century Doric temple on three sides with two main rows of shrubs or small trees, probably myrtle or pomegranate, or both, aligned with the building's columns and separated by narrow unpaved walks. The pattern was completed with small beds of flowering plants and there may also have been ivy or grape-vines growing against the stone precinct wall. The trees or shrubs were grown in pots sunk in pits dug into the bedrock and water was brought by an aqueduct. The garden died of neglect in the 1st century AD with the demise of its watering system. The pattern of straight rows of small trees, shrubs and flowers adhering strictly to an architectural nucleus was probably typical of classical sanctuaries.

Shade-trees were planted not only round temples but also in markets, gymnasia and meeting-places such as Plato's Academy and the Lyceum of Aristotle and Theophrastus. The garden and walk were used as a place of study; the 'peripatetic school' of Theophrastus derives its name from the word *peripatos*, meaning a shaded walk. At his death in 286 BC Theophrastus left his garden to his disciples, making provision for certain slaves to be emancipated provided that they maintained the garden for a period. It was probably used in part to study plants, for in his *Enquiry into Plants* Theophrastus presented the first systematic classification of them in Western literature. Another great philosopher of the 3rd century BC bequeathed his formal gardens to the city of Athens to be used as a public park.

In the 5th century BC travellers had brought back to Greece the first accounts of Persian royal parks. Under Alexander the Great, Greeks camped in the *paradeisoi* of the empire they were overthrowing. In the Hellenistic period, lasting almost three centuries after the death of Alexander in 323 BC, gardens were influenced by these oriental models. Thebes, Kleonal, Sikyon, Alexandria and many colonies in Italy and Sicily boasted lavish public parks with artificial grottoes and fountains. Such a park outside the city of Rhodes had rack-cut steps,

benches and grottoes creating a 'romantic landscape'. The private Hellenistic garden, richly adorned with sculpture, had a *peripatos* wide enough for a litter to pass, with side-lanes framed by trees and flower-beds. In this period, too, cemetery plots, which had long been planted with acanthus and asphodel, grew into funerary gardens, with stands of cypress, poplar or willow and containing stone walls, wells and even dining pavilions.

As the inheritors of Greek culture the Romans drew not only on Hellenistic garden practice but also on the body of knowledge about plants that Greek philosophers had assembled and, furthermore, grew in their own gardens plants that had been favourite species among the Greeks.

Rome

There is a considerable amount of information about Roman gardens, coming from pictorial and literary sources and, most importantly, from physical remains, such as the town and villa gardens engulfed by the eruption of Vesuvius, as well as villas elsewhere, including that of the Emperor Hadrian at Tivoli. In making their own gardens the Romans drew on the experience and example of the cultures with which they were in contact. By the end of the 2nd century BC the Romans had at their disposal the elements that were to constitute their art of gardens, which took such varied forms as the sacred landscape, urban promenades, or meeting places for philosophers and for those dedicated to literary activities.

At the domestic level the most significant development was the modification of the traditional Italian house to accommodate private gardens. In this process the atrium, a courtyard open to the sky and the centre of family life, was transformed into a semi-public reception room while the enclosed space, the *hortus*, which lay beyond, initially devoted to the cultivation of vegetables, become a pleasure-garden. This private area, known as the peristyle from the columns surrounding it, was dedicated to leisure; it was planted with shrubs and flowers and included fountains. The decor of these gardens varied but included themes of a sacred character, especially Dionysiac. There might be herms representing a god or

his followers, statues of fauns, fountains in the forms of grottoes and evergreen plants such as ivy and myrtle, the plants of Bacchus and Venus respectively. The smallest garden was sure to contain a figure of Priapus, the god of fertility and symbol of the life which rises from the ground – which is also the place where the ashes of the dead are laid to rest.

The walls of the porticoes surrounding gardens were often enlivened with paintings (*topia*), including landscapes, seascapes, and, as in the House of Livia on the Palatine, sanctuaries, tombs and statues. These were themes that the gardeners (*topiarii*), generally slaves of Greek extraction, might develop in the arrangement of the garden itself. The art of ornamental gardening, *opus topiarium*, extended far beyond what we understand by 'topiary' but certainly included the shaping of trees and shrubs. Much more typical of Roman gardens than picturesque topiary, however, was luxuriant vegetation, unifying art and nature in a setting where divinity was always present.

From the end of the 2nd century BC there were a great many parks and gardens on a large scale that are known to us from texts and inscriptions. These were established on the hills surrounding the town centre: the Quirinal, Esquiline and Aventine hills, the right bank of the Tiber, and also the 'hill of gardens', now the Pincio. Gradually, however, following confiscation, many of the gardens created by aristocratic families fell into the hands of the emperors and subsequently much of the ground that they had occupied was used for civic buildings.

Two of the best known gardens of the 1st century AD were those belonging to Pliny the younger, his literary letters giving descriptions of the Laurentian Villa on the coastal plain near Rome and the Tuscan Villa, north of Rome in the upper valley of the Tiber. These were 'open' gardens, making use in the first case of views of the sea and in the second of perspectives over cultivated land to hills and mountains. The essence of their design lay in the interpretation of nature and house, and this led to a marked articulation of the different parts of the house and to a multiplication of the façades, frequently provided with porticoes, and to the scattering of little pavilions in the landscape. Around this architectural core stretched the terraces. Sometimes there were *allées* bordered by lawn (the *pratum* at the Tuscan Villa) or by planted areas. The terrace was sometimes called a *xystus* on the model of those used by the athletes in Greek gymnasia. Some elements of these gardens were enclosed, including Pliny's favourite part of the Tuscan Villa, the 'hippodrome', an area laid out in the form of a stadium, its shady boundary formed by plane trees, festooned with ivy and interplanted with box and laurel.

The ensemble of monuments laid out by the Emperor Hadrian between AD 118 and 138 at the foot of the hill of Tibur, now known as Tivoli, demonstrated this Roman manner of landscaping on a magnificent scale worthy of an emperor. It is said that Hadrian, himself fascinated by architecture, aimed to reproduce the buildings and the sites which he had visited in the course of his travels. The villa's buildings were either open porticoes or closed peristyles laid out in gardens with fountains, *bassins* or canal-like stretches of water known as *euripes*. There were also 'promenades' in the form of a stadium, two baths, a Greek theatre, libraries, an odeum (for musical performances), and apartments for guests, soldiers and various services to the court. The pavilions and the open spaces, as well as the villa, were adorned with a considerable number of works of art, including mosaics, paintings, reliefs and statues. A characteristically Roman feature of the layout was the way the undulations of the ground were utilized to establish terraces opening on to vast perspectives over the surrounding countryside while most of the buildings were set in the hollow of a fold so that there was a contrast between intimacy and domination of space.

As a ruin, Hadrian's Villa proved a rich source for the antique sculptures so prized by Renaissance princes of the Church. At a deeper level, the Roman way of relating architecture and garden to one another and both to the broader landscape provided the foundation for the Italian Renaissance garden.

The Canopus, a branch of the Nile delta near Alexandria, was one of the buildings and sites of the empire reproduced at Hadrian's Villa, Tivoli.

Traditional Gardens of Europe and America

From the evidence of surviving gardens, from visual representations and from often incomplete but sometimes surprisingly detailed records, it is possible to assemble a reasonably complete picture of the way European gardens have developed since the Renaissance. Taking a broad view of developments prior to this century, what is immediately striking is the importance that for 400 or 500 years was attached to gardens as emblems of status and expressions of taste. Great talents were employed and great resources lavished on projects that, in many cases, would be considered ambitious even with the advantages of modern technology. However, the extravagance of a project provided no protection from shifts of fashion so that the history of some of Europe's greatest gardens must be seen as a complex process of revision and alteration in which the evidence of some phases may barely survive beneath subsequent overlays.

The major developments since the Renaissance are covered in the following national sections but it has to be admitted that in this arrangement some individual gardens of note have not found a place. This is partly the consequence of changes to national boundaries, partly as the result of the need to condense a great body of material. Among the omissions that are particularly regretted are some of the great gardens of eastern Europe, such as the splendid baroque layout of Eszterháza in Hungary and examples from some of the smaller countries which do not have an entry, such as the extraordinary and magnificent 17th-century estate of Enghien in Belgium. Another group of gardens regretfully omitted are those created by Europeans in places as far afield as India, Brazil, South Africa and Indonesia. European gardens prior to the Renaissance call for special treatment and the following summary attempts to bring together the main strands.

Medieval Gardens

In contrast to what we know of Renaissance and later gardens, our knowledge of medieval gardens is very limited. No garden of the period exists and there are few reliable visual representations of actual gardens, only typical scenes and even those almost all date from after 1400.

Furthermore, horticultural literature from about 500 to 1500 is scanty. Roman gardens are better documented and also they have been better investigated by archaeologists. Substantial archives concerning gardens begin only in the 13th century. What we do know of medieval gardens is a mosaic of scattered facts drawn largely from sources marginal to horticulture.

The calendar for April from the Trés Riches Heures *of the Duc de Berry, executed in the early 15th century
by Pol de Limbourg, shows an ordered landscape and a walled garden.*

The first half of the 9th century stands out as an exception in a long period of obscurity, with several important documents surviving from the epoch of Charlemagne and his immediate successors giving evidence of aesthetic and utilitarian horticulture. Of these one of the most notable is the *Capitulare de villis*, a decree listing 88 or 89 plants to be grown on the Crown estates at all towns in the Empire, during Charlemagne's rule a region comprising most of western Europe from the Netherlands to northern Spain and central Italy, and from the Atlantic to the borders of Hungary. The decree, which includes references to named varieties of apples and pears and distinctively southern plants, is evidence of a fresh approach to horticulture, for nearly a third of the plants listed cannot be found in classical sources.

Another important document is the detailed plan for a model monastery and its garden preserved in the monastic library of St Gall in Switzerland. The gardens comprise an infirmary garden of medicinal herbs, a kitchen garden and the monks' cemetery treated as an ornamental orchard planted with different sorts of trees. Two other interesting pieces of evidence from this period are a short Latin poem by the monk Walafrid Strabo and a gardener's calendar by another monk, Wandelbert of Prüm. Walafrid's *Hortulus* ('The Little Garden'), demonstrates a keen appreciation of plants cultivated with his own hand, including the lily, rose, flag iris and garden sage, appealing not merely to sight but also to the sense of smell.

Charlemagne himself not only had royal gardens for the production of food and medicine but also parks and pleasure grounds, in which he kept animals and birds, including peacocks. He showed a keen personal interest in wine-growing and succeeded in bringing to the vineyards around his palace at Ingelheim, in what is now Rhineland-Palatinate, stock from such distant places as Burgundy, Hungary, Italy, Lorraine and Spain. This transport of living plants on a grand scale is evidence of the recovery of the gardening skills of classical times.

It is significant that there were diplomatic relations between the Baghdad Caliph Harun al-Rashid and the court of Charle-

magne, for the superior botanical knowledge and horticultural skills of the Muslim world were to affect the form of medieval gardens as well as their content of plants. During the Middle Ages, notwithstanding warfare between Muslim and Christian, science crossed frontiers, and pilgrims and merchants who visited Islam brought back reports of the higher civilization which, however reluctantly, they admired. Pleasure-gardens and parks provide a notable example of influence from east and south upon northern Europe.

Until very recently it has been supposed that there was in western Europe no such thing as a landscape garden before the Renaissance. Furthermore, it was accepted as an article of faith that, until late in the 16th century, there was no deliberate sowing or planting of forest trees apart from individual specimens in small gardens. The deliberate creation of acres of wood and coppice, both for utility and pleasure, can, however, be traced back to the 11th century at least.

The 'paradise' or enclosed park was adopted by the Arabs from the Persians of classical times, walled preserves being created in Muslim lands, including North Africa, Sicily and Spain. The European borrowing of the park from the Muslim world was made possible by the historical circumstance of the Crusades. In the second half of the 11th century Geoffrey de Montbray, Bishop of Coutances created such a park beside Coutances in Normandy on returning from a visit to relatives and pupils in southern Italy, to which the influence of Muslim culture had been transmitted from Sicily. It seems probable that the oriental concept of the park, translated to Normandy, was brought to England by the Norman bishops and baronage. By 1110 it is certain that Henry I enclosed a large area with a stone wall around the royal manner of Woodstock in Oxfordshire, creating in the park a menagerie of wild animals.

Lodges and pavilions were a feature of these parks. The most famous of them is the walled pleasance of Everswell, enclosed in the park of Woodstock by Henry II in 1165 for his mistress the fair Rosamond. Its more usual name of Rosamond's Bower was given through the late Middle Ages to a whole class of pleasure-gardens. The word 'gloriet'

is often used to describe a pavilion in a park setting. The word seems to have come to England with Eleanor of Castile and was used to describe the island palace created between 1278 and 1290 in a lake formed around Leeds Castle in Kent. It derives from the Arabic *'aziz*, meaning glorious. One of the pavilions in the royal estate of the arabized Normans at Palermo in Sicily still bears an Arabic inscription; 'Here is the earthly paradise … this is called *al-'aziz*.' The epithet has become the name of the building, La Zisa.

Several different purposes were inherent in the pleasance with its lodges, pavilions or smaller kiosks. Hunting, whether with hounds or bows and arrows, was one purpose but spectatorship was quite as important as actual hunting. Some park lodges were 'standings' like grandstands, for comfortable observation of the hunt and for informal social life. This applied to watching fish caught from ponds and lakes, as well as to the usual taking of game. But the park might also be planted to yield fruit. This was the case, for example, with the improvements made in about 1190 by the Bishop of Auxerre, Hugh de Noyers, to his manor at Charbuy in what is now Yonne.

In England abbots and priors of the great monasteries as well as leading lay figures carried out improvements to estates, but the highest development of the pleasance was at residential castles and at unfortified manor-houses such as Woodstock and Havering-atte-Bower in Essex. A main constant was the inclusion of water in the design. A late example was Henry V's Pleasance in the Marsh created at Kenilworth between 1414 and 1417. This, like earlier examples, was a square area surrounded by double moats, covering nearly 4 hectares (9 acres) altogether with 1 hectare (2½ acres) of garden at the centre. In this were a banquet-house and three other kiosks at the angles, built of timber on stone foundations, with, as the castle accounts reveal, 'Aleyes' or walks. The pleasance was accessible from the castle 1 km (⅔ mile) across the Great Pool, whose waters were brought into the moats.

In France the most famous and best recorded of the pleasances was at Hesdin in Artois. In 1295 Count Robert II of Artois enclosed a very large park with a wall 13

km (8 miles) long and began a 'House in the Marsh' with a gloriet in a great pool, reached by a bridge as at Leeds Castle; it is evident that Count Robert was well aware of Queen Eleanor's works begun some 15 years earlier. The original works at Hesdin included an aviary and a 'chapel of glass', still unfinished at Count Robert's death in 1302 but completed by his daughter Mahaut before 1329.

The pleasance of Hesdin was uniquely famous for the series of water-engines directly based on the early 13th-century Arabic *Book of Mechanical Devices* by Ibn al

Razzaz al-Jazari of Diyarbakir. These engines, kept up for over 250 years but destroyed along with the town, castle and park in 1553, operated surprise jets and showers, a talking owl, and practical jokes, such as dropping visitors into a mass of feathers and blowing soot and flour in their faces before confronting them with mirrors.

It is not altogether clear who was responsible for designing pleasances such as Hesdin, although in this case we do know the names of certain craftsmen associated with some of its features. The master carpenters and masons responsible for the

The little paradise garden painted by a master from the Upper Rhine in the early 15th century provides a valuable insight into the range of plants that might have been found in European gardens in the late Middle Ages.

architectural features were among the very few people then able to make surveys and draw to scale and they, as well as master engineers, carvers and painters, were commonly paid at a higher rate than is known for master gardeners. It is evident that the key to successful design was subtlety in

on Islamic studies of botany and medicine, must be counted the predecessors of what are commonly described as the first botanic gardens, those founded at Pisa and Padua in the 1540s. In Spain the leading physicians who directed them included Muslims, Jews and Christians and there was extensive translation from Arabic of relevant literature. At the medical school of Montpellier in France, founded by Arab physicians from Spain, there was by 1250 a physic garden on the same site as the later botanical garden of 1593. There were gardens of botanical character at Venice in 1333, Prague later in the century (planted by an Italian at the bidding of the Emperor Charles IV) and in the London suburb of Stepney a private garden belonging to Henry Daniel, who boasted of 252 different species of herbs.

Besides the essentially utilitarian gardens there was also the pleasure-garden, which took two forms, according to the space available. Most houses had an enclosed herbarium viewed from above from bedroom windows and fit for outdoor meals or repose. This 'herber' was often square or oblong, within trellised fences, and consisted largely of a lawn. It was intersected by paths, contained a pool or fountain, and was surrounded by borders of flowers and by raised seats of turf. Where the garden was mainly of grass this might be treated as a flowery mead by including daisies and other close-growing plants, an exotic idea that originated in the south. In the borders were red and white roses, madonna lily, flag iris, peony, and a few other bulbous and herbaceous plants, the number of species and varieties increasing century by century. Climbing wild roses, honeysuckle (woodbine), and grapevines covered the surrounding trellis. In the larger gardens, outside this, there might be a 'cloister' or pergola, a tunnel-arbour built on wooden rods or withies and covered with roses, vines or ivy. From the evidence of illustrations there was great variety in design. By 1400 one favourite plan for the noble

proportion and it is precisely this quality that is found in the great buildings of master masons. Though gardeners were perhaps seldom responsible for more than the skilled culture of plants, a few seem to have had a higher status and some of the later royal gardeners probably were experts in the layout of pleasure-gardens.

In addition to the pleasance, several types of garden existed at once. First was the strictly utilitarian garden for food-vegetables and herbs for seasoning, with fruit-trees and nuts as standards or against walls. In second place came the physic garden with medicinal herbs for various conditions, usually in separate beds. This might be on a large scale when it belonged to the infirmary of a monastic house, or be a small adjunct to a private garden, cultivated by the housewife. Physicians and apothecaries commonly maintained their own physic gardens to supplement the costly imported drugs obtained commercially.

A few of these physic gardens, drawing

garden consisted of alternate chequers of turf and garden-bed; in some beds standard flowering trees such as apple or cherry were planted. In other gardens the long raised beds of early tradition – raised to prevent the roots becoming waterlogged whereas in the drier South beds typically were sunken to allow irrigation by flooding – continued as regular features in gardens, sometimes planted with one species in each. Later they were often left largely bare but with plants set out in ornamental pots or trimmed *estrade* shrubs, that is trained in a succession of tiers.

A second form of pleasure-garden in larger grounds was the *viridarium, virgultum*, or orchard, planted not for the supply of fruit but for beauty. Apples, pears, cherries and the occasional quince, medlar, or mulberry, planted among forest trees, provided splendid displays of blossom or fruit for short periods, but at all times shaded space for recreation. There was often a fish-pond or a lake, and in such cases the orchard began to take on the attributes of the pleasance. Ornamental planting of this kind might be associated with architecture, as with the elms planted outside the west front of Wells Cathedral in 1239, and the many sorts of lovely trees planted in the *viridarium* of the Bishop of Le Mans in the mid-12th century, when 'those looking out of the hall windows to admire the beauty of the trees, and others in the garden looking at the fair show of the windows, could both delight in what they saw'.

There is an abundant evidence of the keen interest taken in gardening by monks and especially by nuns and at most major houses there were gardens of all kinds, including recreational grounds planted with trees. However, despite the persistent myth of the 'Cloister Garden', there is no firm evidence that ornamental gardens were made within the main cloisters of monasteries as they have been in continental Europe since the Reformation.

From an early date there were beside large towns public 'meadows' for recreation, planted with trees. Such a garden, with trees arranged in various designs, existed in Milan soon after 1000, and the names of Le Pré-aux-Clercs and Saint-Germain-des-Prés in Paris, the Prater in Vienna and the Prado

of Madrid show how widespread was this tradition. In London by the 12th century there were public gardens with tree-shaded walks around Holywell, Clerkenwell and Clement's Well, where, according to a contemporary chronicler, William Fitz-Stephen, 'great crowds and numbers of students, and young men of the City, walk to take the air in summer towards evening'. Later such gardens catered for sport with butts for archery, bowling-greens, and refreshment booths. By 1314 there was a large park open to the public by the Castle of Helmond in the Netherlands.

Garden architecture and furnishings, as seen in paintings and miniatures, showed considerable variation, but the types were mostly international. Gardens might have a closely boarded fence or vertical pales cut to points; a post-and-rail fence; or most commonly, a fence of diamond (occasionally square) trellis. The raised benches might be of piled and squared layers of turf, but were usually held up by facings of stone or brick, sometimes of wattling or boarding. The earlier pools were simple rectangular tanks with a masonry margin, but later became circular or polygonal in plan and

contained a fountain, which might be a pinnacled architectural structure. Paths were of compacted sand or gravel, or occasionally of stone flags or quarry tiles, often separated from the beds by a low boarding or bricks laid flat, unless the beds were raised behind stone or brick retaining walls. By the 15th century individual trees might have their butt encircled with wickerwork and filled in with soil to form a bench. Pergolas and tunnel-arbours were made of poles or withies and needed frequent replacement and repair. The finest gardens also had low wooden rails to the beds, sometimes coloured, and towards 1500 heraldic beasts appeared, carved in wood or stone; they are a mark of the Burgundian style of the second half of the 15th century, along with 'tester' or shelter arbours trained over seats, and the provision of stone tables for outdoor meals. The beasts were adopted in the English gardens of the early Tudors. Another sign of the Burgundian style was the training of shrubs and small trees in *estrade* form. Contemporary with these developments was the cult of the garden carnation, first evidenced at Valencia in 1640 and thought to have come from Persia

The knot garden, as in this modern version at the Tudor House Museum, Southampton, was usually a geometrical pattern within a square. This last major development of gardens in the late medieval period evolved further during the early Renaissance, especially in northern Europe.

via Turkey and Italy. Various kinds of support were used for the heavy double flowers on weak stems. Individual plants or small trained shrubs might be grown in ornamental pots or in pierced flower-pots with saucers and be placed on beds or along boundary walls, permitting replacement through the season.

The last major development of the Middle Ages was the appearance of the knot, usually a geometrical pattern within a square, but at first composed of heraldic beasts, as described at Richmond Palace in 1460 and thought to have come from Persia and other estates, 'most fair and pleasant gardens, with royal knots, alleyed and herbed; many marvellous beasts, as lions, dragons, and such other of divers kind, properly fashioned and carved in the ground, right well sanded, and compassed with lead; with many vines, seeds and strange fruit, right goodly beset'. It must be emphasized that the artistic sense of the word 'knot' derived from the carved bosses of stone vaulting or wooden roofs and

implies only a circumscribed design of any kind; but soon geometrical patterns, either based on mazes and labyrinths or comparable to family badges of formal design, ousted the animal forms.

Apart from obvious climatic and cultural differences between gardens of North and South, there were specific national characteristics, largely concerned with the main sorts of plants employed. In Andalusia and Naples there could be extensive use of orange and lemon trees, myrtles and, after the middle of the 15th century, the newly fashionable double clove carnation. Cypresses would flourish throughout Italy and southern France, but seldom survived many winters in England and were impossible in central Europe. The pomegranate, though marginally hardy, would not flower well, nor set fruit at all, in the North. Grape-vines, on the other hand, could be grown everywhere as ornamental climbers, and would produce large quantities of dessert grapes even in London. In France, certain southern plants were brought north-

wards: first lavender, then rosemary, the latter finally reaching England with Queen Philippa in 1340. Wallflowers and stocks, already developed in several colours in Moorish Spain by the 11th century, also took time to arrive in England, but were known by the 14th century and may have come direct from Spain with the hollyhock in the train of Queen Eleanor of Castile after her marriage in 1255 to the son of Henry III who was later to reign as Edward I. The garden flora of Germany and central Europe was in some ways distinctive; the best of the early printed herbals were German and it was greater Germany that exercised the strongest influence on English botany and horticulture at the end of the Middle Ages.

Although no detailed lists appear to survive of the plants grown in pleasure-gardens, there is evidence that the trade was highly developed. The choice may have been restricted but the best gardens of the Middle Ages must have made a splendid display.

The Hortus Floridus *(1614) of Crispijn van de Passe, one of the earliest florilegia illustrated with copper-plate engravings, records the greatly increased range of flowers available to Dutch gardeners in the early 17th century. The gardens portrayed, however, retain many late medieval characteristics.*

ITALY

At the end of the 16th century, when Giusto Utens executed this view, Francesco de' Medici's garden at Pratolino enjoyed a European reputation for its waterworks and grottoes.

For nearly two centuries the rest of Europe looked with admiration to Renaissance Italy as the interpreter of the garden tradition of the ancient world. Many of the great gardens that fascinated and enchanted eager travellers from the north — as well as giving pleasure to those for whom they were created – have now been lost completely while the schemes of others have been substantially modified. Nonetheless, enough survive in recognizable form to make possible a fair appreciation of the qualities that have typified the Italian tradition. Fortunately, too, even where neglect and shifts of fashion have caused a garden to be lost or altered beyond recognition,

contemporary accounts, as well as early prints, drawings and paintings, make it possible to form a reasonably accurate idea of Italian gardens in their prime. Harmony and symmetry derived from classical theories, spatial subtleties, ingenious effects, dramatic and poetic qualities – all these have helped to make Italian gardens a recurrent source of inspiration to designers.

THE CLASSICAL INFLUENCE

As early as the 14th century it is possible to detect, for example in the writings of Petrarch and Boccaccio, a fresh delight in the natural world, though this does not

seem to have been translated into new ideas about garden design. The garden of the Villa Palmieri in Florence, as described in Boccaccio's *Decameron*, still seems very much in the medieval mould. It was the study of classical literature, art and history by the Florentine humanists in the 15th century that gave a new dimension to the cultural life of Italy and had a direct effect on the way gardens were laid out.

The most influential formulation of ideas on architecture and design derived from classical authorities was Leon Battista Alberti's *De re aedificatoria libri X* ('Ten Books on Architecture'), completed in 1452 and printed in 1485. The garden of the Villa

Quaracchi, Florence, which lives for us through a description in the diary for 1459 of its owner, Giovanni Rucellai, may have been the work of Alberti himself. Although still medieval in some of its features, the garden conformed to the classically inspired principles he favoured. The house stood on a hillside, commanding a view, the main axis emphasized by an avenue of trees leading down to the River Arno across the Pistoia road. There was topiary, too, in the manner described by the classical writer Pliny the Younger.

The custom of withdrawing to a country residence for study and contemplation (*villeggiatura*) developed in the early 15th century and gave impetus to the design of gardens for rural villas. The Villa Medici, Careggi (now in the suburbs of Florence), transformed from a fortress-like manor by Michelozzo Michelozzi for Cosimo de' Medici, included a conscious imitation of a Roman garden. The Platonic Academy that met at the villa under the leadership of Marsilio Ficino must often have engaged in earnest discourse in this small scented garden furnished with the dark greens of bay, box, cypress and myrtle. Little now remains.

Il Trebbio and Villa Medici, Fiesole

Two Tuscan gardens with schemes by Michelozzo Michelozzi have survived in a reasonable state and give some idea of the way design was changing. Il Trebbio, a Medici hunting lodge at Cafaggiolo which was converted from a medieval fortress in the middle of the 15th century, occupies a commanding hilltop position. The new spirit can be seen in the way the enclosed gardens, with their vine pergolas (one of which still survives) running lengthwise, were conceived as an extension to the villa. The design does not, however, exploit the views the fine position affords.

In contrast, at the Villa Medici, Fiesole, the gardens of which were created a few years later than those of Il Trebbio, two terraces were constructed at some expense to take advantage of the panoramic views. The upper terrace, on which the house stands, provides an extension of the rooms and serves as an outdoor *salon*. The lower terrace, although now laid out as a formal parterre garden, may originally have been

used for growing fruit and vegetables. A feature that has survived more or less unchanged is the *giardino segreto*, to the west of the house. The 'secret garden', to translate the term literally, which persisted for centuries as an important element in Italian garden design, was an adaptation of the medieval enclosed garden room. The secluded *giardino segreto* at the Villa Medici, with its magical views over Florence and the Arno valley, provided an ideal setting for the contemplation and philosophical discussion that sustained the artistic and scholarly circles patronized by the Medicis.

The Belvedere

In comparison with medieval gardens, those laid out in the region of Florence, Siena and Lucca in the 15th and early 16th centuries display a new confidence in the handling of space and, in particular, in the harmonious marriage of architecture and setting. Rome, a city almost in ruins when the Papacy returned in 1417, at first lagged behind,

Despite superficial alterations, the gardens of the Villa Medici at Fiesole retain the form given them by their designer, Michelozzo Michelozzi, in the 1450s. The giardino segreto *gives views over Florence and the Arno valley.*

although imposing buildings were soon being erected. Throughout the 15th century the gardens of Roman palaces were confined to the enclosed courtyard (*cortile*), which gave little more scope for ingenuity than the medieval cloister. Donato Bramante's response to Pope Julius II's commission (1503) for a magnificent new Belvedere Court at the Vatican was, however, revolutionary. Perhaps the inspiration for his bold scheme came from the vast terraces linked by ramps at the Temple of Fortune, Praeneste (the modern Palestrina), constructed under Sulla in the 1st century BC. Whether this is so or not, the sense of theatre that Bramante gave to a very large architecturally enclosed space on a sloping site is certainly inherited from classical architecture. He divided the area into three parts: an arena for the lavish pageants of the papal court, the largest part, formed the bottom level; the middle section consisted of seating looking down on the arena, while the upper level, with a large central alcove, was a formal garden containing a collection of statuary.

In 1580 Bramante's majestic design was drastically altered, cut in two by the library of Sixtus V and with the alcove transformed into a semi-dome. The influence of this scheme was, nonetheless, profound. The theatricality of the dominant central axis running through three levels with the dramatic linking staircases was innovatory. Perhaps just as influential, however, was the revival of the garden as a setting for statuary.

Palazzo Piccolomini and Villa Madama

Little new building or reworking of country residences took place in the vicinity of Rome during the 15th century. Somewhat further to the north, the village of Corsignano was remodelled by Pope Pius II, a humanist with strong antiquarian interests and a sentimental attachment to his birthplace. He renamed it Pienza and the Palazzo Piccolomini which he had built there contains one of the loveliest hanging gardens. From a *giardino segreto*, intimate and apparently enclosed, archways give splendid views over the Val d'Orcia.

The plan for the Palazzo Piccolomini and its garden exploits with real flair an exceptional site; it does not, however, break new ground, as did the first of the Renaissance villas built near Rome but outside the city walls. The Villa Madama, which Cardinal Giulio de' Medici (later Pope Clement VII) had built on the eastern slopes of Monte Mario, was in effect a reconstruction of an imperial Roman villa. Among those involved in the design of this ambitious project, begun in 1516, were Raphael, Antonio da Sangallo the Younger and Giovanni da Udine. What survives – the scheme was never completed and the villa was burnt during the sack of Rome in 1527 – gives only a shadowy idea of the monumental scale on which architecture and garden were integrated. The central element of the design was an open circular court framed by a symmetrical building through which passages radiated at the four points of the compass to loggias. The loggia on the south opened on to the entrance court and the approach by a monumental stairway. On the north there were formal terrace gardens leading to a *giardino segreto*. From the eastern loggia there were spectacular views towards Rome, while that on the west gave on to an open-air theatre of classical Roman design excavated from the hillside. Despite its misfortunes the Villa Madama, conceived more as a complex of courts and loggias for open-air entertainment than as a place of residence, was to have an important and lasting influence on the design of Roman villas and gardens.

DESIGN VERSUS NATURE

A characteristic of Italian gardens that remained a constant at least until the end of the 18th century is already apparent in the Renaissance gardens of Tuscany and Rome constructed in the 15th and early 16th centuries. These were gardens in which the design counted for more than the plants, of which only a very limited range were used and then only as a kind of evergreen architecture. The neglect of the flower garden by designers gives a somewhat misleading impression for, during the early Renaissance particularly, there is ample evidence of a delight and interest in flowers for their ornamental value.

Gardens devoted to ornamental plants have fared badly but Italy's early botanic gardens, the first in the world, have sur-

At the Villa Madama architecture and garden were integrated on a monumental scale that had a profound influence on Roman villas and gardens. This ambitious project, in effect a reconstruction of an imperial Roman villa, was begun in 1516 but never completed. Little remains of this first Renaissance villa built in the vicinity of Rome but outside the city walls.

Among the earliest botanic gardens was that established in Padua in 1545. Its initial purpose was to provide medical students with an opportunity to study medicinal plants. The small beds of the central circular design remain basically unchanged.

CASTELLO

vived. Taking their cue from classical authorities, Renaissance scholars treated the study of plants as an integral part of medicine. The Orto Botanico at Pisa, established about 1543 and generally considered the first, was a *hortus medicus* – a physic garden, intended to help students in their study of plants, the source of the medicines then available. This garden, and those established within a few years at Padua (1545) and Florence (1550), proved more important than their origins might suggest for they gave an impetus to botanical studies throughout Europe, leading to the first systematic classifications not based on medical properties.

THE MANNERIST STYLE

A new mood can be detected in the intellectual and artistic life of Italy after the sack of Rome in 1527. The expression of this mood in architecture and the fine arts, restless and energetic but not easily characterized, is conveniently labelled Mannerism. In garden design it is typified by two major developments, which led to the

creation of some of the most celebrated of all Italian gardens. One of these developments was to charge the garden with allegorical references, generally intended to flatter the commissioning patron. The first example of an iconographic programme of this kind was at the Medici villa at Castello, near Florence, where the garden was begun in 1538. The 'most rich, magnificent and ornamental garden in Europe', as Vasari described it, was intended to glorify the power of the Medicis, newly reinforced when Cosimo became the first Duke of Tuscany in 1537. The designer was Niccolò Tribolo, the work being completed after his death by Bartolommeo Ammanati and Bernardo Buontalenti. However, the allegorical scheme that was expressed in statues and fountains was devised, it is thought, by Benedetto Varchi, a scholar and a friend of the Duke.

Changes in the disposition of the statues, and the loss of some of them, have weakened and confused Castello's iconographic programme. Furthermore, the rectilinear bareness of the garden as it now is reveals its underlying, and typically Tuscan,

The garden of the Villa Medici at Castello survives but the late 16th-century lunette by Giusto Utens shows that once it was more closely planted than it is today. It was laid out from 1538 with an iconographic programme to flatter the Medicis.

conservatism, rather than the magnificence commented on by Vasari. In its time, however, Castello was advanced not merely on account of its allegorical scheme. Here was an early example of the other major development of Mannerist gardens, the introduction of ingenious water displays. The French writer Montaigne, who visited the garden in 1580, described the way the gardener could shower the unwary with water by manipulating a device 'two hundred paces away'. Childish or frivolous though they may seem, *giochi d'acqua* (literally 'water games') such as those at Castello remained important features of Italian gardens throughout the 16th and 17th centuries, commented on with astonished admiration by visitors from the north. The scheme at Castello also included a grotto, a feature perfectly suited to the watery exuberance of Mannerist gardens. In describing the grotto

Montaigne mentions 'all sorts of animals, copied to the life, spouting out by the water of these fountains, some by the beak, others by the wing, some by the nail or the ears, or the nostrils'.

Pratolino

Probably Europe's most famous garden at the end of the 16th century was Pratolino, near Florence, its reputation accounted for by the prodigious mastery over nature demonstrated in innumerable water displays. Virtually nothing survives of the scheme created for Francesco de' Medici from about 1569 to 1581, probably by Buontalenti, and the iconographic programme, which almost indubitably existed, is not known for certain. However, there are full accounts of the chief attractions, especially the grottoes, the largest of which represented the Flood. According to Montaigne, when you sat on a bench to admire the sculpture, 'by a single movement the whole grotto is filled with water, and all the seats squirt water to your backside'. There was no escape from a drenching for as you fled up the stairs the gardener 'may let loose a thousand jets of water from every two steps of the staircase.'

Among the most astonishing water displays at Pratolino were the automata, hydraulic contrivances that made music and noises and gave the illusion of men and animals moving. These were inspired by the extraordinary inventions of the School of Alexandria, principally known through the writings of Hero, a Greek scientist of the 1st century AD. Although his *Pneumatica* and *Mechanics* were not published in Italian translations until 1589, their content was known before this date, as can be seen from the designs of a number of important gardens, including those of the Villa d'Este at Tivoli.

Villa d'Este

The grandeur of this spectacular garden owed much to the competing ambitions of two great princes of the Church. The garden created by Cardinal Ippolito d'Este between 1560 and 1575, slightly earlier than Pratolino, was an answer to the imposing *palazzo* being built at Caprarola by his great rival, Cardinal Alessandro Farnese. On the western side of Tivoli, the hill town where Cardinal d'Este was governor, the land sloped away steeply, affording views south-west across the *campagna* to Rome and north-west to the Sabine Hills. The dramatic potential of this precipitous site was fully realized in a tightly integrated design that was rich in marvellously varied detail. The originality of the scheme is in no way diminished by recognizing the influence of two classical sites, Praeneste and Hadrian's Villa. The latter, an ensemble of monuments erected by the Emperor Hadrian in the 2nd century AD, was only a few miles away, at the foot of Tivoli. The ruins at both these sites had been studied in detail by the architect and antiquary Pirro Ligorio, who played an important role in the design of the Villa d'Este, in particular in advising the Cardinal on an elaborate iconographic programme for the gardens.

The principal entrance was originally at

The Fountain of Neptune at the Villa d'Este, Tivoli. The lavish use of water, including elaborate automata, and the majestic terracing of the steep site make the Villa d'Este, created between 1560 and 1575, the most spectacular of all Italian gardens.

the lowest level, the central axis leading up to the house, which stands at the top of a series of majestic terraces. The main perspectives are formed by cross axes and additionally, in the steepest part, by diagonal ramps. To close the vistas and at points of intersection there were statues and fountains, the lavish water displays being the outstanding feature of the garden.

Even today the fountains of the Villa d'Este are impressive; the Pathway of the One Hundred Fountains, for example, still ranks as one of the most celebrated sights of Italy. This promenade is flanked by three rows of small fountains. At the the back of the middle row were one hundred stucco

The fountain displays of the Villa d'Este are still impressive. Among the best-known sights of Italy is the Pathway of the One Hundred Fountains, consisting of a long promenade flanked by three rows of small fountains. These were originally backed by one hundred stucco reliefs depicting scenes from Ovid's Metamorphoses *but only a few now survive.*

reliefs of scenes from Ovid's *Metamorphoses*. Little remains of these or of the Rometta, the fountain at the south-east and of the terrace which portrayed the Seven Hills of Rome and their major monuments. Other fountains survive but the *giochi d'acqua* and automata that were once a source of amusement and delight have disappeared. The idea for the most ingenious of the automata, the Fountain of the Owl, came directly from Hero, who describes 'birds made to sing and be silent alternately by flowing water'. Chirping birds perched on bronze branches fell silent when an owl began to hoot mournfully. According to Montaigne, the Fountain of

the Dragons produced the sounds of 'cannon-shots and muskets', while from the Fountain of the Organ came a trumpet call followed by a sweet harmony.

Much of the statuary, which, with the fountains, gave the garden its allegorical meaning, came from Hadrian's Villa, unearthed in the excavations carried out by Ligorio for Cardinal d'Este. The significance of this elaborate programme is now difficult to grasp from a visit as many of the statues were removed during the 18th century. Two themes were expressed in the dual dedication of the garden, to Hercules and to Hippolytus. Hercules, from whom the d'Este family fancifully traced its ancestry, symbolized strength, Hippolytus chastity. The elaboration of the programme extended to presenting the spectator with a choice. For example, at the Fountain of Dragons on the central axis, the cross-axis leads in one direction to the Grotto of Diana, representing virtue, in the other to the Grotto of Venus, representing vice.

The Villa d'Este represented the fullest expression of Renaissance ideals in garden design, a fact not easily recognized after so many losses and with the fullness of the planting picturesquely blurring the original scheme. It is still, however, a glorious survival, a majestic theatre filled with the music of water.

Villa Pia

The Villa Pia at the Vatican, designed by Ligorio for Pope Pius IV in 1560, is another highly original garden, though on a much more intimate scale. It is a *giardino segreto*, designed as a papal retreat; the Belvedere Court already provided a grandiose setting for pageantry and public display. Four different buildings, including a three-storey *casino* or pavilion, surround an open paved oval. What makes this garden unique is the harmonious way these richly detailed buildings are grouped in space, linked by a low wall with seats and vases.

Villa Farnese

An even more magical *giardino segreto* was that designed at Caprarola by the architect Giacomo da Vignola for Cardinal Alessandro Farnese. Vignola's main task, begun in 1556, was to transform a fortress into a monumental *palazzo* that would display the taste and wealth of the Cardinal. The two main gardens, completed in 1578, one for winter and the other for summer, were unremarkable. From the summer garden a path leads up to a *casino*. The approach is by a ramp, down the centre of which runs a *catena d'acqua*, a narrow water channel. In front of the *casino*, is a parterre defined by caryatids of human scale; behind lies an open-air room, a simple garden floored with pebble mosaics and backed by trees. The charm of this setting lies partly in the surprise of its discovery, partly in the sharp contrast between its modest beauty and the oppressive grandeur of the *palazzo*.

Villa Giulia

Before working on the Villa Farnese, Vignola had played a part in the design of the Villa Giulia, Pope Julius III's villa on the outskirts of Rome, not far from the Porta del Popolo. Only the internal courts survive but they show a remarkable development in the design of courtyard spaces, in particular in the theatrical treatment of changes of level. A loggia leads from the main semicircular court to two smaller courts at lower levels, these two forming the nymphaeum. This architectural grotto contains four caryatids with water flowing at their bases. What remains is an architectural garden in which complex spatial relations are handled with exceptional confidence. The Villa Giulia is interesting, too, in the way painted scenes (*topia*) are used. This is a Renaissance revival of a practice common in classical gardens.

Villa Lante

If the Villa Lante is the work of Vignola, and it is traditionally attributed to him, this, the best preserved garden of the period, is his masterpiece. Cardinal Gambara, for whom the design was executed (and the work completed by 1573), wanted a summer retreat on the edge of the town of Bagnaia, near Viterbo. The scheme, laid out on a sloping site, consisted of a formal garden arranged in terraces and a park. The main architectural elements, two *casini*, appear as ornaments of the formal garden rather than as the *raison d'être* of the design. The lowest terrace is a square dominated by a fountain, which Montaigne described as 'a high pyramid which spouts water in a great

The giardino segreto *of the Villa Farnese at Caprarola, intimate and human in scale, offers a welcome escape from the oppressively monumental* palazzo *designed by Vignola for Cardinal Alessandro Farnese in the second half of the 16th century.*

The Villa Giulia, near Rome's Porta del Popolo, was built in the 1550s for Pope Julius III. The nymphaeum, an architectural grotto in which four caryatids support the upper level, demonstrates a highly original and theatrical handling of space.

The Villa Lante, Cardinal Gambara's summer retreat on the edge of the town of Bagnaia, near Viterbo, was completed in 1573 and remains less changed than any other Italian garden of the period. This view looks down to the lowest terrace with its fountain and water parterre.

many different ways: one rises, another falls. Around this pyramid are four pretty little lakes, full of pure and limpid water. In the centre of each is a stone boat, with musketeers who shoot and hurl water against the pyramid, and a trumpeter in each, who also shoots water.' The fountain with four youths holding the Montalto device was substituted for the pyramid after 1590, when the property was acquired by Cardinal Alessandro Montalto. The fountain and pools were originally surrounded by flower parterres, which were replaced, probably in the 17th century, by the present *parterres de broderie*.

The central axis, which ascends between the two *casini* to the Fountain of the Deluge on the uppermost level, is accented at numerous points. In the centre of the middle terrace, for example, stands a large stone table with a central trough for cooling wine. Behind this table is the Fountain of Giants, fed by water issuing from the claws of a large crayfish, the Cardinal's symbol. The symbol is repeated elsewhere in the

garden; a sculpted channel in the form of the limbs of a crayfish is also aligned on the main axis, above the Fountain of Giants.

The sense that park and garden are intimately related gives the Villa Lante a special quality. However, most of the fountains that formed part of the original scheme for the park and which underlined this relationship were changed or destroyed after Cardinal Montalto acquired the villa. The survival, more or less unchanged, of the formal garden is remarkable enough.

Villa Orsini

A more extravagantly fanciful garden where Vignola may have played a role is that of the Villa Orsini at Bomarzo. Work on the *sacro bosco*, or sacred wood, as Pier Francesco 'Vicino' Orsini, Duke of Bomarzo, referred to his creation, was carried out intermittently between 1552 and 1580. Giants hewn out of solid rock form part of a complex design that includes now obscure antiquarian and literary references, in particular to Ariosto's epic poem *Orlando Furioso* (1532).

One of the most curious of Italian Renaissance gardens is that of the Villa Orsini at Bomarzo, known by its creator as the sacro bosco *(sacred wood). Giant figures are hewn out of solid rock.*

TUSCANY

During the 16th century gardens outside the Roman sphere of influence in no way matched those of Rome in grandeur or boldness of design. Typically, the gardens of Tuscany reflected the domestic scale of most villas. In execution, however, the gardens could be exquisite, as can be seen from notable examples that have survived. Two that are outstanding for the way they combine a domestic quality with a markedly individual character are the Villa Gamberaia at Settignano and the Villa Capponi at Arcetri. The former, constructed over a long period, includes in a modest area eight different units held together by a grass *allée* and a *giardino segreto*, which extends along the full width of the site. Two units close to the house and separated from each other are secret *boschi* or groves of ilex. The Villa Capponi, completed about 1572, has an even smaller garden that is clearly designed for personal use rather than entertainment. The elements consist of a grass terrace giving superb views over Florence, an enclosed parterre garden and two walled gardens in descending levels.

A more severe garden is that of the Villa Bombicci at Colazzi, beautifully sited on the edge of a ridge of hills south of Florence. The design is now attributed to Santi di Tito, although it was long associated with Michelangelo. Built in 1560, but never completed, it displays a subtle balance of proportion and harmony with its surroundings. A conspicuous feature is a fine cypress avenue that leads up to the villa past a pool which reflects the eastern façade.

Boboli Gardens

The initial design of the nearby Boboli Gardens provides a striking example of Tuscan conservatism. The terrain and the unfinished Pitti Palace were acquired by Cosimo I de' Medici in 1549. In the same year Niccolò Tribolo designed the central axis, simply making the naturally existing hollow behind the palace into an amphitheatre and laying out thick plantations on its banks. The utilization of the space as a garden theatre dates from the 17th century, when the plantations were cleared and tiers of seats installed. The first use of the amphitheatre for festivals was in

The garden of the Villa Gamberaia at Settignano, though small in scale, consists of numerous elements ingeniously united in a coherent composition. The parterre water garden has been modernized but in keeping with the garden's overall character.

July 1637, when an equestrian ballet was performed to celebrate the marriage of Ferdinand II de' Medici to the Princess of Urbino.

Much else in the gardens, including the setting of the Isolotto, took its present form in the 17th century. This feature, which is supposed to be based on the Maritime Theatre at Hadrian's Villa, now looks curiously out of scale; the statue on the island formerly stood outside the Pitti Palace. La Grotta Grande is a survival from the late 16th century and is the most

At the Boboli Gardens behind the Pitti Palace in Florence the Piazzale dell'Isolotto, the Ocean Fountain, is approached by the long western axis. The 17th-century setting is said to have been inspired by the Maritime Theatre at Hadrian's Villa, Tivoli.

fantastic grotto of this period that has come down to us. Buontalenti, in his day the leading director of lavish entertainments (*spettacoli*), designed the upper storey of the entrance façade and the three grottoes of the interior.

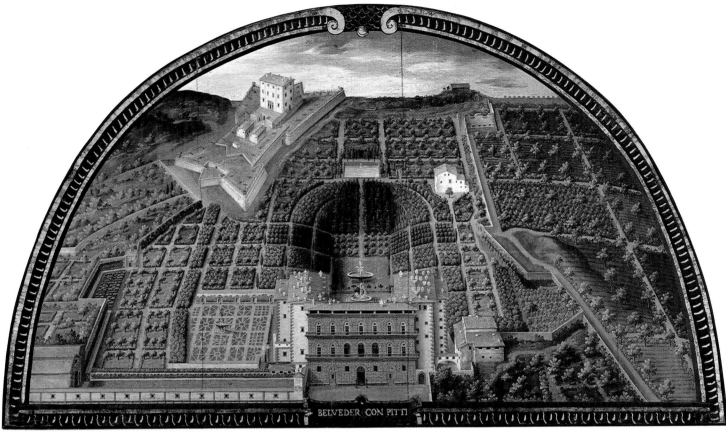

BELVEDER CON PITTI

Villas Bernardini and Corsi-Salviati

Another Tuscan garden, the Villa Bernardini at Saltocchio, which dates from about 1590, also has a grand formal axis cutting through woodland. Although the idea had already been realized at the Boboli Gardens, the *boschi* at Bernardini have an added delight: on either side of the central grass avenue are two parallel rectangles of once thriving woodland, within each of which was a sequence of unexpected little spaces.

Exceptional among Tuscan gardens, in that it is laid out on a flat site, in the Arno valley, is the Villa Corsi-Salviati at Sesto. Furthermore, the garden was made in five different periods of history. The estate, bought by Jacopo Corsi in 1502, consisted of a small Tuscan house and simple garden of grass squares for bowls. There were minor adjustments in 1593, major alterations in 1644 which established the present groundplan, and baroque additions in 1738 aimed at counteracting the flatness by giving flamboyancy to the skyline. In the 19th century a romantic landscape of lake, mound and mock castle was added. The gardens were restored in 1907, a green theatre being incorporated in the formal design.

VENICE AND GENOA

Two other great centres of power in the 16th century provide few examples of Renaissance gardens. In Venice itself virtually nothing survives. We know, though, from literary and visual evidence, of the Venetians' love of outdoor rooms with loggias, pergolas, flower-beds, dividing screens, elaborate seats and sculptures. Space was always scarce so it was largely on the city perimeter and on islands like Murano that gardens were established.

Little even remains of villa gardens in the Veneto. One of the most magnificent of these was that designed by Andrea Palladio for his friends the brothers Barbaro at Maser. The gardens of the Villa Barbaro, which were constructed during the 1560s, are described in detail in Palladio's *I Quattro Libri di Architettura*. Little remains of the original layout, with its arbours and parterres, its boundary wall topped by stone warriors and the access drive flanked by Olympic gods. Remarkably, however, the

The lunette by Giusto Utens, dating from c. 1599, *is the earliest complete view of the Boboli Gardens. It shows clearly the natural horse-shoe shape behind the* palazzo *where the plantations were later cleared for the ampitheatre.*

giardino segreto has survived. A rectangle, part lawn and part small-stone paving, is enclosed on three sides by the villa, while on the fourth a large pool reflects a semi-circular exedra ornamented with stucco statues. The *giardino segreto* of the Villa Barbaro is Roman in spirit.

One of the most famous 16th-century gardens of the Veneto, the Giardino dei Giusti at Verona, was laid out in a typically Tuscan style, with terraces, fountains and grottoes. During the 19th century the garden was redesigned but several noted visitors have left descriptions of it. Thomas Coryat writes in *Crudities* (1611) of a 'second paradise . . . beautified with many curious knots, fruits of divers sorts and two rowes of lofty cypresse trees, three and thirty in ranke'. Goethe, who visited the garden in 1786, also commented on the size of the cypresses but now only one or two of these great trees survive.

Giardino Barbarigo

One of the Veneto's most extensive gardens is the Giardino Barbarigo at Valsanzibio near Padua, laid out for the Procurator Antonio Barbarigo and traditionally dated 1669. This is now the Villa Pizzoni Ardemani and is also known as the Villa Donà dalle Rose. The huge domestic garden might be a maquette for a seemly town plan with its green streets and enclosures, its modest villas as the civic centre, and its submission to the natural amphitheatre of the Euganean Hills in which it is set. The major west-east axis leads from the hills in a series of pools to a water-gate at the lowest point, the original entrance by canal from Venice. The north-south axis, only slightly less important, links the arms of the amphitheatre with avenues which climb the hillside and is ingeniously modelled to contain the modest *casino* and exaggerate the perspective from it. The avenues were destroyed in the Second World War but have since been replanted.

Planned round these two axes and circuited with a pleached lime walk, the garden is an approximate rectangle that has within it a number of exciting enclosures. These include a maze (recently restored to its perfect square), a unique oval rabbitry (the Garena), Diana's Bath and the Fountain of the Swan.

The prosperity that Genoa enjoyed after the founding of the republic in 1528 led to a building boom, particularly with the laying out of the Strada Nuova (now Via Garibaldi) in 1550. The steepness of the hillside made the creation of large gardens impossible. Of the small urban gardens that were once numerous only a baroque example, that of the Palazzo Podesta, remains to show the use of the restricted spaces behind the *palazzi*. The largest of the 16th-century Genoese gardens belonged to the Palazzo Doria, built for the founder of the republic, Admiral Andrea Doria. The site, just outside the city walls, allowed the creation of an extensive terraced landscape from the hillside to the sea. The gardens were the setting for formal entertainments and celebrations, their focal point being a large statue of Neptune in the lower garden, near the harbour. At the end of the 16th century this stucco figure was replaced by a marble fountain of Neptune on a sea chariot surrounded by Dorian eagles. This survives on its original site but the gardens were swallowed up as the city expanded in the 19th century.

ROMAN BAROQUE

The fascination with spectacle and optical illusion that was such a marked characteristic of Roman architecture in the 17th century inevitably influenced the design of gardens. Nonetheless, the major achievements of baroque Rome were in town planning and church design, not in gardens. The vast parks that were laid out in Rome itself from the beginning of the 17th century consisted mainly of plantations. The buildings, and the formal gardens around them, were a subordinate part of the layout. This is the case, for example, at the Villa Borghese, laid out after 1605 for Cardinal Scipione Borghese. The existing gardens, overlooking the Piazza del Popolo, are only a fragment of the complex, which originally had a circumference of more than 7 km (4 miles). *Allées* intersected extensive plantings of trees, leading to statues, fountains, grottoes and lakes, but there was no overall symmetrical plan. The formal gardens, created between 1617 and 1619 around a *casino*, were of a more traditional Renaissance style. They included parterres, a *giardino segreto* and an alfresco dining room designed as a temple. Another of the great parks created in the 17th century was that of the Villa Doria-Pamphili, laid out in 1650. Here, too, the *casino* with its formal garden was a relatively minor incident in the overall design. Both of these parks were remodelled during the 19th century in the then fashionable English romantic style. When the new landscape of the Doria Pamphili had matured, the park inspired artists like Corot.

Roman baroque landscape art is not to be found at its most triumphant in the city itself but at Frascati, the old Tusculum, some 25 km (16 miles) south-east of the capital. The country villas that had been built there from the end of the Roman Republic had fallen into decay during the Middle Ages. With its rediscovery in the second half of the 16th century, the area once again became a fashionable place where it was possible to escape the heat of the Roman summer. The villas constructed there, although ingeniously varied in their detail, had several points in common. The

Despite the expense of laying on a supply of water, extravagant fountains and giochi d'acqua *were major features of the baroque gardens at Frascati, outside Rome. The water-theatre at Villa Mondragone was installed by Scipione Borghese after he bought the property in 1613.*

The terraces and staircases at the Villa Garzoni in Collodi rise spectacularly to a great cascade, whose rocks are fashioned like an elongated giant. The cascade itself parts the woods and disappears against the statue of Fame deep in the bosco *at the summit.*

slope on which they were sited falls away to the north, affording views over the *campagna* to Rome. The villas were in fact ranged as though the city exercised a powerful magnetic force. The sites had to be carved out of the steep wooded hillside and the amphitheatre that generally resulted from the excavations formed an ideal setting for elaborate water displays. Although the cost of piping water in was high, the hills having no adequate natural reserves, fountains, cascades and *giochi d'acqua* were major features. The *giardino segreto* and parterres were other common elements.

Villa Torlonia
Many of the Frascati villas have suffered from neglect and, in World War II, bomb damage. The Villa Torlonia, for example, survives as an undistinguished public park, the villa itself having been destroyed in 1944. The philosopher and philologist Annibale Caro, who rediscovered Frascati,

established a 'modest Tusculum' here in 1563, taking Cicero as his model. The magnificent cascades that brought the garden fame were installed by Scipione Borghese in 1607. Water fell through a series of basins to feed a powerful jet that played in front of a wall decorated with numerous fountains. Originally this retaining wall contained 10 niches but the number was increased to 22 after 1621. Each niche had a fountain rising from a shell-shaped basin and on the piers between the niches 24 urns spouted water. The approach to this spectacle from the villa was through a *giardino segreto* and a flower parterre, once richly adorned with statues. In a subsequent phase of work, begun in the 1680s, a long, narrow terrace was created that gave an ever-changing set of perspecives to the spectator approaching the *casino*. The water theatre at the Villa Mondragone was another commission executed for Scipione Borghese, who acquired this property in 1613.

Villa Aldobrandini
The best preserved of the baroque gardens of Frascati belongs to the Villa Aldobrandini. The main work was carried out here between 1598 and 1603, for the elderly Pope Clement VIII (Ippolito Aldobrandini). The villa occupies an imposing position overlooking the town and the *campagna* but the drama lies behind it. A semi-circular wall cut into the hill contains five niches, each housing a statue and each with a water-jet rising in front of it; in the central niche Atlas carries the globe. On the central axis behind the wall water falls down a staircase before flowing through the Aldobrandini emblem, a star, to form a veil-like shower over the figure of Atlas. Because the space behind the villa was so restricted the flower parterre was placed to one side and the *giardino segreto* on a lower terrace. In the 17th and 18th centuries one of the most famous features of the garden was the Stanza dei Venti, a garden salon with ingenious *giochi d'acqua*. The diarist John Evelyn, who visited the gardens in 1645, wrote of the *giochi d'acqua*: 'in one of these Theatres of Water, is an Atlas spouting up the streame to an incredible height, & another monster which makes a terrible roaring with an horn; but above all the representation of a storm is most naturall, with such fury of raine, wind and Thunder as one would imagine ones selfe in some extreame Tempest'.

Villa Garzoni
Although each has its own distinctive character, the gardens of Frascati form a remarkably homogeneous group. In this respect they are perhaps untypical of baroque landscape art in Italy as a whole. The influence of Rome is, however, pervasive. It is strikingly apparent, for example, in the garden of the Villa Garzoni at Collodi in Tuscany. In 1652 the Garzoni family began the transformation of a medieval fortress into a country villa. In order to take full advantage of a dramatically steep hillside the new garden was separated from the villa by a road, but it has been swung in such a way that the lower parterre can be seen from the windows. The parterre, furnished with twin circular pools and family heraldry in box, is outlined with double scalloped hedges. From this level steps and staircases

on the main axis link three promenade terraces, ascending spectacularly to a great cascade. This surges out of the woods, in which stands, as the culminating point, a statue of Fame. The cascade, whose rocks are fashioned in the form of a giant, widens as it ascends, giving an impression of elongation when seen from above and abruptness when seen from below. On the uppermost terrace there is a charming garden theatre and, beside the statue of Fame, an 18th-century bath-house with separate compartments for men and women.

Villa Marlia

Another fine baroque garden in Tuscany is the Villa Marlia at Lucca. From 1806 to 1814 this was the summer residence of Elisa Baciocchi, Napoleon's sister, who enlarged the garden laid out by the Orsetti family in the late 17th century. A series of open-air rooms, apparently carved out of the woods and walled by hedges of clipped yew, lies to the east of a large green esplanade for exercising horses that extends in front of the villa. Among the most beautiful and evocative of these is a well-preserved open-air theatre. Terracotta statues of Columbine, Harlequin and Pulcinella silently wait for the auditorium to fill.

The calm of Villa Marlia's green enclosures, especially its theatre and water-garden, is perhaps less typically baroque than the dramatic features linking formal areas to the natural landscape that are to be found in many other Italian gardens. At the Villa Cetinale near Siena, for example, a powerful single axis extends from a colossus of Hercules in front of the house through lessening degrees of formality to an avenue rising on a wooded slope, eventually culminating at a hermitage on the skyline. At the Villa Crivelli in Lombardy the Scala del Gigante, an avenue of cypresses, marches across the landscape until it fades into distant woodland. The link between the formal garden and the natural landscape at the Villa Cicogna in Piedmont is one of the finest water-staircases in Italy.

Isola Bella

The best-known, and the most fantastic, example of the baroque marriage of the contrived and natural is Isola Bella. It is one

Although the architectural form has been blurred by the foliage of trees, Isola Bella on Lake Maggiore still seems like some fantastic galleon drifting across the lake against a backdrop of blue mountains. The baroque villa lies at water level and to the east of it a series of terraces rises to a pyramid (left) bristling with sculpture.

of a group of three small islands on Lake Maggiore that all enjoy magnificent views of distant snow-clad mountains. Isola Madre nearby was dramatically landscaped in the mid-16th century, possibly encouraging the design of Isola Bella itself. The transformation of this rocky island into a flowered and leafy galleon apparently drifting across the lake was begun for Count Carlo Borromeo in about 1630 and completed after his death in 1670. The villa lies at water level on the western end. East of it rise ten terraces,

The main feature of the park at La Reggia, Caserta, is the cascade and canal, lying on the central axis of the grandiose palace built for Charles III. The cascade begins more than 3 km (2 miles) from the palace.

The Villa Pisani at Strà has one of the best preserved gardens along the Brenta canal in the Veneto. Following Venetian practice, the gardens were laid out behind the house, a long canal forming the central vista.

bristling with sculpture, that culminate in a flat-topped pyramid. The fullness of the planting as it is now softens the rigorous geometry imposed on the natural form but adds enchantment to one of the loveliest spots in all Italy. Lake Como, too, had splendid baroque gardens, such as those of the Villa d'Este and the Villa Carlotta, but in these northern lakes nothing matches the poetic originality of Isola Bella.

THE DECLINE

In the late 17th century Italian garden design began to lose its creative energy. There is very little from the 18th and 19th centuries in any way comparable in originality with Italy's Renaissance and baroque masterpieces. The decline coincided with the rise as a dominant influence throughout Europe of the French formal garden perfected by Le Nôtre. However, there were relatively few imitations in Italy of this grandiose transformation of a formality deeply rooted in the Italian tradition. The most perfectly preserved example is found at the Villa Crivelli Sormani-Verri, Castellazzo, in Lombardy. This was laid out by a Frenchman, Jean Gianda, early in the 18th century on the site of a garden in the grand Italian manner. Although modest in scale, this is recognizably French in character, with elaborate parterres in front of the villa's main façade, clipped trees and such classical French elements as *cabinets* of trimmed hedges.

A French-inspired garden on a truly monumental scale was that designed in the mid-18th century by Luigi Vanvitelli for Charles III, Spanish King of Naples. The financial resources were inadequate to complete the vast project that was begun at La Reggia, Caserta. The main feature, a cascade and canal, even though not finished as planned, gives some idea of Vanvitelli's extraordinarily ambitious scheme. While the sheer extent of the palace and gardens is impressive the characteristic Italian harmony of proportions is lacking.

The transformation of the Villa Pisani at Strà in the Veneto by Napoleon's Italian Viceroy, Eugène de Beauharnais, has left another example of French influence. The gardens of the impressive villa fronting a long curve of the Brenta canal were begun in 1735 by Girolamo Frigimelica for the Doge of Venice, Alvise Pisani. Some elements survive of the original gardens, laid out according to Venetian tradition behind the house. These include a maze, gazebo and fine wrought-iron *grilles*. The *trompe-l'oeil* planting of the park is, however, distinctly French in character.

The most dismal aspect of the 19th century is not simply the feebleness of the *giardino inglese*, a fashionable though pathetically pale imitation of the English landscape garden, but the neglect of many major gardens of earlier periods. It is fortunate that in this century the restoration of some of these has allowed a fuller appreciation of one of the richest and most important garden traditions of Europe.

THE NETHERLANDS

This version of Bruegel's 'Spring' by Abel Grimmer conveys the spirit of Dutch Mannerist gardens of the 16th century, medieval in structure, elaborate in ornamentation.

Throughout northern Europe the Dutch garden has played a significant role in the development of landscape architecture. This is particularly true of the Dutch Renaissance garden, which developed during the 16th century and was anticipated in the ideal and emblematic garden described by the Dutch humanist scholar Erasmus in *The Godly Feast*, published in 1522. Although in large part deriving its composition from the Italian humanist garden, it was imbued with an aura of Christian piety. The square pleasure garden was enclosed on three sides by a gallery supported by marbled pillars which housed a library and an aviary. The gallery's frescoed walls portrayed in *trompe-l'oeil* a permanent microcosm of the animal and plant world. A 'fountain to refresh and cleanse the soul', whose marble channels divided the garden in half, was surrounded by separate beds of choice and fragrant plants, each accompanied by a motto. Beyond the gallery lay a kitchen garden with rare herbs, flanked on one side by a turf meadow and on the other by an orchard containing 'many exotic trees' and beehives.

Hans Vredeman de Vries
By the end of the 16th century such Erasmian components as galleries, fountains and parterres for rare plants were incorporated into the garden designs of

Hans Vredeman de Vries, the first Netherlander to conceive of the garden as an art form. The Dutch Mannerist garden, of which he was the most influential exponent through the publication in 1583 of a garden pattern book (*Hortorum viridariorumque elegantes et multiplicis formae*), remained medieval in structure although it included elaborate Flemish Mannerist ornament. His gardens are characterized by a series of separate trellised or galleried plots adorned with highly intricate parterres, topiary, arbours and fountains, the designs of which were a personal interpretation of the classical orders. Of particular significance to the development of European gardens was his use of *parterres de pièces coupées*, also known as parterres of cutwork, in which the pieces of the design are flowerbeds intended for the display of individual rare and exotic plants. De Vries had an international reputation, his commissions including designs for gardens and fountains for the Duke of Braunschweig at Wolfenbüttel and for Emperor Rudolf II in Prague, and garden pavilions and *trompe-l'oeil* panels of garden vistas in Antwerp and Hamburg. As intricate as his strapwork designs, the de Vriesian parterres were employed throughout northern Europe during the 17th century, notably in the Hortus Palatinus in Heidelberg and, in a modified form, at the Trianon de Porcelaine at Versailles. His gardens are reflected in designs in numerous works, including Crispijn van de Passe's *Hortus Floridus* of 1614.

Plant introductions

Such was the renown of Dutch horticulture in the 17th century that there was a demand throughout Europe for skilled gardeners, plants and horticultural treatises from the Netherlands. The establishment of the Leiden University botanic garden in 1587 and the appointment of Carolus Clusius (also known as Charles de L'Ecluse) as its director in 1594 had given a great impetus to the study of medical and ornamental plants. Clusius was instrumental in introducing into cultivation many plants from the eastern Mediterranean, Spain, Portugal, Austria and Hungary. His introduction included tulips, of which the cultivation led to a brief period of feverish speculation – tulipomania – between 1634 and 1637. In the de Vriesian parterres of 17th-century gardens the rare and exotic introductions were not planted out in groups but admired as single specimens. In the early part of the century these small, variously shaped beds, divided by paths and sparsely planted with floral treasures, were central to the house, as portrayed by van der Passe, but later they were set in separate enclosures.

THE DUTCH CLASSICAL GARDEN

The aspirations of the new Dutch republic, freed from Spanish domination in the early 17th century, were symbolized in the development of an indigenous classical style that in garden design eclipsed de Vriesian Mannerism. The origins of this style lay in the principles of symmetry and harmonious proportion which, through the writings of the 15th-century humanist scholar Alberti, had greatly influenced the development of

The Leiden Botanic Garden (above), founded in 1587 as a physic garden and re-planned and planted by Clusius as a true botanic garden from 1594, has a long record of distributing newly introduced plants to other gardens.

Through his introductions and botanical studies Clusius helped to lay the foundations of the Dutch bulb industry. The displays at De Keukenhof (right) near Lisse demonstrate the achievements of the industry today.

garden design in Italy. The influence of these principles in the Netherlands can be seen in a plan, dating from about 1620, of the Buitenhof of Prince Maurits in The Hague. Maurits, Prince of Orange and Stadholder of the republic, was a renowned military scientist who had already applied classical principles to the design of army camps and fortifications; he may himself have executed the plan of Buitenhof. In this case an abstract design of circles within squares is translated into a walled rectangle or double square, each square containing a circular *berceau*, an elaborate trellis on which plants were trained. The two *berceaux* were linked to one another by a rectangular pavilion containing *trompe-l'oeil* frescoes. The symmetry of the design was underlined by the arrangement of eight arbours, four square and four circular, outside the *berceaux*. The *parterres de broderie* within the *berceaux* were some of the first examples of this elaborate kind of decoration in the Netherlands.

An interpretation of classical principles that reflected the real character of the country is to be found in Dutch canal gardens. In these the influence of France and Italy was tempered by conditions peculiar to the Netherlands. The rectilinear outline contained by water was closely related to the medieval system of land distribution in low-lying marshlands, where regularly spaced, long, narrow strips were separated by indispensable drainage canals. An enclosure of trees and hedges was an essential shield for the garden's vegetation in a landscape exposed to strong winds. The flatness of the terrain made the creation of terraces and cascades difficult and, in any case, the attitudes of the ruling bourgeoisie did not favour monumental grandiose layouts. Even the princely gardens of the provincial governers, the Stadholders, were modest in scale. The inspiration of Virgil's *Georgics* may be detected in the utilitarian and horticultural areas of these gardens, though what mattered more was the Calvinist ethic of a man's duty to employ the products of nature provided by the Maker. Furthermore, there were rapid advances in Dutch horticultural science, which were quickly taken up by the owners of estates. The 17th-century vogue for country-house poems, moralistically didactic and reflecting

the Erasmian spirit in the way the products of nature are given an emblematic value, give an insight into the status of the garden in this period.

The dilettante architect and landscape gardener Prince Frederik Hendrik began rebuilding the castle of Honselaarsdijk and laying out its gardens in 1621. In its proportions and symmetry Honselaarsdijk was the prototype of the Dutch classical canal garden.

Honselaarsdijk

The prototype of the Dutch classical canal garden, and one which served as a model throughout the 17th century, was Honselaarsdijk, south of the Hague. In 1621, Prince Frederik Hendrik, who succeeded his brother Maurits as Stadholder in 1625, began rebuilding the castle and laying out the gardens, which together formed an architectural unit. Within a rectangular plan enclosed by canals and trees, the moated castle and gardens were aligned on a central axis, along which were ranged three compartments, consisting of parterres, circular hedged walks and orchards. An Italianate semicircular piazza and grand avenue flanked by trees and canals extended this axis beyond the palace's entrance. The plan's proportional relationship of width to length was 3:4, reflecting ideas on symmetry and harmonious proportion derived from Alberti. Subsequent developments included

the creation of two parterres by the French designer André Mollet in about 1633 and, by 1680, under William and Mary, further changes that gave the layout a more baroque allure. The gardens were destroyed in 1815.

Hofwijck

At Hofwijck, near The Hague, the Dutch diplomat-poet Constantijn Huygens created a country house and gardens that were a highly personal interpretation of classical and Calvinist ideals. The symmetrical and elongated form of the gardens was intended to correspond to the proportions of the Vitruvian human figure, whose perfection of form reflected God's creation. In the layout, executed between 1639 and 1642 with the collaboration of the architect Jacob van Campen, the moated villa represented

the head, an orchard flanked by avenues represented the chest and arms and for the legs and knees there was an elongated wooded area with a mount in the centre. This anthropomorphic plan symbolized in moralistic terms the path of redemption, with a progression from the terrestrial world of the woods, through the perfect world of the Edenic orchard, to the contemplation of God in the villa. The informal planting of trees within the rectangular framework, intersected and surrounded by canals, was one of the earliest examples in the Netherlands of a less rigid formality.

Italianate classical influences were developed in less idiosyncratic gardens than Hofwijck by van Campen and other architects. These included Pieter Post and Philips Vingboons, both of whom published their plans for country houses and their gardens. Huis ten Bosch, which was laid out by Pieter Post for Frederik Hendrik in 1647, recalls the Villa d'Este at Tivoli. One of the most remarkable Dutch classical gardens was that created at Vrijburg Palace,

At Huis ten Bosch the Dutch architect and painter Pieter Post designed the most Italianate of all the gardens created by Prince Frederik Hendrik. This view by Jan van der Heyden shows it about 20 years after 1647, when it was laid out to a unified conception of sober simplicity.

Mauritsstad (Recife) in Brazil by Johan Maurits of Nassau-Siegen while he was serving as Governor-General of the colony from 1637 to 1644. Maurits incorporated within a unified plan botanical and zoological gardens, pleasure and kitchen gardens.

Wooded parks

Quite different in character to these classical gardens were the wooded parks laid out by Johan Maurits between 1647 and 1678 at Cleves, near the Dutch border, in Germany. At the time he was serving as Stadholder to the Elector of Brandenburg. Five unique parks, evoking sacred landscapes and displaying a 'wild regularitie', were linked to each other and to the city by a network of avenues. Baroque in concept and Mannerist in detail, each had a distinctive character bearing the personal stamp of Johan Maurits. The New Deer Park, for example, laid out on a wooded hillside, contained a series of terraces, forming an amphitheatre, with ponds, statues, and a Palladian semicircular gallery designed by van Campen. The axis was extended into the surrounding countryside by a canal flanked by lime trees. The various trophies erected throughout as focal points were a unique feature of these parks. In emulation of the Romans, Johan Maurits placed his tomb along a road at Bergental, which, as the last of the parks, was laid out between 1670 and 1678, and there he spent his final days in a hermitage.

THE FRANCO-DUTCH GARDEN

The changes made at Honselaarsdijk shortly after the marriage of William and Mary in 1677 reflect the growing influence of French baroque gardens. This influence did not, however, result in the eclipse of the Dutch classical garden but rather in an adaptation to it of the dominant central axis and ornamental flourish of the French baroque garden.

The development of the Franco-Dutch style, the term by which this hybrid is described, owed much to the collaboration of the architect Jacob Roman and the French Huguenot artist and designer Daniel Marot in gardens at de Voorst, Zeist and Het Loo. In these examples, the sober, flat rigidity of Roman's classical plans was

The great gardens at Het Loo, created by William and Mary between 1686 and 1695, have recently undergone a major restoration. The labyrinthine tunnels, clothed in hornbeam, contained in the Queen's garden hark back to the Mannerist designs of Hans Vredeman de Vries.

enlivened by Marot's ebullient baroque ornament. The gardens at Het Loo, Apeldoorn, represent the ultimate expression of William and Mary's gardening taste in the Netherlands.

Het Loo

As the most lavish of Dutch gardens, Het Loo was renowned for its ornamentation and, in particular, for its fountains and cascades. According to a description published in 1699 by an English visitor, Walter Harris: 'The Gardens are most Sumptuous and Magnificent, adorned with great variety of most noble *Fountains*, *Cascades*, *Parterres*, *Gravel Walks*, and *Green Walks*, *Groves*, *Statues*, *Urns*, *Paintings*, and pleasant Prospects into the Country ... a work of wonderful *Magnificence*, most worthy of so *Great* a *Monarch*; a Work of prodigious expence, infinite variety, and curiosity.'

With its central axis aligned on the palace, the enclosed Great Garden was divided by a cross-walk, flanked by canals

and oaks, into a terraced Lower Garden and a more distant Upper Garden. The Lower Garden contained eight square parterres and in the centre of the garden was the Venus Fountain, situated on the junction of the main axis and a cross-walk that divided the parterres into two sets of four. At each end of this cross-walk were cascades and on either side of the Venus Fountain were fountains depicting the celestial and terrestrial globes. The Upper Garden, which was begun in 1692, terminated in a sweep of colonnades; before being moved to this position they had connected the house with its wings. The main feature of the Upper Garden was the King's Fountain, set in a large octagonal basin, with a jet spouting water to a height of 13m (43 ft). The King's and Queen's gardens lay under the respective royal apartments on either side of the building, the Queen's garden being notable for its labyrinthine hornbeam tunnels.

Instead of *bosquets* or woods, a series of intimate *giardini segreti* was laid out around

At Het Loo the Lower Garden is divided up into eight square parterres. The Venus Fountain is at the centre of a cross-walk which terminates at either end in cascades. Along the cross-walk are two fountains, that of the celestial globe, shown here, and that of the terrestrial globe.

the Great Garden, including orangeries, mazes and kitchen gardens. In the park, beyond the Upper Garden on the east side, was an aviary, the Grove of Saturn (with six radiating avenues), nurseries and many water features. Most of these features, as well as the Lower and Upper Gardens as laid out in the time of William and Mary, were lost when the park was landscaped by Louis Napoleon in 1807. In recent years the gardens have been magnificently restored and were opened as a museum in 1984.

Although Het Loo was unique in its magnificence, its components could be found in many other gardens of the late 17th and early 18th centuries. Renaissance vestiges such as geometrical forms of topiary, *berceaux*, mazes, and trellis arbours were combined with *parterres de broderie* and Italo-Franco fountains and sculptures, while deer-parks, menageries and aviaries were incorporated in the parks. Tea pavilions situated along moats or canals were common features, as were orangeries.

As the most lavish of Dutch gardens, Het Loo was renowned for its ornamentation and, in particular, its fountains and cascades. A contemporary account describes over 50 types of waterworks.

Zorgvliet

By the end of the 18th century every country house of note displayed orange trees and other exotic plants in tubs, which were placed around circular or oval terraced basins in separate enclosures. The orangery was necessary to provide protection for plants during winter. One of the most elaborate was at Zorgvliet outside The Hague, a property acquired by Hans Willem Bentinck, who was created Earl of Portland and became superintendent of William and Mary's gardens in the Netherlands and England in 1689. The monumental semicircular orangery at Zorgvliet, built in about 1675, terminates the main axis leading from the modest villa, which had been the residence of a popular Dutch poet and statesman, Jacob Cats. Zorgvliet is interesting in that Bentinck retained two dominant Mannerist features of Cats's garden – a Mount Parnassus and a circular maze with a mount, both of which were surrounded by terraced walls. On the advice of Johan Maurits, he extended the gardens to include a meandering stream and dunes, whose natural beauties were considered an essential part of the geometric plan. Adornments of the garden included extravagant Italianate grottoes and cascades, *treillage* arbours and portals, and

elongated *parterres de broderie*, but the layout lacked cohesion.

Rosendael and Petersburg

The Franco-Dutch garden spread quickly to other European countries, particularly England, Germany and Russia. In marked contrast to the Franco-Dutch garden, however, was Rosendael, near Arnhem, with a wooded layout on a hilly site recalling Johan Maurits's Italianate parks at Cleves. Also different in conception were the gardens of the wealthy bourgeoisie laid out along the Vecht River in the province of Utrecht. The intimacy, charm and playful nature of their layout anticipated the rococo. Many simulated stage settings, with walls of yew framing house and garden. Nearly all had tea pavilions on the riverside. A typical example was Petersburg (often visited by Peter the Great of Russia when he was in the Netherlands), which was created in 1717 to a design by Simon Schijnvoet. A series of island rooms contained aviaries, orangeries with Russian bath-houses, ponds and ornate fountains, statues and numerous pavilions.

ART OR NATURE?

A change in attitude towards the relationship between art and nature is reflected in garden design in the early 18th century, particularly in gardens laid out near Haarlem by members of the Amsterdam bourgeoisie. In these Régence layouts, created from about 1720, the house was subordinate to the garden, of which the main structure of woods engulfed the building and nearly eclipsed the parterres. Instead of a single static viewpoint, there were transverse or radial avenues piercing the woods and terminating in a variety of scenic focal points in the garden. Idealized and self-contained landscapes were created within the enclosed confines of the garden, excluding any direct connection with the surrounding countryside. *Allées*, still ponds, grass parterres and other expanses of lawn were typical features. Pieter de la Court van der Voort, the first garden theorist of the Netherlands, expressed the ideals of the Régence garden in a work first published in 1737 which gave advice on the laying out of grounds for small country houses.

Waterland

A notable and early example of these gardens, dating from about 1720, is Waterland near Haarlem. The emphasis was, typically, on the natural rather than the artificial, with trees as the principal structural element. The design, conceived as a labyrinth, was laid out on an irregular piece of ground of about 12 hectares (30 acres). The main feature was a large pond, from which five avenues radiated through woods to terminate at a variety of pictorial elements. These included an intimate green room with a triumphal arch, a Turkish tent, and a camera obscura projecting moving pictures of boats on a nearby lake. The presence of these last two features was quite unprecedented at the time, one evoking distant lands and the other representing science in the service of nature.

Duin-en-Berg

The earliest example of an asymmetrical plan within a geometric framework was Duin-en-Berg, laid out about 1730 along the dunes to the north of Haarlem. Dense woods were pierced by winding walks and rectilinear *allées*, intersecting at oblique angles. There were statues, *bassins*, mounts and mazes, but also, skilfully integrated against the backdrop of woods, meadows and orchards to combine the useful with the beautiful.

The recently restored shell gallery at Rosendael was probably designed by Daniel Marot, a French Huguenot, who became the principal exponent of the Franco-Dutch style.

Beeckestijn

The intricate artificiality of the rococo gardens designed in about 1730 by Daniel Marot was the antithesis of the natural simplicity of the Dutch Régence woodland gardens. A synthesis of these two styles is evident after 1750 in such early Dutch landscape gardens as Beeckestijn in Velsen. A plan of 1772 by J.G. Michael, the first landscape architect of the Netherlands, reveals the influence of Stephen Switzer and Batty Langley, the English writers on gardening, who were both advocates of a more natural style. The formal layout was retained at Beeckestijn but with sinuous paths between rigid avenues of trees, meandering walks through an ordered group of oaks, and serpentine paths around flowering shrubs on a lawn. An extension of the garden on the west was a more daring stroke, the centre-piece, a cornfield, being framed by trees and paths set in undulating patterns and by a meandering brook. Evocative buildings included a Gothic temple and a hermitage.

An elaborate topiary twist suggests an early phase in the history of the castle gardens at Twickel. Many changes of taste have been registered here since the transformation of the early 17th-century Renaissance garden.

Twickel

By the end of the 18th century the French picturesque garden had become a major influence. The enclosed landscapes that this inspired included winding walks, artificial hillocks in woods, meandering streams, irregular lakes, serpentine canals, wheatfields and orchards, cattle and sheep. These elements served as frameworks for scenes evoking different times and places and moral sentiments. Arcadian presentiments of death or pastoral gaiety were associated with various architectural forms, the pattern book of G. van Laar providing examples in *anglo-chinois* taste with appropriate settings. At Twickel, in Delden, a garden expressing this taste was created in about 1790. Earlier in the century the Renaissance square garden had been developed into a baroque rectangle. To accommodate the picturesque *anglo-chinois* garden, the canal around the rectangular framework was enlarged to form a lake and sinuous waterways. These contained a 'French wood' with a hermitage in a tree, an 'English park', and remnants of the Renaissance orchard. Outside lay a deer-park, a mount and buildings including a gardener's cottage, a chapel, and, along the lake, a fisherman's hut.

THE ROMANTIC LANDSCAPE PARK

The later transformations at Twickel reflect changes of taste in the 19th century. In about 1830 Jan David Zocher the younger, the grandson of J.B. Michael and the most eminent Dutch landscape architect of the century, created a romantic landscape park there. In his simplification, the emphasis shifted from the picturesque architectural elements, of which nearly all were removed, to water and trees. The style developed by Zocher, who skilfully adapted his designs to each individual site, drew on English landscape designs by Brown and Repton but were modified by French and German interpretations of the landscape park.

The subsequent landscaping at Twickel by Eduard Petzold was in the picturesque manner that Prince Pückler-Muskau had developed in Germany. Another addition was formal parterres laid out by the French landscape architect Edouard André, who, in 1886, at Weldam Castle, carried out the first reconstruction of a 17th-century Dutch garden.

Vondelpark

During the 19th century, in the Netherlands as in other European countries, there was a growing awareness of the need for public open spaces. Among the earliest to be created were 'public walks' laid out on the great dikes of towns such as Haarlem, Breda and Utrecht. Vondelpark in Amsterdam, designed by J.D. Zocher the younger and his son L.P. Zocher, was the first true public park in the Netherlands and is still the city's largest. It was partially laid out by private enterprise in 1865 and was completed in 1877. The narrow strip of marshland, with watercourses intersecting and surrounding it, was planted with groups of trees to create unexpected vistas. Because of the high water-table little remains of Zocher's planting except for several oaks and willows, and subsequent developments have modified the landscaping.

FRANCE

A view of about 1685 by P.D. Martin showing the gargantuan Orangerie at Versailles, below which lies the Pièce d'Eau des Suisses.

In the European tradition the French grand manner represents garden design at its most ambitious. Monumental scale, rigorous order, richness of detail and splendour are the hallmarks of a style that was widely imitated in the courts of Europe but never more magnificently realized than in the gardens created in France during the reign of Louis XIV. Many of these gardens have been lost but the distinctive French character of the surviving and re-created examples can be appreciated even when only the main lines remain to convey the grandeur of their conception.

The story of French gardens is not, however, encompassed in the Golden Age of the Sun King. The gardens made during the evolution of the grand manner, in which the theory and practice of Italian Renaissance garden design was a vital stimulus, are in themselves of considerable interest, though for our understanding of them we must rely almost entirely on visual and documentary records; and the gardens of the 18th and 19th centuries, whether created in reaction to the grandiose schemes of the mature baroque or whether in response to the romantic spirit that was first mani-

fested in England, bear the clear imprint of the national genius.

RENAISSANCE GARDENS

Although French rulers of Naples and Sicily had direct experience of Islamic and Italian gardens as early as the 13th century, there is little evidence of change in the static character of medieval French gardens until well into the 15th century. Then, however, the transformation of the medieval pattern was largely due to Italian influence. During this century a number of Frenchmen engaged in campaigns waged in pursuit of French claims to Naples and, somewhat later, Milan, had an opportunity to see Italian gardens. They were especially impressed by the cultivation of exotic fruits such as oranges and lemons and by the novelty of Italian Renaissance ornament.

Gaillon

When, in 1495, Charles VIII returned from pressing his claim to Naples, he brought back with him a number of Italian artists and craftsmen with an expertise in gardening matters, including a Neapolitan priest, Pacello da Mercogliano. Charles's chief residence was Amboise and it is possible that Pacello da Mercogliano helped in the design of the garden there. More certain is the role he played at Blois and Gaillon. At the latter he advised Georges d'Amboise, Archbishop of Rouen and minister of Louis XII, on the layout of a garden that acquired considerable celebrity. An upper garden was made between 1502 and 1509 with a gallery on one side giving views over the Seine. There were square beds planted with flowers, fruit trees, or box and rosemary cut into figures. One square showed the arms of France delineated in small plants while another was in the form of a labyrinth. A prominent feature on this terrace was a wooden pavilion sheltering a marble fountain that had been brought from Italy. Similar pavilions and fountains were to be found at Amboise and Blois. A curious and unique feature at Gaillon was Le Lidieu, a private retreat in the park, with a chapel, a house and a garden. Further work was carried out in this area after 1550 by Cardinal de Bourbon, with the construction of a canal and rock hermitage and the building of a sumptuous *casino*, the Maison Blanche. The gardens were redesigned by Le Nôtre and only the terraced site of the upper garden survives.

Blois

At Blois, which was adopted as a royal residence by Louis XII and Anne de Bretagne, Pacello da Mercogliano had charge of the main garden until his death in 1534. Although the site gave fine views to the south over the Loire, the large garden, laid out between 1499 and 1515 on two levels, was located west of the château. The level area of the lower garden, which was supported by high walls and surrounded by a wooden gallery, was divided into ten rectangular compartments laid out in geometric patterns. In contrast to the symmetry of this scheme, the approach to the main axis from the château was first by a bridge across a moat, then by a dog-legged turn. Contemporary accounts mention vegetables and fruits, including oranges and lemons grown in tubs. In winter these were kept in a wooden shed 'which protects them from snow and malicious winds'. This shelter was possibly the first of the many orangeries that were to be built in France.

The major influence exercised by Italy was not, however, in the introduction of exotic fruits and Renaissance ornament; Italy led the way in extracting from the classical past models and theory for the construction of buildings and gardens. In particular, the Vitruvian theory, reformulated by Alberti, of beauty as a harmony of all the parts resulted in an architectural approach to garden design. In France a shift towards such an approach is clearly seen early in the 16th century. At Bury, for example, where the château and garden were probably constructed between 1511 and 1524, the garden was placed some 5 m (16 ft) below the level of the main rooms as the climax of an axial approach through a *cour d'honneur* and the main entrance to the principal building.

Fontainebleau

Under François I numerous Italian artists and craftsmen worked in France, particularly at the king's favourite residence, Fontainebleau. The appeal of this site, which takes its name from a spring of fresh water that gave rise to the town, lay in its setting, surrounded by a picturesque forest strewn with giant boulders. There had been a hunting lodge there since the 12th century, and possibly even earlier. The main form of the grounds as laid out for François I between 1528 and 1547 is still recognizable, despite many changes of detail. He made the causeway that leads from the forest to the château and, west of this, the trapezoid lake, which forms the focus of the Cour de La Fontaine, the centre of his additions to the château. East of the causeway he made the Grand Jardin, approximately square but divided into two unequal parts by a canal, while north of the palace was a private garden, the Jardin de Diane, with access from the royal apartments. The Grotte des Pins, which takes its name from the Jardin des Pins, an area west of the lake planted with pines by François I, is one of the earliest examples of an architectural grotto in France. It may have been designed by Primaticcio, an Italian in the service of François. The three-arched façade with crude giants emerging from the rock still survives.

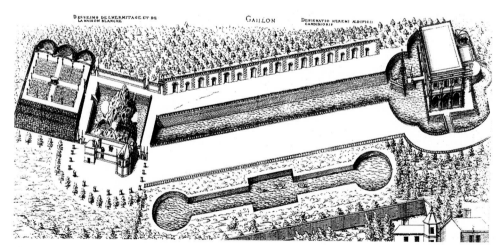

The gardens at Gaillon were among the most celebrated of the French Renaissance. A Neapolitan priest, Pacello da Mercogliano, who came to France in 1495 with Charles VIII, advised on the design executed for Cardinal Georges d'Amboise.

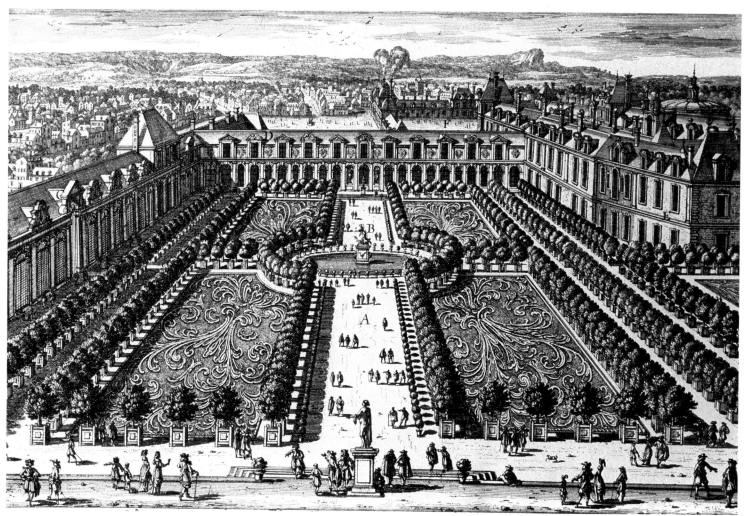

Since being transformed into a major royal residence by François I, there have been many changes at Fontainebleau. This view engraved by Perelle shows the Jardin de Diane, redesigned by Le Nôtre in 1645, and to the north the Orangery of 1647.

Ancy-le-Franc

Partly because of the allowances made for the nature of the site and for the buildings that already existed, Fontainebleau was not in the time of François I a totally harmonious marriage of architecture and garden. A much more tightly integrated layout, though on a smaller scale, was at Ancy-le-Franc in Burgundy. This was designed by Sebastiano Serlio, one of the Italians invited to France by François I, but the work was completed by another architect, probably French. Château, gardens and *bosquets* were held within a rectangular plan very much on the Italian model of villas such as the Medici villa at Castello. An unprecedented feature at Ancy-le-Franc was a raised terrace forming a promenade with a view of the gardens.

Serlio had little opportunity in France to

At Fontainebleau, surrounded by a picturesque forest, François I was able to indulge his passion for hunting. The main lines of the grounds, including the lake, though changed in detail, are still recognizably those formed under François between 1528 and 1547.

practise as a garden designer but he had considerable influence through his treatise *Tutte l'opere d'architettura*, published in four books between 1537 and 1547. The fourth book contained the first designs for ornamental parterres to be printed in France, although the practice of laying them out existed long before this date.

Anet

Ancy-le-Franc was unmistakably Italian in character but another garden, also begun in the 1540s, shows an individual synthesis of the Italian Renaissance and native French traditions. This was Anet, one of the most celebrated of French Renaissance châteaux, designed by Philibert de L'Orme for Diane de Poitiers, Duchesse de Valentinois. As at Bury (though at Anet the scale was grander) the main garden was the climax of an axial

Philibert de L'Orme, architecte du roi, *designed the château and gardens for Diane de Poitiers at Anet, synthesizing the Italian Renaissance and native traditions in an individual style. Little survives of the 16th-century arrangement, which was superseded in the 1680s by a much vaster layout designed by Le Nôtre.*

approach that passed through the entrance, *cour d'honneur* and château. From a terrace, spectators looked down on compartments laid out with heraldic designs representing Diane de Poitiers' ancestry and royal connections. The garden was enclosed on the remaining three sides by stone galleries, with pavilions in the north-east and north-west corners. Between them a room for bathing and entertaining opened into a crescent-shaped basin formed from the castle moats. The site was marshy and de L'Orme showed considerable ingenuity in the pioneering way he used water ornamentally in basins and canals while providing an adequate drainage system. In imposing a symmetrical layout on a site encumbered with old buildings de L'Orme established the architect's responsibility for laying out grounds.

Chenonceaux

De L'Orme also worked for Diane de Poitiers at Chenonceaux, a romantically sited château standing in the River Cher with gardens bordering the water on either side of the forecourt. The massive terrace to the east constructed between 1551 and 1555 enclosed an extensive level area divided into regular beds and planted with fruit trees, vegetables and flowers. A circular fountain was added when Catherine de Medici took possession in 1560 and she also had a large garden made on the south bank of the river. The château was restored in the 19th century and the gardens on the north bank of the Cher are at present laid out in a modern interpretation of the French classical style, with *broderies*, flowers, standard hibiscus and clipped box.

The influence of Catherine de Medici

Catherine de Medici, wife of Henri II, mother of François II and Charles IX and regent during the latter's minority, had a passion for building, on which she spent extravagantly despite the almost continuous civil wars that troubled France. For her, gardens were important in themselves and as venues for diplomacy and elaborate festive occasions. The gardens of her most far-reaching enterprise, the Tuileries, were, for example, the setting for a lavish entertainment given to the Polish ambassadors in 1573, when they came to present the crown of Poland to the future Henri III.

Although much of the work done for Catherine de Medici has been lost or obscured by subsequent modifications, as at the Tuileries, she left her mark on a number of gardens. At Fontainebleau, for instance, the private garden north of the palace – formerly the Jardin de Diane but in the time of Catherine called the Jardin de la Reine – was transformed between 1560 and 1563 with the construction of a carved and painted free-standing gallery by a team of artists under Primaticcio. At Fontainebleau, too, a retreat with dairy for private entertainment, the Mi-Voie, was created in the park.

The Tuileries

The Tuileries, now one of the principal promenades of Paris, were created by Catherine de Medici between 1564 and

Philibert de L'Orme also worked for Diane de Poitiers at Chenonceaux, in its setting astride the River Cher one of the most romantic of French Renaissance châteaux. Subsequent work, including an elaborate rock fountain, was carried out for Catherine de Medici, who took possession in 1560.

1572. The site, which was formerly used for manufacturing bricks and tiles, had been acquired by François I to build a palace, a project delayed until Catherine de Medici embarked upon it. Although she left the palace incomplete, she used the gardens, which, until 1664, were separated from it by a wall and public road. The layout of the *allées*, dividing the area into rectangular compartments, persists. However, in Catherine's day the regularity of the layout was offset by considerable variety in the planting of the rectangles, some with fruit trees or groves in quincunx, others containing features such as a labyrinth and a giant sun-dial. Somewhere, probably attached to a building, there was a ceramic grotto by Bernard Palissy, the French potter and writer. The compartments nearest the palace were laid out with dwarf shrubs and flowers in ornamental designs and surrounded, in the customary way, by a low fence of trellis, with arbours at each corner. Beyond these, the three main *allées*, running east-west, were planted with fir, elm, and sycamore respectively.

The planting was supervised by Bernardo Carnessecchi; the chief gardener was Pierre Le Nôtre, a member of a gardening dynasty that in the reign of Louis XIV was to produce a designer of real genius, André Le Nôtre. Indeed, between 1666 and 1671 André transformed the garden, which had already been remade for Henri IV between 1594 and 1609. His monumental scheme, with the Grande Terrasse along the river, the wide central *allée* and an avenue extending in the direction of Saint-Germain-en-Laye, forms the basis of the main axis of modern Paris, stretching from the Louvre to the Arc de Triomphe in the Place de l'Etoile. The palace itself was burnt down during the Commune of 1871.

Saint-Germain-en-Laye

The fountains and waterworks of late 16th-century Italian gardens such as those of the Villa d'Este at Tivoli and Villa Lante were much admired by French travellers. The dramatic terrace site of the Château-Neuf at Saint-Germain-en-Laye, overlooking the Seine west of Paris, was exploited for waterworks on the model of those at Pratolino. The project had been begun for Henri II by Philibert de L'Orme but the work was completed between 1599 and 1610, during the reign of Henri IV. Terraced gardens descended to the river in seven stages and ground made unstable by quarrying was buttressed by massive ramps, of which the upper one still survives. Old excavations beneath were turned into galleries and grottoes furnished with water-powered automata. The fourth terrace and the roofs of two galleries at right angles to it formed a continuous promenade looking down on the Jardin en Dentelles, laid out with the royal monograms. The galleries terminated in two pavilions, of which one survives. Neglect, rebuilding and subsequent urban development have destroyed the terraces but it is possible from a commanding position on the promenade made between 1669 and 1673 to get an idea of the potential of the site.

The hydraulic engineer who designed the elaborate set-pieces as well as the machinery for animating the automata was Thomas Francini, who had been invited to France from Italy by Henri IV. He and the brothers who came with him took the name Francine and founded a dynasty that was to play a major role in the design and supervision of waterworks in French gardens. François de Francine, the son of Thomas, was to create the fountains of Versailles.

The Mollet dynasty

The Mollets were another dynasty of royal gardeners that became established during the reign of Henri IV. Claude Mollet (the first of two prominent members of the family to bear the christian name Claude) had served his apprenticeship at Anet under his father and in 1582 had laid out there the first *parterre de broderie*. The designs for

The steeply sloping site of the Château-Neuf at Saint-Germain-en-Laye provided scope for elaborate waterworks of the kind that had given fame to Italian gardens such as the Villa d'Este and Villa Lante. Perelle's engraving (c. 1665–70) shows an unexecuted project for the parterre.

this were devised by Etienne du Pérac and replaced the heraldic designs in the main garden. Claude became gardener to Henri IV in 1595 and for him he executed a number of designs. At Fontainebleau, for instance, he laid out a *parterre de broderie* on the Jardin de l'Etang, a square island formerly adjoining the Cour de la Fontaine on the north side of the lake; it was destroyed in 1713. This is one of the first places where the planting was done in box. His rather solid parterre dressings for Fontainebleau, Saint-Germain-en-Laye and the Tuileries are illustrated in Olivier de Serres's *Théâtre d'agriculture* (1600), a book which first drew attention to the need to compensate for optical distortion when gardens were to be seen from a particular point of view.

The Luxembourg Gardens

The *parterres de broderie* illustrated in Claude's own posthumous work, *Théâtre des plans et jardinages* (1652), are in the more refined style of his sons, the style that became associated with classic French garden design. *Parterres de broderie* in this light and elegant manner were laid out for Marie de Medici at the Luxembourg Palace in Paris, where work was begun in 1612. Jacques Boyceau, who designed these, in-

corporating the monogram of Marie de Medici, has been credited with the invention of the style only because his own *Traité du Jardinage*, published in 1638, includes the earliest representation of garden decoration in this manner.

Since the time of Marie de Medici the Luxembourg has undergone many changes. Now the palace houses the Conseil de la République and the gardens are one of the most frequented open spaces on the left bank. A curious survival from the 17th century is the Grotte de Luxembourg, a substantial architectural fountain in rustic style. When the Rue de' Medicis was made in 1862 this was moved from its position against buildings, where it closed a vista, and is now a free-standing feature at the head of a canal.

BOTANIC GARDENS

In an account of the development of the French classic style it is easy to overlook the interest in botany and in the ornamental value of plants. Botany and medicine went hand in hand, the inquiry into the medicinal value of plants being the prime motive for studying them closely. The first botanic garden in France, the Jardin des Plantes at Montpellier, was made by Richer de Belleval between 1593 and 1607. An original feature was the oblong mount (still in existence), with terraces facing north and south to provide microclimates. Parallel to this, plants were arranged in long troughs and labelled with numbers referring to a catalogue. Access to the various parts of the garden was through arches inscribed according to the habitat or use of the plants to be studied.

The garden, destroyed in 1622 and subsequently remade on a smaller scale, declined in importance after the Jardin Royal des Plantes Médicinales was established in Paris by Guy de la Brosse, physician to Louis XIII, in 1626. The royal garden, later the Jardin des Plantes, was laid out formally, with medicinal herbs grown in parterres. La Brosse gave popular lectures demonstrating their use. The garden today still follows the basic original design, although it has been slightly enlarged. It is used mainly as an amenity park and zoo in the centre of Paris.

The head gardener of the royal garden

was Vespasian Robin, son of Jean Robin, a noted botanist, herbalist and gardener, whose own garden was famous for the number and variety of flowers it contained. He was in regular contact with another great student of plants, the humanist Nicolas-Claude-Fabri de Peiresc. At his small garden at Aix-en-Provence de Peiresc collected rare plants and at the family home north of Toulon he made a large garden with areas reserved for flowers, medicinal plants and exotics. Such men were at the forefront of botanical and horticultural developments in France during the 17th century.

THE CLASSIC FRENCH STYLE

The great political power wielded by Cardinal Richelieu, principal minister to Louis XIII and virtual ruler of France, brought with it vast financial resources. Without them he could not have embarked on the ambitious project of making his family home into the greatest house in Europe and combining it with a new town of overall regularity. The location for the realization of this town-planner's dream was an unpromisingly flat and marshy valley formed by the River Mable in what is now Indre-et-

The Luxembourg Gardens in Paris have long been among the most frequented open spaces of the left bank, as can be seen in this 19th-century view by Albert Edelfelt. The palace and gardens were begun in 1612 for Marie de Medici, partly inspired by the Boboli Gardens in Florence, where she had lived in her youth.

Loire. The plan was conceived in 1628, the design was drawn up by Jacques Lemercier and the work supervised until 1639 by Pierre Lemercier, Jacques' brother. The house, garden and town, incomplete at the Cardinal's death in 1642, were finished by his great-nephew, Armand Jean Vignerot du Plessis, Duc de Richelieu.

Richelieu

The château of Richelieu set new standards of magnificence, not only in extent but also in the detail of the ornamental gardens and the sculpture programme. The hierarchy of courtyards leading from the entrance extended for nearly 460 m (500 yd), while behind the château the main axis was closed only by a *grille* in a great semi-circular hedge flanked by architectural grottoes. The canalized River Mable formed a second major axis at right angles to the main one, the first instance of a second major axis being used in a garden plan of this scale. The water from the canal fed the moats surrounding the château, the parterre and the town itself. These survive but only a pavilion and two architectural grottoes remain as relics of Richelieu's palace, on the site of which there are now cornfields and plots of land belonging to an agricultural centre run by the University of Paris.

Rueil

Among other projects carried out by Cardinal Richelieu, the garden at Rueil was justly famous. Louis XIV coveted it and sent André Le Nôtre to look at it when he made Versailles. The garden, enlarged by Richelieu after he bought the property in 1633, was visited by the English diarist John Evelyn in 1644, fourteen months after Richelieu's death: 'though the house is not of the greatest, the gardens about it are so magnificent, that I doubt whether Italy has any exceeding it for all rarities of pleasure'. One of the main features was a large architectural cascade, the prototype of others at Saint-Cloud and Chantilly, for which the waterworks were devised by Thomas Francini. Only a few vestiges of Richelieu's garden survive, to be found now in the grounds of the Sandoz Group at Rueil-Malmaison.

André Le Nôtre

In the formal landscaping of grounds on the scale of the château of Richelieu – with, theoretically, the possibility of infinite extension in any direction – symmetry, implying perceptible boundaries, had to give way to a balanced arrangement about an axis. Effective use of the extended axis, as in the work of Le Nôtre, depends on choosing a site with differences of level. The flatness of Richelieu offered no advantages. Le Nôtre may have learned how to exploit the levels of a site from the example of the architect François Mansart. The latter's first work of any consequence for garden design was the château of Balleroy in Calvados, carried out between 1626 and 1636. Here he made a new village street at right angles to the old one, giving an extended approach to the château across a shallow valley. At Maisons, a country house commissioned in 1642, the château stands on a terraced platform above the Seine, free-standing with all approaches kept as open vistas; *sauts de loup*, trenches preventing trespass, mark boundaries but do not interrupt the view. The main rooms looked south-east across the *grand parterre* (now restored), with the axis continuing in an avenue on the far side of the Seine.

The genius of Le Nôtre lay not in the invention of a new style but in the absolute

The large architectural cascade at Rueil was one of the major features of Cardinal Richelieu's famous garden. Designed by the Italian Thomas Francini, it was the prototype of others at Saint-Cloud and Chantilly. It is shown here in an engraving by Perelle after Silvestre.

At Vaux-le-Vicomte the great canal makes a dramatically unexpected second axis. On its far side, facing the Grandes Cascades, is the Grotte, a massive wall with niches containing rockwork cascades.

mastery of a repertory that was already well known and widely used, at least in its parts. In 1651 André Mollet published *Le Jardin de plaisir*, which set out the classic concept of French garden design: a hierarchy of *parterres de broderie, parterres de gazon* (turf) and *bosquets* arranged according to a strictly regular plan. Le Nôtre adapted this formula to the necessities of the site, choosing the ground for his great sweeping vistas dominating the landscape, with secondary axes at right angles to the main one, often used to dramatic effect.

Vaux-le-Vicomte
Le Nôtre's first great garden was Vaux-le-Vicomte, created for Nicolas Fouquet, *surintendant des finances* to Louis XIV. Fouquet wished to make the small estate of Vaux, which he had inherited from his father, worthy of his position. He was a perceptive patron of the arts and at Vaux showed real flair in bringing together the architect Le Vau, the painter Le Brun (who had responsibility for the decoration of Vaux) and Le Nôtre. They were assisted by Claude Robillard, *fontainier*, and the flower-gardener Antoine Trunel.

The château, raised on a platform surrounded by moats, is integrated with the courtyards and offices into a perfectly proportioned whole, with gardens framed in trees descending the gently sloping site to the valley of the Anqueil. Water is carefully disposed in basins to catch reflections and subtle use is made of changing levels. From the house the central axis continues beyond the valley in a vista terminated by a colossal statue of Hercules without any hint of the second major axis formed by the great canal, over 900 m (984 yd) long, that crosses

The original design for Nicolas Fouquet at Vaux-le-Vicomte, in which Le Nôtre played a major role, provided a setting for lavish entertainments. Fouquet's downfall followed shortly after the spectacular reception celebrating the completion of château and garden in 1661.

it. This axis is dramatically revealed on reaching the Grandes Cascades, whose existence below the line of approach is also unsuspected. Facing the Cascades on the far side of the canal is the Grotte, a massive wall with seven round-headed niches containing rock-work cascades, flanked by two grotto-like recesses with giant reclining river gods. The Grotte supports a balustraded terrace from where, with the Grandes Cascades in the foreground, the gardens and château are seen to great advantage.

The symmetry about the central walk is broken by secondary axes at right angles to it running east to west. The middle, and principal, one of these is a walk crossing below the *parterre de broderie*, with gates on the west, leading to the kitchen garden (*potager*), and on the east rising in a stairway of fountains called the Grilles d'Eau. This axis is reinforced by two canals on either side of the steps leading to the third parterre, whose central walk was formerly lined with fountains and known as the Allée d'Eau.

At Vaux it is balance rather than symmetry that gives the gardens their integrity. In this, and in its conception as a setting for lavish entertainment more suited to princes than to private individuals, Vaux is the immediate precursor to Versailles.

In August 1661, on the completion of the château and gardens, Fouquet invited the king to a spectacular reception to show his creation in all its magnificence. Blind to the resentment that his ostentatious way of life might arouse in Louis, he saw too late that he had overreached himself. At the moment of accepting invitations to Vaux, the king was planning his host's downfall. A fortnight after the lavish entertainment, Fouquet was arrested and charged with peculation and high treason. He spent the rest of his life in prison.

The gardens went into decline almost immediately after their brief moment of glory. Most of the statuary and even some of the trees were taken by Louis XIV for his own gardens. So collapsed, decayed and impoverished were the gardens when the château was acquired by Alfred Sommelier in 1875 that the restoration he put in hand amounted to little less than a reconstruction. Now, however, apart from Versailles,

Vaux is the finest and best kept example of a classical French garden.

Versailles

The scale and magnificence of French garden design during the reign of Louis XIV, represented by Versailles, became the model of Europe, if not the world. The estate had been acquired in 1632 by Louis XIII, who had enlarged the existing hunting lodge and enclosed a park. The Duc de Saint-Simon (whose views must be set in the context of his marked antipathy to Louis XIV and his policies) described the original site as 'the most sad and barren of places, with no view, no water and no woods'. The king's choice of Versailles as the seat of the government and the court had much to do

with his distrust of the nobility and his dislike of Paris. The palace and gardens were to be the symbol of his own conception of the role of the French monarchy, in which the nobility were to be reduced to a position of dependence on his own good favour. Colbert, the king's chief minister, warned Louis of the great difficulties and expense confronting him in realizing his plan. Louis was undeterred. 'It is in the difficult things', he wrote in his memoirs to his son, 'that we show our quality.'

Louis took the sun as his emblem and it was to provide the iconography for the whole layout. Apart from the actual mythology of Apollo, this theme could be made to embrace such topics as the hours of the day, the seasons of the year, the four quarters of

A painting by Cottel of 1688 shows La Salle du Bal at Versailles, sometimes referred to as the Bosquet des Rocailles, on account of the thousands of shells imported from Madagascar for its decoration. This is one of the many bosquets created among the numerous trees planted either side of the Tapis Vert.

the globe and the seven ages of man. Since Diana was Apollo's sister, scenes of hunting could be included, appropriate to a dynasty devoted to the chase.

It was Louis's good fortune to be served by men of the foremost quality in all fields. At Versailles these included the architects Le Vau and Hardouin-Mansart, the artist Le Brun, who had responsibility for the sculpture programme between 1665 and 1683, and Le Nôtre. The château was rebuilt three times and on each occasion the gardens were modified. This fact alone makes it difficult to apportion credit but it was Le Nôtre who ordained the layout of the Grand Design. He gave the land a new shape, now making use of the natural

declivity of the site to form a series of terraces, now hollowing out a vast amphitheatre for the Parterre de Latone, now clothing the slopes with woods and hedges, within which were contrived green enclosures (*cabinets de verdure*) of astonishing architectural elaboration.

Le Nôtre took the points of the compass for his main axes, making the long perspective from the windows of the Grande Galerie, a view extending as far as the eye can see, to the setting sun. To the north he sheltered the gardens from cold winds by a tall hedge (*charmille*) that formed a continuation to the walls of the palace. To the south he opened the vista to the summer sun, across the terrace of the Orangerie.

At Versailles the main vista, conceived on a heroic scale, leads from the Parterre d'Eau, which lies beneath the window of the Grande Galerie, by way of the Parterre de Latone (the Bassin de Latone is shown in the foreground) down the Tapis Vert to the Bassin d'Apollon and so to the canal.

Versailles had limited natural water and yet the sort of garden Le Nôtre planned required copious supplies. A network of reservoirs was created west of Saint-Cyr and in 1680 construction began on a gigantic pump, the Machine de Marly. Fourteen enormous water-wheels forced the waters of the River Seine up the 162 m (177 yd) of hillside to the Aqueduct de Marly at a rate

Although the gardens of Versailles were in an almost constant state of evolution for a period of more than fifty years, from the outset Le Nôtre's Grand Design called for an extravagant use of water. At Versailles itself the supply was inadequate for the prodigious number of fountains and great ingenuity was required to bring water from a distance.

Below: *The Machine de Marly, the construction of which began in 1680, was a gigantic pump whose 14 enormous water-wheels forced the waters of the Seine up to the Aqueduc de Marly,*

which then fed a reservoir supplying the gardens. Even with the machine in operation, not all the fountains could play simultaneously.

Right: *The main axis of the gardens runs westward from the Grande Galerie to the Canal. A subsidiary axis running north-south, shown in a painting by J. B. Martin, begins at the Bassin de Neptune, designed by Le Nôtre in 1679 but not completed until 1741.*

Although numerous changes were made at Versailles after Louis XIV's death, the broad lines of Le Nôtre's layout were not fundamentally altered. An addition of the late 18th century, the Petit Trianon, shown here in a painting by Claude Louis Chatelet extravagantly illuminated for an entertainment, indicates, however, the marked shift in taste during the following century in favour of a freer, lighter style.

of some 5,000 cu. m (6,540 cu. yd) of water daily. An even more colossal undertaking, involving diverting the waters of the River Eure, was abandoned when the 30,000 soldiers detailed as the task force were recalled to service at Neustadt. Thanks to the hydraulic expertise of François and Pierre de Francine there were 1,400 fountains to be supplied and although those nearest the palace displayed for most of the day, the use of the others had to be rationed. Elaborate instructions were given to the *fontainier* Claude Denis to ensure that the fountains came on just before the king arrived in any particular part of the gardens.

The largest of the *pièces d'eau* is the great cruciform Canal, the long arm of which lies on the main axis, the cross piece forming a secondary axis. In Louis's time the waters were busy with a flotilla of sumptuously decorated small ships ready to take the court on evening excursions. The Pièce d'Eau des Suisses is the largest of the arti-

ficial lakes. Named after the regiment of Swiss Guards who were employed on the excavations, it was begun in 1678 and is closely linked with the gargantuan Orangerie constructed by Hardouin-Mansart. Madame de Sévigné noted the 'prodigious mortality of the workmen, whose bodies are carried out every night by the cartload'; the men were killed by the marsh gas released by their colossal excavations.

Once the new contours had been established the process of refinement and redecoration continued until the end of the reign. The area immediately adjacent to the château was left open and flat as a series of parterres, a necessary intermediate stage between the architecture of the façades and the *bosquets*, the ornamental features enclosed by trees. Beyond the *bosquets* stretched the park and beyond the park was the landscape of nature. It was virtually only in the parterres that flowers were planted and although the real flower garden was at

Trianon, the three great parterres at Versailles accounted annually for 150,000 plants.

From the Parterre d'Eau, which lies beneath the windows of the Grande Galerie, the main perspective of the gardens leads by way of the Parterre de Latone down the Tapis Vert, sometimes known as the Allée Royale, to the Bassin d'Apollon and so to the Canal. The statuary announced the main theme of the decorative ensemble. Latona, mother of Apollo, is shown appealing to Zeus for protection against the peasants of Lycias, who were pelting her with clods of earth. Zeus retaliated by turning them into frogs. The Bassin d'Apollon shows the moment of sunrise; the chariot of the sun is labouring to get clear of the water before it breaks forth upon another day. These and the many other fountains, as well as numerous free-standing pieces of sculpture, amplified the allegorical programme. A remarkable achievement at Versailles is that although some 70 sculptors were employed in the gardens, under the tutelage of Le Brun they formed a school of artists working in an astonishingly homogeneous style.

Throughout Louis's reign there were many changes to the *bosquets*, involving enormous labour in the planting of trees. One of the most remarkable of the *bosquets* was the Salle du Bal, sometimes known as the Bosquet des Rocailles after the thousands of shells specially imported from Madagascar to decorate it. The sloping ground had been hollowed out to form a steep-cut arena, with cascades tumbling down from tier to tier between gilded *guéridons*, small ornamental tables on which candelabra could be placed, bringing the magic of candlelight to the nocturnal festivities of the court.

The horticultural extravagance of Versailles reached its climax at Trianon, at the north end of the Canal. Louis was a passionate lover of flowers. The Parterre des Fleurs, one of his first embellishments of his father's hunting-lodge at Versailles, had been moved to Trianon when work began on the palace. The focus at this new location was provided first by a pavilion in the 'Chinese' taste, the Trianon de Porcelaine, covered in blue and white Delft tiles, subsequently replaced by the Trianon de Marbre or Grand Trianon.

The gardens at Trianon were an attempt to defy the natural seasons. Orange trees were planted not in tubs but in the soil. When winter came a greenhouse was raised over them. Flowers were bedded out on the coldest days and replaced, if necessary, during dinner, so that Louis could enjoy a summer garden on a January afternoon. The gardener, Le Bouteux, a nephew of Le Nôtre, kept the almost unbelievable number of 1,999,000 flowerpots and the navy was used to bring flowers from warmer lands.

Although pared of much of their extravagance, the gardens of Versailles are still essentially those of Louis XIV, Le Nôtre and Le Brun. Louis XV did little except at Trianon. Although Louis XVI replanted all the trees and made important modifications, the pressure to recast the whole area in the form of *jardin à l'anglais* was resisted. The replantation of 1775 respected the broad outlines traced by Le Nôtre.

Marly

To escape the enormous palace where he lived in public, Louis XIV built retreats. Work at Marly began after the king had chanced upon the site in 1679. Le Nôtre and Le Brun worked on the project but the principal hand in the highly original design was that of Hardouin-Mansart. The buildings were disposed in a long, horseshoe-shaped valley opening to the Seine, the king's house occupying the focal point and 12 pavilions for the guests lining either arm of the horseshoe. The low ground in the centre was cast into terraces and a series of monumental lakes was created on the main axis. On three sides, high, wooded hills enclosed the site; on the side open to the valley the land fell away, revealing a magnificent prospect towards Saint-Germain. However, privacy was secured by the skilful use of ground levels; it was only to those privileged to enter the precincts that the whole glorious layout of Marly was reavealed.

In the area immediately surrounding the château everything was closely packed and heavily overhung by high banks and steep woods. In each corner was a *cabinet de verdure* with a highly ornamental fish-pond tiled in porcelain. To the south of the château was the Petit Parterre, from which a noble flight of stairs led to an all-encircling pergola, which linked the château with its pavilions. Behind this a great cascade, known as the Rivière, tumbled tumultuously down a steep avenue. Finding it too costly to maintain, Louis XV replaced it by a grass slope. To the east of the Rivière the precipitous contours were used to create the Roulette, a switchback railway on which ran an ornately gilded toboggan.

The gardens were constantly altered and elaborated but their special character survived. Diderot identified it as 'the contrast between the delicacy of art in the bowers and *bosquets* and the rudeness of nature in the dense bank of trees which overhangs them and forms the background. This continual transition from nature to art and from art to nature produces a truly enchanting effect'. Marly was finally destroyed by Napoleon but the strangely beautiful trees remain and the site has been restored so that the broad outlines may still be traced.

Chantilly

Although the grand manner was especially suited to creating a setting for the Sun King's Court, the style was applied to many other gardens. At Chantilly the 'Grand Condé', Louis II de Bourbon, greatly increased the size of the park that had been created between 1522 and 1567 by Anne de Montmorency. In 1663 he employed Le Nôtre and a team of artists to lay out grounds on a vast scale. Le Nôtre himself looked on what he did there as among his greatest achievements, for he succeeded in imposing regularity on a very irregular site. The main axis ran south-north, parallel to

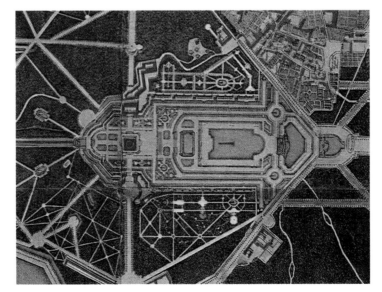

The plan of Marly was hardly less formal than that of Versailles, but here Louis XIV was able to entertain selectively in a way that was impossible where almost all aspects of court life were public. Twelve pavilions for guests lined either arm of a horseshoe-shaped valley, with the King's house occupying the focal point.

the façade of the château, and extended into the forest at either end. A new approach led to the terrace, built in the time of Anne de Montmorency, east of the château, from where the whole scheme was revealed. Monumental steps, with colossal river gods in niches on either side, led to the Grand Parterre. In the foreground stood a fountain, the Grand Gerbe, and beyond it the Manche, a branch of the Grand Canal, which formed an east-west axis. Either side of the Manche were two vast compartments, with round and oval basins. On the far side of the Grand Canal the axis terminated in a bay and crescent-shaped

theatre, the Vertugadin, formerly lined by busts of the twelve Caesars. Other features at Chantilly included architectural cascades, now lost, although Le Nôtre's Grand Parterre and Canal have been restored.

The move to simplicity and intimacy

Among other gardens where Le Nôtre and his associates worked were Sceaux for Colbert, Dampierre for the Duc de Chevreuse and Anet for the Duc de Vendôme. Dezallier d'Argenville's *La Théorie et la pratique du jardinage*, first published in 1709, codified the practice of Le Nôtre and his school but in the revised edition of 1722

a theoretical justification is given for a less contrived approach to garden design. Expensive and elaborate artefacts should give place to 'the noble simplicity of steps, banks, ramps of turf, natural arbours and simple clipped hedges'. A tendency to simplification began before 1700. Nonetheless, for the first three quarters of the 18th century regularity in garden design remained the rule. Some fine provincial examples survive, for instance Jallerange at Besançon, and the restored garden of La Motte-Tilly, Aube.

Under Louis XV gardens of a more intimate character were favoured, compared with the grandiose schemes of Louis XIV. The contrast in taste can be seen in comparing Marly and the Petit Trianon, conceived by Gabriel for the Marquise de Pompadour, Louis XV's mistress, but completed after her death. The large royal gardens of the past, such as the Tuileries and Versailles, had virtually become public gardens. Their 18th-century successors were the municipal promenades like those at Nîmes and Besançon and the extension of garden design to town planning as at Nancy.

LE JARDIN ANGLAIS

Classical taste in France never stifled the desire for rural nature in the countryside, even for wild nature, hence the importance of the forest of Fontainebleau in French culture. However, the change from an architectural to a more 'natural' style that was first apparent in England, culminating there in the great landscape parks of 'Capability' Brown, did influence the design of French gardens. One of the first to introduce the English taste for landscape gardening was the political philosopher Montesquieu, who had visited England in 1729. He had been most impressed by the use of large areas of grass in English parks and told Lord Charlemont, who, in 1746, visited him at his château of La Brède in

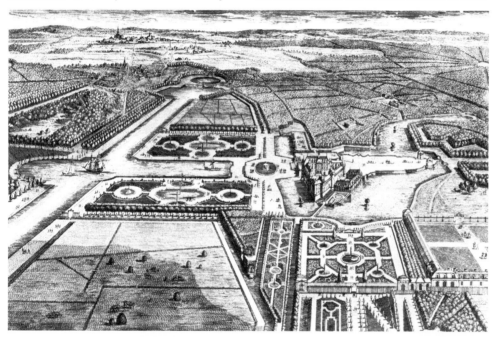

From 1663, after completing work on Vaux-le-Vicomte but before starting at Versailles, Le Nôtre was employed by the 'Grand Condé' to redesign the grounds at Chantilly. His great achievement was to impose regularity on a marshy irregular site, with the main axis running parallel to the façade of the château.

At Sceaux, Louis XIV's minister Colbert called on Le Nôtre to design the gardens and park. The elaborate cascades that formed part of his design brought their tumultuous waters to the great pièce d'eau *of the Octogone.*

Bordeaux, 'I have tried to put your country's taste into practice here and to set out my grounds in the English way'.

The knowledge of the English style in France was, however, largely second-hand and the literary sources fostered the idea that English gardens were derived from the Chinese. As a result the French version of the English style was often called '*les jardins anglo-chinois*'. Buildings in the Chinese style naturally formed part of the fashion. A surviving example is the Pagode de Chanteloup (1775-8), inspired by Chambers's pagoda at Kew and built as a dominant feature in a park combining irregular layout with great classic vistas.

In the second quarter of the 18th century, many *jardins anglais* were created as small gardens attached to formal layouts. This was the case at Chantilly, where in 1774 a meadow east of the Grand Parterre was transformed into a *jardin anglais*. Various features, including ponds, lawns, a flowered trellis and an orchard were enclosed in a wood with winding paths and streams. The Parc Balbi at Versailles, begun in 1786, is another example of the same fashion.

In other instances the *jardin anglais* was interpreted in a much broader way, with the laying out of large estates ornamented with buildings in an exotic style. One of the most curious is the Désert de Retz, laid out by Baron de Monville between 1774 and the Revolution. The house was perhaps the strangest of its buildings, for it looked like the shaft of a colossal broken column. The first residence had been the Maison Chinoise, an example of oriental exoticism inspired by the publications of William Chambers.

A perfect example of the romantic interpretation of the *jardin anglais* is the vast landscape created for the Princesse de Monaco at Betz, an estate she acquired in 1780. The *fabriques*, the buildings constructed to set the tone of the garden, included some in the neo-Gothic taste, the first of their kind in France.

One of the most influential gardens with an irregular layout was Ermenonville, where the Marquis de Girardin combined picturesque beauty with rural management. When he visited England in 1763 he found that the concept of the *ferme ornée* corresponded with his own idea of how an estate

Vue Perspective de la Colonne.

The Désert de Retz is one of the strangest and most poetic creations inspired by the taste for the jardin anglo-chinois. The house itself has the appearance of a colossal broken column, within which there are apartments on three floors.

At Ermenonville the Marquis de Girardin combined picturesque layout and rural management in the manner of the English ferme ornée. Rousseau's tomb on the Ile des Peupliers became a place of pilgrimage and inspired similar features in other European gardens.

should be organized. Jean-Jacques Rousseau spent the last two months of his life at Ermenonville and was buried on the Ile des Peupliers, a site that became one of the best-known pilgrimages in France.

EMPIRE STYLES AND THE 19TH CENTURY

The French architectural style of gardening was temporarily curtailed by the Revolution, partly because it was associated with the *ancien régime*, but also because the emigrés who returned to France found it more convenient to restore their neglected estates and parks in the English manner. At Liancourt, for example, which had possessed one of the most admired of early 17th-century gardens, enlarged and surviving, despite neglect, until the after the Revolution, the old layout was swept away in favour of a model estate *à l'anglaise*.

At Malmaison, the favourite residence of the Empress Joséphine, the gardens were laid out, as so many others, in the English style. Using Napoleon's influence and with the help of a series of eminent botanists, Joséphine collected plants from all over the world. The garden has been immortalized by the illustrations of the celebrated Belgian artist Pierre-Joseph Redouté. The most familiar are those from *Les Roses* but his other illustrations, including those in *Les Liliacées*, demonstrate the brilliance of his work and the range of plants grown at Malmaison.

Although early in the 19th century the major influence may have been from English practitioners of the landscape style, such as Humphry Repton, it was the Frenchman Gabriel Thouin and his codification of *le jardin anglais* that determined its development throughout the 19th century. In his search for a practical method, Thouin combined a functional scheme of walks linked to a vast circular *alée* round a lawn punctuated with vegetation. This was the style of the brothers Bühler, who created many parks and gardens, including the Parc de la Tête d'Or at Lyons and the Jardin Thabor at Rennes.

Hausmann's modernization of Paris under Napoleon III provided an opportunity for the creation of a number of public parks and in these the *jardin anglais* was adapted for the provision of promenades for recreation. The two names most closely associated with these public parks are the landscape architects Jean-Charles-Adolphe Alphand and Jean-Pierre Barillet-Deschamps. They both played an important role in the development of the Bois de Boulogne, which Napoleon III gave to the city in 1852. Masses of rock were used to give variety to a site that for the most part was flat and Barillet-Deschamps added pines, cedars and other trees arranged in clumps to leave open clearings and vistas. At Buttes-Chaumont, a park laid out in the Belleville district and begun in 1864, the site, on old quarries, was naturally hilly and the garden created there by Alphand and Barillet-Deschamps is one of the most picturesque in Paris.

Typical features of Barillet-Deschamps's 'decorative horticulture' were wide paths with ample curves, ground shaped into little dells in the middle of hollow lawns, and trees in bold isolation or leaning over round flowerbeds or clumps of shrubs. It was widely applied to landscape engineering by Alphand and his circle and subsequently, and less effectively, to small private gardens.

The Parc Monceau was another example of collaboration between Alphand and Barillet-Deschamps. One of the first examples of a *jardin irrégulier*, it had been laid out from 1773 by Carmontelle and had contained an astonishing accumulation of *fabriques*. A few of these survived the restoration by Alphand and Barillet-Deschamps in 1861. In the Parc Monceau Barillet-Deschamps pioneered bedding with subtropical plants of large, variegated or otherwise ornamental foliage. His experiments gave an impetus to the use of patterned beds, a fashion that began in England. French gardeners adopted both carpet and flower bedding without distinguishing between them; the resulting composite form was known as *mosaïculture*, a style of gardening which flourished in the late 19th century and which is still widely practised in France. There was a strong fashion for zoomorphic and emblematic shapes after 1878, when examples had been shown at the Exposition Universelle.

At the close of the 19th century a reaction against the irregularity of the English style and a revived interest in Le Nôtre resulted in many restorations and reconstructions in the 17th-century manner. One of the loveliest, devised before the First World War for the Marquise de Ganay by Achille Duchêne, is Courances.

From the end of the 19th century Achille Duchêne, with other members of his family, played an important role in restoring French parks and gardens in the classic style. Courances in Essonne demonstrates mastery of a tradition that is still vital.

THE BRITISH ISLES

The paintings of Thomas Robins the elder, such as this view of a Chinese pavilion at Woodside House in Berkshire, reveal details of English gardens in the third quarter of the 18th century.

The revolution in garden design that began in England in the early 18th century has left its mark on the landscape in almost every corner of the British Isles. The loosening of formal garden geometry that started in England also profoundly influenced the making of gardens in many other parts of the world, the English manner enjoying great popularity in the late 18th and 19th centuries especially.

The success of the landscape movement has to some extent contributed to a distorted view of the history of gardens in England and other parts of the British Isles. The great formal layouts of the 17th century have been lost almost in their entirety and the hardly less ambitious gardens of the Victorian period are only now being favourably reassessed. Yet these two periods are a reminder that ordered architectural gardens also belong to the tradition of garden-making in Britain.

As in other parts of the world, the survival of historic gardens is under threat and their maintenance or restoration often depend to a remarkable degree on the commitment of a few individuals. Nonetheless, in mainland Britain and Ireland there are many gardens of exceptional quality to which the public has access. In many cases these gardens are outstanding for their planting as well as their design, this part of Europe having played a major role in the

introduction of new species and varieties of horticultural merit.

RENAISSANCE GARDENS

In England the static tradition of the medieval garden was probably first jolted by influences coming from the Court of Burgundy. At Richmond Palace (1497–1501) the gardens of the first Tudor monarch, Henry VII, were designed with a series of enclosures linked by covered walks and galleries, which probably followed the Burgundian style.

Burgundian influence on court life continued in the dazzling ostentation of the early years of Henry VIII's reign, yet when Henry took to building palaces and gardens the major influence was from his great rival, François I of France. The evidence is slender but it seems that the privy gardens of Hampton Court Palace (1531–4), Whitehall (completed 1545) and Nonsuch Palace (1538–47) had much in common with each other and, for example, with those at Fontainebleau. The gardens, square and laid out in quarters in open and closed knots, were situated below the state apartments. Each garden had a central fountain and was surrounded by covered walks. What gave Henry's gardens a uniquely English character was the lavish use of gilt and painted wooden decoration based on the dynastic heraldry of the Tudors. This gaudy underlining of Tudor legitimacy must have given these gardens a curiously medieval appearance despite the obvious impact of new Renaissance ideas.

Elizabeth I did not continue Henry's ambitious building programme but during her reign the pleasure-garden became a major feature of the many country houses built by wealthy and powerful aristocrats –

for example, the important garden created between 1563 and 1567 by Robert Dudley, Earl of Leicester, during the modernization of medieval Kenilworth castle in Warwickshire. To locate this garden beneath the castle windows was not possible but a terrace provided a view down on to it. The square, divided into quarters planted with fruit trees and herbs, had at its centre a fountain with a bear and ragged staff, Leicester's personal device, forming a decorative finial.

Theobalds Park

Even more ambitious were the gardens created at Theobalds Park in Hertfordshire between 1575 and 1585 for William Cecil, Lord Burghley, an enterprise in which the herbalist John Gerard may have had a hand. Elizabeth I frequently stayed at Theobalds; its palatial scale was a compliment to her and an indication of Burghley's status. The Privy Garden, situated below the private apartments, was laid out with hedges, arbours and knots divided by raised walks. The Great Garden, on a truly grand scale, being more than a hectare (2½ acres) in extent, lay beneath the state apartments. It was surrounded by a moat and divided into nine knots, the central one containing a fountain. Busts of Roman emperors, a marble obelisk, a sundial and knots representing the royal arms were among the features incorporated. Later additions included a mount. Although the layout owed much to French influence, the decorative detail was probably in the elaborately intricate style of Netherlandish Mannerism, a style that was to become highly influential in northern Europe largely through the pattern book *Hortorum viridariorumque elegantes et multiplicis formae*, published in 1583 by Hans Vredeman de Vries.

A panoramic view, c. 1555, by Anthonis van Wyngaerde of Hampton Court, as seen from the Thames, shows the Privy Garden peopled with the King's Beasts, heraldic models, painted, gilded and mounted upon posts or pedestals. Similar decoration was used at Nonsuch Palace and Whitehall.

Salomon de Caus

Direct royal patronage of the arts was once again re-established during the reign of James I, whose accession in 1603 marked the beginning of a new openness to outside influences. Salomon de Caus, a garden designer who was employed by both the Queen, Anne of Denmark, and Henry, Prince of Wales, was a French Huguenot engineer who had studied in Italy and knew the gardens of Pratolino, famous at the time for their prodigious and ingenious waterworks. He was also familiar with the waterworks executed by the Francine brothers for Henri IV in France. In 1615 de Caus published *Les Raisons des forces mouvantes*, which set out the principles of hydraulics on which the waterworks of 17th-century gardens were based. The details of the works de Caus carried out between about 1609 and 1612 at Somerset House, Greenwich Palace and Richmond Palace are not known precisely. It is likely, however, that they included waterworks and grottoes, though perhaps less elaborate than those of his most famous garden, the Hortus Palatinus at Heidelberg, created after he left England in 1613.

Wilton House

The spate of garden building that had occurred at the time Salomon de Caus was active in England picked up again in the 1620s and 1630s with the arrival of Isaac de Caus, Salomon's brother or nephew.

Among the most important projects in which he was involved was the creation of an elaborate garden for the fourth Earl of Pembroke at Wilton House, Wiltshire, begun in 1632 and recorded in de Caus's own publication, *Le Jardin de Wilton*.

The main garden was laid out in a large rectangle with three major divisions running transversely. The division nearest the house consisted of four compartments of *parterres de broderie*, an early English example of the elaborately patterned parterres of French inspiration. The central division was the Wilderness, a formal plantation through which the River Nadder ran a sinuous course, and an oval circus with a statue of a gladiator at its centre formed the third. The broad central path running through these divisions culminated in the garden's most celebrated feature, a grotto located beneath a balustraded terrace, from which the spectator could look down on the garden and out into the parkland.

Inigo Jones

Inigo Jones, who also played a role at Wilton, was, with André Mollet, one of the dominating figures in garden design during the reign of Charles I. On visits to Italy he had imbibed Palladianism and Renaissance assumptions of the unity of building with the 'Arts of Design'. In the fashionable court masques for which he designed scenery he first demonstrated Italianate concepts of planting, landscaping and building. After 1614, when he returned from a visit to Italy with Lord Arundel, he remodelled the grounds of Arundel House, partly as a setting for antique sculpture. His major innovation in this project was the introduction of formal gateways between different gardens.

André Mollet

In an international career as a leading gardener that included work in England, the Netherlands and Sweden, as well as his home country of France, André Mollet gave wide currency to the elegant flowing forms of the *parterre de broderie*. In England he worked at St James's Palace early in the reign of Charles I and again, towards the end of his life, after the Restoration. Henrietta Maria, wife of Charles I, also employed him in the early 1640s to replan the

The gardens at Wilton House in Wiltshire have undergone many alterations since they were first laid out about 1632 by Isaac de Caus for the fourth Earl of Pembroke. This aerial view by de Caus looks down the main vista to the architectural grotto.

gardens at Wimbledon House. There had already been two major phases in the creation of these gardens and in Mollet's layout much of the formal planting of the second phase, including a lime walk, was retained. However, most of the old Elizabethan gardens were swept away and in their place four parterres were laid out, two with fountains and *parterres de broderie*. Other features added were a maze and a wilderness, both planted with young trees, the latter consisting of a plantation cut by gravel walks into ovals, squares and angles.

THE FORMAL GARDEN

In his book *Le Jardin de plaisir* (1651) André Mollet advocated avenues terminating at semi-circles in front of palaces. He planted just such an avenue system, aligned on Whitehall Palace, with lime trees in St James's Park for Charles II shortly after the king's restoration in 1660, though there was a canal on the axis rather than the approach road. Another version was made on an even vaster scale for the east front of Hampton Court.

In 1664 a large platform, intended for a parterre, was terraced into the rising slope in the park behind Greenwich Palace. André le Nôtre supplied the design, though

he did not visit the site. The scheme was abandoned, but not before the platform, radiating avenues of elms and other avenues had been installed.

The French passion for rides and avenues had established itself in England and many members of the court followed the example set by the monarch. In the 1680s vast schemes were created at Badminton House in Avon and at Boughton House in Northamptonshire. At the latter the Duke of Montagu intended to make an avenue extending to London, some 100km (62 miles) away. More modest, but still impressive, was the elm avenue 5 km (3 miles) in length created at Windsor in 1683.

An outstanding garden in the French style from late in the century is Bramham Park in West Yorkshire. The house and garden were begun by Robert Benson (later Lord Bingley) in 1699. Throughout much of the 18th century the garden was embellished with temples and other features but much dates from Benson's time: the high beech hedges, the *allées*, the green spaces (*salles de verdure*) at their intersections, the Broad Walk, the parterre (now the rose garden), and the T-shaped canal. The pond at the far end of the parterre once took the flow of a 30-step French fountain.

John Evelyn

The man who introduced the word 'avenue' into the English language was John Evelyn, who at the time of the Restoration was one of the few Englishmen with any proficiency in garden design. In the 1640s he had travelled extensively in Italy, France and Germany, recording in his diary the state of the arts, especially of gardening, in each country. The garden he created at Sayes Court, where he settled in 1652, was French in character, with elaborate groves, a large orchard and a terrace flanked by holly and barberry hedges. Experiments with different kinds of trees at Sayes Court laid the basis for his *Sylva* (1664), which through subsequent expanded editions remained the standard textbook on the propagation, planting and use of trees into the 19th

century. Evelyn's translation of French works on gardening and his original works were of considerable influence in forming the taste of his time. He was also directly involved in the design of a number of gardens. Those he made in 1652 for his brother at the family home of Wotton in Surrey were in the Italian manner, a parterre with fountain being laid out between the house and the hill to the south, the latter cut into a terraced mount, with a portico and grotto at its base. The natural philosopher's garden he designed for Henry Howard at Albury Park in Surrey during the 1660s was also of Italian inspiration. It included a vast upper terrace, a tunnel or 'Pausilippe' (alluding to that near Virgil's tomb on Mount Posilippo), waterworks, canals and vineyards. The design was markedly Roman in character, especially in the nymphaeum or alcove with niches in the centre of the terrace.

Elsewhere, however, Evelyn drew on French models. In the 1660s he assisted Lord Cornbury in planning and planting the park at Cornbury House, Oxfordshire;

the design incorporated groves, a great avenue across the park to the adjoining Wychwood Forest and a broad vista eastwards. At Euston Hall in Suffolk, where Evelyn advised on the enlargement and planting of the park in the 1670s, his work included the creation of avenues on the east and west axes.

Ham House

Only a few vestiges survive of most of these 17th-century gardens but at Ham House, Richmond, gardens of the same date as those at Euston Hall have been reconstructed since 1978. Evelyn visited the house and garden in 1679 and recorded that 'the Parterres, Flower Gardens, Orangeries, Groves, Avenues, Courts, Statues, Perspectives, Fountains, Aviaries, and all this on the banks of the Sweetest River in the World must needs be surprising'. The reconstructed garden on the south side consists of a long terrace, squares of grass divided up by gravel walks, and a geometric wilderness of hornbeam hedges and small trees, derived from the *bosquets* of French gardens. The east side of the house is laid out as a parterre of dwarf box hedges, forming triangular or diamond-shaped beds which are planted alternately with cotton lavender and English lavender and flanked by arbours. The preference for plain grass parterres of the kind to be found in the south garden at Ham was thought of by foreigners as peculiarly English and dates from before the Civil Wars.

London and Wise

In the last two decades of the 17th century and the early years of the 18th the foremost exponents of the formal style were George London and Henry Wise, partners in the Brompton Park Nurseries in Kensington. This nursery had initially been founded by London with three other partners, including Moses Cook, formerly head gardener to the Earl of Exeter, with whom in the late 1660s Cook had re-created at Cassiobury Park in Hertfordshire the atmosphere of a French château set in a forest. The nurseries produced not only what John Evelyn called 'a very brave and noble assembly of the flowery and other trees … evergreens and shrubs', but also vegetables, herbs, fruit trees and flowers. It became the most

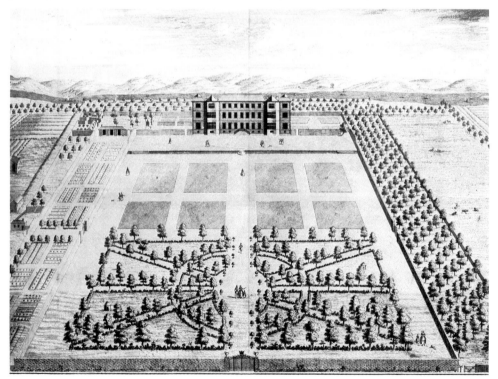

The garden at Ham House, Richmond, on the outskirts of London, was laid out in 1671. The area to the south of the house shown in this 17th-century engraving and that to the east have recently been reconstructed. The geometric wilderness is seen in the foreground.

The engraving by Kip, after Knyff, of Chatsworth House in Derbyshire shows one of the most grandiose layouts of the early 18th century, including the great parterre laid out by the last of the great English formalists, London and Wise, between 1687 and 1706.

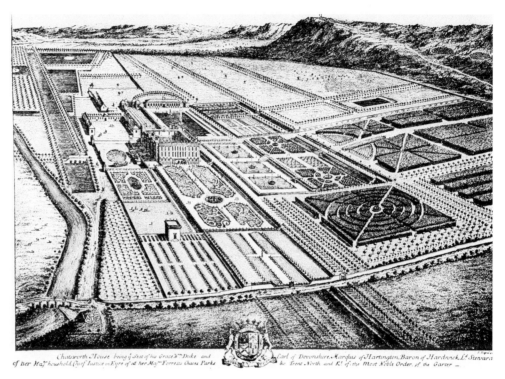

Chatsworth House being ý Seat of his Grace ý:w Duke and ... Earl of Devonshire, Marquis of Hartington, Baron of Hardwick, L:d Steward of her Ma:ties houshold, Chief Iustice in Eyre of all her Ma:ties Forrests Chaces Parks &c Trent North and K:t of the Most Noble Order of the Garter

important nursery in England, furnishing the gardens designed by the partners and many others as well.

The great formal gardens in the French manner created individually or jointly by London and Wise have in most instances been destroyed by subsequent landscaping. This was the fate, for example, of gardens at Longleat House and Chatsworth. At Melbourne Hall in Derbyshire, however, the garden created for Queen Anne's Vice-Chamberlain, Thomas Coke, is a remarkable survival, complete with parterres, geometrically shaped pools, *allées*, pleached walks and classical statuary. Among English gardens a unique feature is the domed and lacy ironwork 'Birdcage' arbour of Robert Bakewell dating from 1706, two years after the date of the London and Wise contract.

On the accession of William III in 1689 London was made Royal Gardener, a position he retained until replaced by Wise at the accession of Queen Anne in 1702.

DUTCH INFLUENCE

In the Netherlands William and Mary had already laid out an ornate garden at Het Loo, distinctively Dutch in character but drawing heavily on the French formal tradition. Their gardening tastes were furthermore reflected in the works carried out at Kensington Gardens and in alterations at Hampton Court. At Kensington, London laid out an intricate geometrical garden to the south, half in parterre with clipped evergreens (a distinctive mark of William's taste) and half as a wilderness.

Hampton Court
In Bushy Park, on the northern boundary of Hampton Court, the quadruple lime avenue (called the 'Chestnut Avenue' when rows of horse chestnuts made it a quintuple avenue in 1699) was laid out early in 1689 with a new north front in mind. In the event Sir Christopher Wren's works were confined to a new east end, and the rest of George

It was in the reign of William and Mary, from 1689 to 1702, that Hampton Court achieved its full glory. The gates (as here, giving on to the park) and 12 panels for the Fountain Garden, executed by the Frenchman Jean Tijou, are of outstanding quality.

London's garden works were laid out accordingly. A parterre, designed by Daniel Marot (who had worked at Het Loo), filled the semicircle. It was an elaborate example of the Franco-Dutch style with *broderie* edged with dwarf box and enriched with pyramids of yew and globes of holly, and incorporating 13 fountains. The semi-circle was enclosed by iron railings, giving outwards views, while in the park two new avenues gave a huge *patte d'oie* centred on the east front.

South of the palace the 'glass-case garden' was devised for tender exotics, Queen Mary's special interest. To the north, the old orchard became an intricate wilderness, including the famous maze.

The works carried out between 1699 and 1702 by William alone (Queen Mary had died in 1694) included extending the Privy

Garden to afford a better view of the Thames. Twelve wrought iron panels by Jean Tijou were erected between this garden and the river side. The new Broad Walk and the Terrace gave promenades of a mile in length terminating at a bowling green enclosed by four pavilions. The gardens were virtually complete at the king's death in 1702.

Queen Anne, who is said to have disliked the smell of box, directed Henry Wise to undo much of William and Mary's parterre work. In 1707 the Fountain Garden lost most of its fountains and was grassed over. However, in 1710 she had the canal dug around the Fountain Garden.

At Kensington Gardens the Queen also made changes, in 1704 adding the Upper Garden and in 1705 making the Royal Paddock, an enclosure for deer and antelope, from Hyde Park. The Upper Garden consisted of three woodland quarters, a mount and a hollow. The latter, formerly a gravel pit, was regularized to form two symmetrical flights of terraces, liberally adorned with clipped evergreens.

Dutch influence in the late 17th century was not confined to the gardens of William and Mary. An interesting survival is Westbury Court Garden in Gloucestershire, which the National Trust has restored since it acquired the property in 1967. The canals, a tall summerhouse dominating the low-lying site, the intricate topiary, the sense of enclosure and independence from the house and, above all, the horticultural emphasis on ornamental and useful plants are more Dutch than French in character.

The development of the english style

Intellectual, economic and social factors contributed to a reaction in the second decade of the 18th century against the fussiness of Dutch gardens and the severe geometry of the French style. The growing discontent with formality was first expressed in the writings of Ashley Cooper, third Earl of Shaftesbury, and in the essays of Joseph Addison. Shaftesbury gave the lead in promoting the concept of the Man of Taste and, in presenting Nature as a new ideal, symbolic of humanistic and liberal

principles, provided the philosophical basis for the idealized landscape gardens of the mid-18th century. Writing in the *Spectator* Addison asked, 'Why may not a Whole Estate be thrown into a kind of garden by frequent plantations? ... If the *natural* embroidery of the meadows were helped and improved by some small additions of Art ... a man might make a pretty Landscape of his own possessions'. At his own small estate of Bilton in Warwickshire he put this idea into practice by the introduction of irregular plantations and winding streams.

Another man of letters who promoted the cause of the natural garden was Alexander Pope. In an essay on gardening in the *Guardian* (1713) he urged a return to the 'amiable simplicity of unadorned nature', rejecting the balance, regularity, and artificiality of formal gardens and elaborate topiary work. Much later, in the verse *Epistle to Burlington* (1731), he proclaimed his cardinal rule: 'In all, let Nature never be forgot ... Consult the Genius of the Place'; in other words, local topography should suggest the character of the garden. From

1717 his own garden at Twickenham, exemplifying his principles of 'pleasing intricacy' and 'artful wildnes', enhanced his considerable influence among a wide circle.

Intellectual and literary influences alone would not have launched a revolutionary movement. The early years of the 18th century saw great improvements in agriculture and landowners benefited from a series of Acts of Parliament that enabled them to enclose large areas of common land. New and better roads and lighter vehicles made travel easier, encouraging expeditions for pleasure rather than necessity. There was, moreover, the impetus given by the Palladian revival in architecture, which provided an important stimulus to the remodelling of old houses and the building of new, to which a landscaped setting was widely accepted as complementary. The first half

The engraving by Kip, c. 1707, of Westbury Court in Gloucestershire shows the formal garden created by Maynard Colchester in the preceding ten years. In many respects the garden is more Dutch than French in character, particularly in its horticultural emphasis.

of the 18th century was essentially a period of improvement and that word in fact became a synonym for the laying out of parks and gardens. This climate was propitious for the development of new ideas of garden-making.

Sir John Vanbrugh

One of the most influential forums for progressive ideas was the Kit-Cat Club. Among the distinguished figures who belonged to this select coterie were the authors Joseph Addison and Richard Steele, the architect Sir John Vanbrugh and landowners such as the Duke of Newcastle (Claremont), the Earl of Carlisle (Castle Howard), Viscount Cobham (Stowe) and General John Dormer (Rousham) who were to make important gardens in the new landscape style. Though never a professional landscape gardener, Sir John Vanbrugh has been claimed as a pioneer of the English

landscape movement, for in the design of buildings he showed an intuitive feeling for their setting. There is no evidence that he ever planned a garden layout but it is probable that at the least he was a powerful stimulus to innovative gardening in the first quarter of the 18th century through his association with major figures and his involvement in the development of Castle Howard and Stowe, two gardens which set the pace in the new art of landscape design. Thomas Brown Duncombe may have been advised by Vanbrugh to site his house at Duncombe Park in North Yorkshire so as to take advantage of views over the landscape. In any event, the creation there of the irregular terrace between 1713 and 1718 was a landmark in the development of the English natural style. In the 1750s this was complemented by a further terrace built a mile away overlooking the ruined Rievaulx Abbey.

At Castle Howard in Yorkshire the architect Sir John Vanbrugh set the Temple of the Four Winds on the Terrace Walk, which follows the line of the old village street, at an oblique angle to the house. This was a significant departure from rectilinear layouts.

Castle Howard

In comparison with Duncombe, the landscape at Castle Howard was on a truly heroic scale and very much the creation of an amateur, the third Earl of Carlisle. At an early stage he had considered plans by London for a formal layout of canals and four broad avenues but this scheme may already have seemed old-fashioned to the Earl. The Castle Howard conceived by Carlisle and his architect Vanbrugh was from the outset vast in scale, theatrical and epic. Horace Walpole, writing in 1772, was moved to comment: 'Nobody had told me that I should at one view see a palace, a town, a fortified city, temples on high places, woods worthy of being each a metropolis of the Druids, the noblest lawn on earth fenced by half the horizon, and a mausoleum that would tempt one to be buried alive.'

The first step in creating the landscape had been to set the house parallel with, rather than at right angles to, the approach so as to create a broad open view. The conception was not realized immediately. Until about 1723 Vanbrugh was occupied with creating the approach on the north side of the house, which passed via an obelisk through the Pyramid Gate, on either side of which was later built the bastioned park wall. The rejection of a regular star-shaped pattern of walks, in the conventional manner, for Wray Wood (such as had been featured in London's original proposal) was decisive for the development of the 'natural' style. Between 1718 and 1732 it was turned into a labyrinth of tangled paths, enlivened by various fountains.

Of similar importance was the line taken by the Terrace Walk at an oblique angle to the house, following the direction of the old village street. At the end of this wide grass walk Vanbrugh set the Temple of the Four Winds, finished in 1728, two years after his death. The scenic climax of the whole is provided by Hawksmoor's Mausoleum, which was begun in 1729.

Cirencester Park

The success of the publications of Stephen Switzer, beginning in 1715 with *The Nobleman, Gentleman, and Gardener's Recreation* (enlarged and reissued in 1718 as *Ichnographia Rustica*), is a measure of the eagerness for new ideas on improving estates, and of Switzer's own influence. For a time he had worked in the Brompton Park Nurseries of London and Wise, and may also have played a part in the laying out of Wray Wood at Castle Howard, before coming under the spell of the new trend in design and establishing himself as a writer. He argued that a whole estate was to be the subject of design, the house and the estate being linked by one or two great axial lines (his 'boldest strokes'). All other parts of the estate garden would be positioned with regard to use, the qualities of the ground, the prospect, and to agricultural improvement or forest plantation.

Cirencester Park in Gloucestershire, one of the largest landscape gardens of the early 18th century, is the most perfect example of Switzer's 'Rural and Extensive Gardening' and its general design is probably due to him. Nonetheless, Lord Bathurst as owner was keenly interested in the execution and the detail of the design. The house is unusually close to the town of Cirencester and is separated from it only by a large forecourt enclosed by an enormously high yew hedge. The structure of the landscape design is one of great lines and woodland, punctuated by a few buildings. Bathurst, who was knowledgeable about trees, was possibly influenced by Pope's gardening precepts in the way he laid out the woodlands. Pope, who visited Cirencester in 1718, enthusiastically approved of the way the irregularly shaped woods were interspersed with fields and open spaces. His link with Cirencester is commemorated by a small classical pavilion, known as Pope's Seat, in the avenue.

Charles Bridgeman

One of Switzer's early recommendations was that 'all the adjacent country should be laid open to view' and that gardens should no longer be enclosed with walls 'by which the eye is as it were imprisoned and the feet fettered in the midst of the extensive charms of nature'. These views may well have been in part responsible for freeing the outlook of his one-time colleague in the Brompton Park nurseries, Charles Bridgeman. Bridgeman is certainly one of the key figures in the evolution of the English landscape garden. Although, said Horace Walpole in 1780, Bridgeman still 'adhered much to straight walks with high clipped hedges, he had many detached thoughts, that strongly indicate the dawn of modern taste'. The ha-ha, a dry ditch used to conceal the boundary of an estate or landscape, was not Bridgeman's invention; the device was first used in France in the 17th century. Bridgeman's 'capital stroke', as Walpole correctly assessed, was to use the ha-ha extensively. 'No sooner was this simple enchantment made than levelling, mowing and rolling followed. The contiguous ground of the park without the sunk fence was to be harmonized with the lawn within; and the garden in its turn was to be set free from its prim regularity, that it might assort with the wilder country without.'

Claremont in Surrey shows the work of a succession of great landscape designers of the 18th century. The amphitheatre, a unique survival, now restored by the National Trust, was designed by Charles Bridgeman for the first Duke of Newcastle.

Bridgeman was able to combine work on a number of private estates with, from 1728 to 1738, the official post of Royal Gardener to George II and Queen Caroline. Much of Bridgeman's contribution to the royal gardens consisted of preserving the existing layout rather than initiating new and adventurous schemes; under him Hampton Court and Windsor retained their formality. Even in work for private clients the formality was sometimes only slightly eased, but elsewhere he could be much more adventurous.

Claremont

At Claremont in Surrey Bridgeman was one of the first of a succession of great landscape gardeners adding to and adapting what went before rather than sweeping all away to begin again. He was engaged by the Duke of Newcastle to extend the grounds of the country retreat acquired from Sir John Vanbrugh, whom the Duke, when he bought the property, had retained to design a new house and garden. A plan of 1725 shows the layout, the core of which, Vanbrugh's Belvedere and bowling-green with serpentine walks through the surrounding woods, still survives. Bridgeman made a round pond, later to become the lake, and the superb turf amphitheatre, a unique survival, fully restored in the late 1970s by the National Trust.

Stowe

The most magnificent of the private estates on which Bridgeman worked was Stowe in Buckinghamshire, the seat of Richard Temple, the first Viscount Cobham. Stowe was the most celebrated English landscape of the day. Bridgeman seems to have begun his activities there in 1713, working alongside Vanbrugh. Stowe remained at the growing point of taste throughout the 18th century and the sumptuous set of views which Bridgeman commissioned from Rigaud and Baron, published by Sarah Bridgeman in 1739, the year after her husband's death, give an idea of Bridgeman's contribution. They show a remarkable fusion of formal, transitional and progressive elements within a cohesive and dramatic layout, the underlying geometry of which had been developed asymmetrically.

Bridgeman, perhaps inspired by Vanbrugh, exploited the awkwardness of the

Vanbrugh, Bridgeman, Kent and 'Capability' Brown all worked at Stowe in Buckinghamshire, the most celebrated and influential English garden of the 18th century. The Temple of British Worthies was one of nearly 40 buildings in Lord Cobham's great landscape park.

site, adapting as key features the existing irregularities and, in one of the earliest extensive uses of the ha-ha, related the garden to the farmland beyond. His layout incorporated an adventurous and judicious use of walks, regular and irregular planting, waterscape, and numerous temples and garden features, many of them embodying personal, literary, historical, religious and mythological themes. Many of the ideas that were developed at Stowe must have come from Lord Cobham himself. This does not, however, detract from the contribution of a designer who was conversant with the progressive thinking of the day and who led in expressing new ideas in garden design.

William Kent

The freeing of garden design from the last traces of formality, a process in which Bridgeman had played such an important part, was completed by William Kent. He had begun his working life as a coach painter but he early attracted the attention of patrons, who enabled him to travel in Italy. The understanding he gained there of landscape painting proved invaluable when, under the patronage of the third Earl of Burlington, he turned his attention to architecture and gardening, for he was able to visualize with a painter's eye the setting of a house as a series of pastoral scenes. The landscape designs that he later carried out

suggest that, as well as having absorbed from Claude Lorrain and Salvator Rosa a feeling for the picturesque scene, he was strongly influenced by the masque designs of Inigo Jones, an edition of which he had published in 1727.

Unlike his professional predecessors, who had practical as well as theoretical knowledge of garden layout, Kent's approach was essentially visual. He relied heavily on foremen and artisans to carry out his garden schemes and to translate into practical terms his drawings for buildings. In spite of these drawbacks, Kent's success both as an architect and landscape gardener was immediate.

One of the first gardens in which he had a hand was at Chiswick House, Lord Burlington's Palladian villa on the edge of London. He replanted the grove which led to an exedra with statues of Roman emperors and introduced a more naturalistic note in the lawn between the villa and the lake, at the end of which he built a cascade. Alexander Pope, who gave Kent encouragement as a designer, was quick to acknowledge the originality of Chiswick. In his view Burlington was the first owner of importance to 'consult the genius of the place' and to respect its natural contours. One of Kent's first buildings was, significantly, the Shell Temple at Pope's miniature Twickenham estate.

At several other estates, Kent worked

with, or followed shortly after, Bridgeman. At Claremont, for example, the Duke of Newcastle turned to Kent after Vanbrugh's death. In this case Kent retained the essence of Vanbrugh's and Bridgeman's layouts but reduced the formality and made an irregular lake and a Cascade. The Grotto which survives today, on the site of Kent's Cascade, dates from the 1750s. In some cases it is not certain that Kent was landscape designer as well as architect. This is the case at Stowe, where the Elysian Fields were laid out 'after Mr Kent's notions', with the avoidance of all straight lines and the creation of a sequence of 'natural' pictures. There were buildings by Kent and the garden design was probably his too, but there is no certain evidence.

In other instances, such as Euston Hall in Suffolk and Holkham Hall in Norfolk, some of Kent's buildings survive and also his drawings for the grounds. Those for Euston show his typical use of clumps of trees, criticized by Horace Walpole as making a lawn look 'like the ten of spades'. The park of Esher Place in Surrey, where in Walpole's view 'Kent is Kentissime', was broken up for development in the 1930s and only the residual Tower house and grotto remain. But at Rousham House in Oxfordshire the grounds as laid out by Kent have miraculously survived, rather overgrown perhaps but untouched by shifts of fashion.

Chiswick House on the outskirts of London was the influential Palladian villa begun for Lord Burlington in 1725. The Orangery, shown in a painting by Pieter Andreas Rysbrack, c. 1729–30, was part of the new romantic pictorial landscape around it.

Rousham

In 1738 Rousham was one of the first places to realize Addison's idea of 'a whole estate thrown into a kind of garden' and Pope's notion of 'calling in' the surrounding countryside. The statues look out over the River Cherwell to an eye-catcher outside the boundaries, linking the garden to the gentle, undulating Oxfordshire scene. For buildings within the grounds Kent used the classical style but for distant buildings, such as the eye-catcher, he made use of picturesque Gothic. The Praeneste Terrace, a seven-arched portico, is an allusion to the Temple of Fortune at the Roman town of Praeneste, the modern Palestrina, a site much visited on the grand tour. To appreciate fully the sequence of idyllic scenes that make up the garden, it is important to follow the circuit as Kent intended. Fortunately this is known from an estate plan of 1738 and a letter of 1750 written by the gardener. It is clear from the latter that Rousham was intended first to be seen as a *ferme ornée*, that is to say a farm laid out for enjoyment with paths running beside hedgerows made ornamental with a mixture of shrubs and herbaceous plants, with the garden hidden behind a screen of evergreens. The first seat was placed to view the Gothicized house across the ha-ha and grazed field. The path then winds through woodland to the Cold Bath glade and along the stream to the Temple of Echo. The climax of the walk was the Venus Vale, a long valley with a chain of ponds, intended to be seen from below, forming a *trompe-l'oeil* effect of cascades running down the hill.

'Capability' Brown

In his lack of practical expertise Kent was the antithesis of 'Capability' Brown, his successor as the foremost exponent of landscape gardening. Lancelot Brown (known as 'Capability' on account of his references to the 'capabilities' of the places on which he was consulted) already had a knowledge of building and gardening work when, in the early 1740s, he came to the notice of Lord Cobham, whose gardens at Stowe were then regarded as among the finest in the country. In 1741 Brown became head gardener and within a short time he was also acting as clerk of the works

and paymaster. In the execution of Kent's designs for buildings and in the laying out of the grounds, where the design was in Kent's style though the guiding hand was probably that of Cobham himself, Brown absorbed Kent's theories and manner of composition. Another influence was James Gibbs, an architect who worked for over 20 years at Stowe and was responsible for several of the numerous buildings that formed part of this great landscape park.

Before his death in 1749 Cobham had helped Brown with recommendations to

Rousham in Oxfordshire was one of the earliest and most admired English landscaped gardens. As it stands it is entirely the work of William Kent. The Venus Vale comes as the climax to the circuit that Kent intended.

friends and relatives. By the early 1750s it was apparent that Brown was the new master of landscape gardening, able to provide not only the designs but also the directions necessary for their execution. Although he continued to subscribe to Pope's dictum that the success of landscape

One of 'Capability' Brown's earliest works, in the middle of the 18th century, was the landscaping of Petworth House in West Sussex for Lord Egremont.

The view shows the house from across the extensive lake, which was formed by damming up a stream.

At Blenheim Palace in Oxfordshire the little River Glyme, crossed by Vanbrugh's monumental bridge, was canalized in the 1720s, with a cascade created beneath the bridge. The cascade and canal were drowned by the two large lakes created by 'Capability' Brown in 1764.

lay principally in 'the contrasts, the management of surprises, and the concealment of the bounds', Brown was no mere imitator of his predecessors. His landscapes, conceived in broad, bold sweeps on a scale far beyond that on which Kent had worked, utilized large expanses of water and the planting of trees by the thousand in belts and clumps.

Among the earliest examples of Brown's work are Petworth House in West Sussex and Warwick Castle in Warwickshire. At Petworth, where the design was drawn up for Lord Egremont while Brown was still at Stowe, notable features include the extensive lake formed by damming up a stream. Recent work confirms that most of the trees were already there when Brown started work. He thinned and regrouped them and planted more.

The finished work at Warwick Castle, where Brown was employed by Lord Brooke from the 1740s to the 1760s, was much praised by Horace Walpole, enabling Brown to develop his country-wide practice. The old formal garden 'without the castle wall', which was in existence when Queen Elizabeth visited the castle in 1576, was removed and the ground shaped, taking account of the mount and framing a view to the Castle Park. Trees were planted as belts, clumps, and specimens, notably cedars of Lebanon. A new carriage drive was made and the courtyard levelled and turned into lawns with Scots pine planted to complement the picturesque scene. In the 1750s Brown was also commissioned to begin the improvements to Castle Park across the River Avon, though here the park was not completed until the 1780s.

For 35 years Brown dominated the profession, his numerous commissions obliging him in the 1760s to take on two draughtsmen for the initial surveying that his work entailed. In many instances, his landscapes could only be created by sweeping away or drastically modifying existing layouts. At Chatsworth in Derbyshire, for example, where Brown worked for the

Between 1722 and 1742 John Aislabie created at Studley Royal in Yorkshire the finest formal water garden in England. The Temple of Piety stands beside the Moon Ponds, one round and two crescent-shaped, that are among the water features fed by the River Skell.

brugh's bridge, were among Brown's most ambitious water features and, backed by a skilfully shaped landscape planted with belts and clumps of trees, resulted in what is sometimes regarded as Brown's finest work. Early in this century the ninth Duke of Marlborough reintroduced formal features in the immediate vicinity of the Palace, in particular the water terraces on the west front designed by Achille Duchêne.

The Brownian formula, though varied to suit the topography of different sites, remained remarkably consistent throughout his career, as can be seen by comparing early works with one of his last commissions, Heveningham Hall in Suffolk. In 1781 Brown drew up plans for the then owner, Sir Gerard Vanneck. Although Brown's sudden death in 1783 cut short his own supervision of the work, much of what he proposed was carried out, including the formation of one of the proposed lakes. He was probably also responsible for the planting of several cedar trees which remain in the foreground of the nine-bay orangery, although the design of the building itself is attributed to James Wyatt.

The amateur tradition in the 18th century

In his lifetime Brown had no serious rival in the field of landscape gardening. The amateur tradition in the 18th century was, however, strong and to it we owe some of the finest and most interesting of British gardens. An early example is at Studley Royal in North Yorkshire. The gardens were created by John Aislabie, who had retired to his estate in 1722 after being ruined by the bursting of the South Sea Bubble. The River Skell was used to create a magnificent formal water-garden, including a large lake, grotto springs, a long formal canal and the Moon Ponds – one round and two crescent-shaped – beside which stands the Temple of Piety. The well-wooded steep hillside above the water has a vista walk, approached by a long, twisting grotto

fourth Duke of Devonshire, he destroyed almost all of the vast formal garden, one of the outstanding examples of the early 18th century, and also widened and altered the course of the River Derwent. At Blenheim Palace in Oxfordshire Brown swept away

formal features such as the 'military' state garden with bastions and curtain walls that had been designed to complement Vanbrugh's elaborate architecture. The two large lakes created by damming the canalized River Glyme, one either side of Van-

Painshill in Surrey was owned by Charles Hamilton between 1738 and 1773 and in this time he developed a masterly natural and picturesque landscape that had considerable influence. As well as the Gothic temple there were buildings in various styles.

tunnel. The ruins of Fountains Abbey, one of the noblest monastic ruins in Christendom, came into the possession of Aislabie's son 50 years after they had become visually incorporated in this romantic landscape of outstanding beauty. The approach through the park from a small hamlet is by a long broken avenue of trees aligned on the towers of Ripon Cathedral, some 3 km (2 miles) away, the park having originally been a formal layout. The house was burned down in 1946 but there remains a magnificent stable block by Colen Campbell and, also by him, a Banqueting House which forms part of the garden layout.

In Scotland, one of the leading figures in the political and artistic life of Edinburgh at the beginning of the 18th century was Sir John Clerk. He was an enlightened land-owner, who from the 1720s to the 1740s made important experiments in garden design at Penicuik House in Midlothian. After returning from a trip to London, which he had made especially to see gardens, he began to turn Penicuik into a sort of *ferme ornée*. By the 1730s he had made through his estate a circular walk that took in a grotto, the Cave of Hurley (made with the cave of the Cumaean Sybil in mind), and a little summer-house, 'Claremont'. The creator of this poetic landscape was influential in advising such friends as Lord Hopetoun at Hopetoun House.

Better-known examples of the *ferme ornée* are Woburn Farm in Surrey and The Leasowes in West Midlands. The former was created by Philip Southcote from 1735. The farm was two-thirds pasture with cattle and sheep and one-third arable. Around the fields and connecting temples and garden buildings were sand-walks with, on one side, a herbaceous border backed by mixed shrubs added to the old hedgerow. South-cote himself described it in about 1752: 'All my design at first was to have a garden on the middle high ground and a walk all round my farm, for convenience as well as pleasure: for from my garden I could see

The grounds at Stourhead in Wiltshire were laid out by Henry Hoare II over a period of 30 years in the middle of the 18th century. The landscape centres on a lake, the circuit walk taking in a grotto and buildings designed by Henry Flitcroft.

what was doing in the grounds, and by the walk could have a pleasing access to either of them where I might be wanted.'

The creator of The Leasowes, William Shenstone, strove to establish his reputation from the landscape garden or *ferme ornée* he made between 1745 and 1763. In this he was successful, drawing many distinguished visitors, but his project caused him to overspend disastrously. The visitor followed a prescribed route, which presented scenes of grandeur, beauty, and variety. Latin inscriptions and dedications invoked classical associations and urns dedicated to the memory of friends provided a desirable tinge of melancholy. There were also

garden buildings, a grotto, bridges, cascades and waterfalls, and the ruins of a priory.

Another amateur who spent more on extensive garden works than his income allowed was Charles Hamilton. In 1738 he obtained a crown lease of Painshill in Surrey, where he developed a masterly natural and picturesque landscape. Partly park and partly pleasure-grounds centred round a lake, Painshill presented a series of set-pieces, both visually and in moods: there were classical scenes, with a Temple of Bacchus in a colourful setting, a Roman mausoleum in a rough dreary setting, and a rustic hermitage set in a dark and gloomy

wood. There were also illusions: the lake, for example, was made to seem larger than it was, and the circuit undulated considerably to give the visitors a number of different angles and heights to look at it from.

Hamilton planted many exotics, especially conifers from North America, and made much use of colour, both in flowers and shrubs. The buildings were a mixture of classical, Gothic, rustic and oriental but the most extravagant effect was created by the grotto of crystal spar. The whole garden is now being restored by the Painshill Park Trust.

Of all the great 18th-century English landscapes created by amateurs, Stourhead in Wiltshire has survived most nearly intact, despite the overlays of succeeding generations. The grounds were laid out over a period of about 30 years by Henry Hoare II, after the death of his second wife in 1743. The circuit walk is set away from the Palladian house, built by the first Henry Hoare, and centres on a lake formed by damming the River Stour. The descent from the house and the circuit of the lake offer a sequence of scenes that reflect Henry Hoare II's wide reading and excellent eye for art. The buildings, which were made in sequence round the lake, were mostly designed by Henry Flitcroft. The Pantheon, a domed

At Stourhead the view across the lake from the Pantheon takes in the five-arched bridge built in 1762, with Stourton church and village in the background. This forms what Henry Hoare called 'a charming Gaspard picture'.

rotunda screened by a recessed portico, symbolizing the classical ideal, dominates the scene, while the Temple of Apollo looks down on what Horace Walpole described as 'one of the most picturesque scenes in the world'. In this landscape the inspiration of the paintings of Claude Lorrain, Poussin and Salvator Rosa are more strongly evident than in any other surviving 18th-century landscape.

The new master of the landscape movement

The man who eventually inherited Brown's reputation as the leading professional landscape gardener was Humphry Repton. Although he had no orthodox training for the profession which he assumed in 1788, he was a man of culture who had taken an amateur interest in the subject and acquired a good deal of practical knowledge of trees and land management while living on his own small estate in Norfolk. His rapid success was in large measure due to the attractive manner in which his recommendations were presented to his clients. The proposals, in manuscript form, were bound in leather and interspersed with drawings, often with movable flaps showing the grounds before and after improvement. He ultimately claimed to have produced over 400 of these so-called Red Books (from the colour usually adopted for the binding), but less than half that number can now be traced.

Repton's concept of landscape design was, by his own admission, based on that of Brown, but his plantations tended to be thicker, while the small buildings in the grounds were frequently of a rustic rather than a classical character. Later he adopted an element of formality in the immediate vicinity of the house, using terraces with balustrades and steps, or trellised enclosures for flowers. He took a particular interest in details such as lodges and cottages, conservatories and 'winter galleries', which were covered walks for exercise in bad weather. His schemes, however, were seldom on so extensive a scale as Brown's and did not involve massive construction work of the kind undertaken for many of Brown's landscapes.

Often his commissions were to introduce additional features in a landscape created by Brown several years earlier. This is the case at Holkham Hall in Norfolk, where he laid out a new pleasure-garden, and at Wimpole Hall in Cambridgeshire, where he was responsible for enclosing a small piece of ground before the north front.

Of the many commissions executed by Repton two gave him particular satisfaction. For Woburn Abbey in Bedfordshire he produced an unusually large and handsome Red Book for the sixth Duke of Bedford in

Humphry Repton, working with his son John Adey Repton, was responsible for the conception of house and garden at Sheringham Hall in Norfolk. As at other properties, the proposals were set out in a Red Book with before and after views. On the left is a view before, from the proposed site looking east, and, above, the same view after.

1802. His proposals included enlarging the stream to form a serpentine river and making a private garden for the family, a 'dressed flower garden', and an American garden (that is to say, an area planted with introductions from North America), in addition to further planting in the park. Other changes included replacing an existing bridge by one of more modest proportions and the erection of a rustic retreat, known as the Thornery. Repton was later able to say that his proposals had 'nowhere been so fully realized as at Woburn Abbey'.

Both the house and grounds at Sheringham Hall in Norfolk were the conception of Humphry Repton and his son John Adey Repton. In the Red Book prepared for the owner, Abbot Upcher, in 1812, the elder Repton remarked that the site had 'more of what my predecessor called *Capabilities*' than any other which he had encountered. 'This', he added, 'may be considered my most favourite work.' The old house on the outskirts of the village was abandoned and 'an appropriate gentlemanlike residence', completed a few months after Humphry Repton's death in 1818, was built in a more picturesque situation against a wooded hillside with distant views of the sea.

18TH CENTURY DIVERSITY

A short-lived phenomenon of the mid-century was the rococo garden, a small-scale intricate garden with effects of rockwork, shellwork, rusticity and, sometimes, flowerbeds in patterns. Some of these gardens were recorded in the watercolours of Thomas Robins. The leading rococo designer was Thomas Wright, who worked at Badminton and elsewhere. Gardens of this type survive at Bowood (the cascade valley), Hampton Court House and Painswick, Gloucestershire.

Architecture played a considerable part in the 18th-century garden, and leading architects of the day displayed an astonishing range of styles, from Gothic to classical, from Chinese to rustic. Both the Gothic and Greek revival movements started in gardens. Buildings could be used for associative as well as decorative effect. Other artefacts included sculpture and bridges, the most delightful being the Palladian bridges at Prior Park, Stowe and Wilton.

Kew

A prolific designer of garden buildings in the second half of the 18th century was the architect Sir William Chambers. He had visited China twice, in 1744 and 1748, at a time when there was a growing vogue for chinoiserie, and in 1757, just as he was laying out the Botanic Gardens at Kew for Princess Augusta, he published his *Designs for Chinese Buildings*. The numerous buildings he designed for Kew included not only examples in the Chinese style but also a mosque, a Palladian bridge, 20 classical temples and the Great Stove, then the largest hot-house in existence, all of which were illustrated in *Plans of the Gardens and Buildings at Kew* (1763). Of those remaining today the ten-storeyed pagoda and Roman 'ruined' triumphal arch are outstanding.

Kew, it should be added, developed as a botanical garden during the reign of George III, who in 1771 appointed Sir Joseph Banks, President of the Royal Society and a central figure in an international network of botanists and other scientists, as horticultural and botanical adviser to the gardens. However, after Banks's death the fortunes and standing of the gardens declined until the appointment in 1841 of Sir William Hooker as director. He was the first of a succession of directors who established

Kew's modern reputation as one of the world's leading institutions concerned with the study of plants. Its scientific role is supported by exceptionally rich living collections and its grounds incorporate many reminders of a long history. Two of the most splendid 19th-century additions are the Palm House, erected in the 1840s and designed by Decimus Burton and Richard Turner, and the Temperate House, also designed by Burton and begun in 1860, though not completed until 1898.

REACTION AGAINST THE LANDSCAPE STYLE

Repton published three volumes in which he set out at length his views on almost every aspect of landscape gardening. Rather to his surprise, he found himself embroiled in a controversy with Richard Payne Knight and Sir Uvedale Price (authors of a didactic poem, *The Landscape*, and *Essays on the Picturesque*) on the nature of the picturesque. The principles of landscape planning to which Brown and subsequently Repton had subscribed were bitterly attacked by both men, with whom Repton had hitherto been on friendly terms. The picturesque controversy continued acrimoniously into the first ten years or so of the 19th century even though the landscape movement had

clearly reached its zenith by this time.

Uvedale Price gave advice on the laying out of several landscapes according to picturesque principles and his *Essays on the Picturesque* proved an influential work. However, among early examples of the genre one of the most truly picturesque creations was Hafod in Wales, which was laid out by Thomas Johnes, a cousin of Richard Payne Knight. The estate was in the valley of the River Ystwyth, where lush pastures were surrounded by bleak mountains. To take advantage of the cascades on the mountain streams Johnes created an extensive system of rides and walks and planted more than two million trees on the mountains. He was disappointed, though, in not realizing his original vision of a smiling peasantry in a smiling country and few of his improvements now survive.

Among the gardens directly inspired by the principles outlined by Uvedale Price was that created by William Beckford, in the early years of the 19th century, for his Gothic Fonthill Abbey in Wiltshire with its famed American plantation, still to be seen though in decay. However, Mount Edgcumbe in Cornwall, a spectacular sea-girt landscape laid out to take advantage of picturesque views, was Price's particular favourite. Scotney Castle in Kent is an outstanding example of a late Regency

At Mount Edgcumbe in Cornwall, on a site which affords views hardly equalled in Britain, the first Earl of Mount Edgcumbe devised walks and grounds in a manner that delighted the influential connoisseur of the picturesque, Sir Uvedale Price.

garden laid out in the picturesque manner by Edward Hussey II with some advice from W.S. Gilpin. The new house was sited looking down on the ruined castle and moat and over a wide pastoral valley. The boldest effect was created by opening a quarry between the new house and the ruin, subsequently richly planted with rhododendrons, azaleas and Japanese maples.

Hawkstone in Shropshire is a late 18th-century picturesque garden where a sandstone cliff rises 100m (300ft) from the plain, and the precipices caused Dr Johnson to tremble with fear. Other attractions included a labyrinthine grotto inside the cliff and a live hermit.

MIXED AND FORMAL STYLES IN THE 19TH CENTURY

The initial plans for Scotney were drawn up in 1836, when the picturesque was already in decline. Since the beginning of the century an increasing number of writers had been lamenting the destruction of the old formal gardens by the 18th-century landscape designers and there was a shift in favour of the preservation and restoration of those that survived. At Levens Hall in Cumbria the amazing display of topiary was recut as early as 1804.

John Claudius Loudon, a prolific writer on garden subjects who was aware of a middle-class readership owning small or medium-sized gardens, must be counted an important influence on the return to formality in garden design during the 19th century. The idea that gardens should be different from the natural landscape and recognizable as works of art provided Loudon with a philosophical support for the taste in regular gardens he had acquired during his European tours in the second decade of the century. In place of pictur-esque gardening, Loudon proposed the idea of the 'gardenesque' style – that is, a style in which each individual plant is allowed to develop its natural character as fully as possible. The term did not become current in garden literature until after Loudon's death in 1843 and then it was not used in Loudon's sense but described a style of garden layout characterized by rampant eclecticism and lack of artistic unity.

Alton Towers

By far the best example of the gardenesque style in the sense in which the term came to be used was Alton Towers in Staffordshire. Loudon's own verdict on it – 'The work of a morbid imagination joined to the command of unlimited resources' – shows clearly that it did not conform to the style that he was proposing. His own plans for the garden had been rejected. The grounds were laid out between 1814 and 1827 by the fifteenth Earl of Shrewsbury as an elysium in the Churnet valley. Among the many garden buildings erected in the steeply sloping romantic setting are a domed conservatory, a three-storeyed Gothic prospect tower and the cast-iron Pagoda Fountain. Alton Towers is now a pleasure-park, but much of the original garden is well maintained.

Biddulph Grange

Biddulph Grange, also in Staffordshire, is another celebrated example of the mixed style and is one of the most innovatory gardens of the 19th century. The design of James Bateman's garden, only 6 hectares (15 acres) in extent, provided a framework of picturesque settings that allowed for the variety of conditions he needed to grow the wide range of plants he was collecting. The various parts, though secluded from one another, were linked with great ingenuity. An Egyptian court, with its flanking sphinxes and monumental entrance under a yew pyramid, is joined by a dark passageway to the Cheshire cottage, which leads into a pinetum. From a cave in the glen a winding flight of steps in a dark tunnel leads to a Chinese garden, the most striking of all the garden scenes at Biddulph, which still contains some of the original plant introductions of Robert Fortune. The garden is now being comprehensively restored by the National Trust.

The extraordinary display of topiary, shown here in a photograph of c. 1880, is today the chief feature of Levens Hall in Cumbria. The gardens and park were laid out between 1689 and 1712. Many of the original trees still stand but the topiary was recut in 1804.

The remarkable garden created by James Bateman at Biddulph Grange in Staffordshire provided a framework of picturesque settings for a wide range of plants. The Chinese garden, known as 'China', *was planted with bamboos and maples, its features including a temple in a willow-pattern setting, dragon parterre, Great Wall, look-out tower and joss-house.*

Sir Charles Barry

The notion that all garden styles were potentially valid and had to be judged by their own rules gave way gradually to a firmer view of the style most suitable for the English country house. Repton had promoted the idea that English gardens from the 16th century had been based on an Italian style, of which the French and Dutch styles of the later 17th century were merely variants. The Italian became the preferred style for a mansion of olden times or for a modern facsimile, the Italian revival being pioneered by James Wyatt in his terrace garden at Wilton House in the first decade of the 19th century. Sir Charles Barry, who popularized the style, took his inspiration from authentic features of surviving Italian Renaissance models and the fashion he established was a dominant feature of country-house garden design from the 1840s to the 1860s.

The first of his gardens were those he laid out between 1834 and 1842 for the Duke of Sutherland at Trentham Park in Staffordshire. Here he coped with the difficulties of a flat site between the house and the lake (which had been considerably enlarged by 'Capability' Brown) by creating a series of low terraces with elaborate parterres of flowerbeds, fountains, statues, vases, stone balustrading and stone temples and pavilions.

Cliveden and Shrubland Park

In a number of commissions Barry was fortunate to be dealing with sloping sites that offered considerable dramatic potential. At Cliveden in Buckinghamshire, for example, the present house and terrace he designed is on the superb site overlooking the River Thames that was first exploited by the Duke of Buckingham in 1666. Below the imposing terrace is the famous balustrade brought from the garden of the Villa Borghese in Rome, a later and appropriately authentic addition made by the first Viscount Astor in 1896. The Italianate terraces Barry designed for Shrubland Park in Ipswich, Suffolk, in the early 1850s are another example of his use of architectural terracing; a great staircase, dividing into a crescent at the bottom, connects a balcony garden and two terraces. From a loggia on the lower terrace, further steps descend to the informal park.

Cliveden in Buckinghamshire has undergone many changes since the site was first exploited in the second half of the 18th century by the Duke of Buckingham. The Long Garden, containing statuary and topiary box and yew, was created in the late 19th century by the first Viscount Astor.

Barry's practice was to leave the planting of the gardens he designed to the head gardeners. The bedding system, in which flowerbeds are planted with different subjects at different times of the year, was developed on a grand scale in the great Italianate gardens like Shrubland Park and Cliveden. The impressive parterre stretching out below the terrace at Cliveden is a simplified version of a 19th-century design. John Fleming, who became head gardener to the Duke and Duchess of Sutherland after 1849, is credited with being the first to adopt the bi-annual bedding system, in which a spring bedding of bulbs and biennials is followed by a summer planting of pelargoniums, petunias, verbenas, calceolarias and other tender plants.

William Nesfield

While Barry found the inspiration for his Italianate buildings and gardens in Renaissance models, William Nesfield, who came to prominence after the landscaping he carried out at the Royal Botanic Gardens at Kew from 1844 to 1848, turned to old

The impressive parterre at Cliveden is a simplified version of a 19th-century design made for the Duke and Duchess of Sutherland after they acquired the property in 1849. The balustrade just visible in the foreground was brought from the garden of the Villa Borghese in Rome.

gardening literature, primarily works of the late 17th and 18th centuries. Although his stylistic range was varied, he was best known for his parterres in the 17th-century style, using intricate patterns of box tracery on gravel beds. During the 1850s his interest in Tudor precedents grew and led him to experiment with parterres laid out in the patterns of monograms and with beds

relying on coloured gravels rather than plants. Most of his decorative work has been destroyed, including the Royal Horticultural Society's garden at Kensington, where his reliance on gravels provoked strong criticism from horticulturalists and initiated a reaction against him. However, examples of his parterres survive at Holkham Hall in Norfolk and Broughton Hall in

North Yorkshire. At the latter his parterre of a scroll and feather design in box on coloured gravels was turned into a lawn in the 1870s but largely restored at the turn of the century.

Drummond Castle

The re-creation of gardens in a 17th-century style has been a recurrent theme of Scottish gardens in the 19th and 20th centuries and Drummond Castle in Perthshire is an outstanding early example. Lewis Kennedy, who worked at Drummond from 1818 to 1860, was probably responsible for the design. This consists of a long rectangle laid out below the castle and house, divided by diagonals to form a very elongated St Andrew's cross. The design is tightened by the creation of a central square contained within two main walkways, this area itself being divided by a central path. The present simplification of the compartments formed by these lines reveals the underlying structure rather starkly, but originally there was a happy confusion of shrubs and herbaceous plants filling the beds.

PUBLIC PARKS

The first advocate of public parks for the rapidly developing cities of the early 19th century was John Claudius Loudon. At the beginning of the 1820s he compared Britain unfavourably with other European countries: 'our continental neighbours have hitherto excelled us in this department of gardening; almost every town of consequence having its promenades for the citizens *à cheval* and also *au pied*'. In London there were royal parks such as Hyde Park (open to the public since the 1630s) or Richmond Park but in general the ordinary citizen did not have access to public areas affording 'a free wholesome air, and an ample uninterrupted promenade'. What made the creation of public parks possible was a widespread belief that they would be instruments of social reform. Loudon thought that they would 'raise the intellectual character of the lowest classes of society'.

The first public garden that fulfilled Loudon's ideal of a garden of public instruction was Derby Arboretum, completed to his design in 1840. Its outstanding

Drummond Castle in Perthshire is an early example of the revival of an old style of design, effectively recreating the idea of a 17th-century Scottish garden rather than restoring an original layout. Lewis Kennedy, who worked at Drummond between 1818 and 1860, appears to have been responsible for the design and execution of the garden.

feature is the way sinuous artificial mounds enclose the space, solving the problem noted by Loudon that 'there is no distant prospect, or view beyond the grounds, worthy of being taken into consideration before laying them out'. Derby was successful in Loudon's terms as a plant collection, exemplifying his notion of the gardenesque style of planting.

Birkenhead Park

The pioneering but small-scale work at Derby was followed in 1843 by the first major public park, Birkenhead Park in Liverpool. Sir Joseph Paxton's design, which owed little to earlier landscape garden design, provided a brilliant solution to the requirements of a public park (as opposed to a public arboretum or botanical garden), in particular the paths and drives within the park and the circulation systems linking the park with the city. On a swampy, low-lying and extremely unpromising site, he created two lakeside areas strongly enclosed by planted artificial mounds up to 10 m (33 ft) high. The lakes were sinuous in outline, very unlike the serpentine curves of Brown's, and in each lake islands were placed to restrict the expanse of water visible at one glance. The paths, which wound towards and away from the water's edge, contributed to the effect by offering the pedestrian a frequently changing series of views. Even at the path junctions, the intrigued pedestrian is prevented from seeing more than a few metres ahead by massed rock formations and solid planting. The circulation system separated the pleasure traffic within the park from the commercial traffic of the town in such a way that the business of the town was not hindered and the views within the park were unspoiled.

After this promising start the design of English public parks is disappointing. Although most areas of London and the northern industrial towns had a newly created public park by the end of the 1860s, the unattractive character of most of the original sites proved too much of a challenge. The difficulties were often compounded by delays in construction caused by economic and political factors. The Crystal Palace Park at Sydenham (created in 1853), where Paxton supervised the re-erection of his glass masterpiece designed for the Great Exhibition of 1851 and laid out terraced grounds, is one of the few later public parks that matches Birkenhead in quality.

Forms of bedding

The bedding system that had first been developed in private gardens was soon applied to public parks. Between the late 1860s and the 1880s two other forms of bedding were particularly popular. Subtropical bedding used tender plants (a development made possible by advances in greenhouse technology), with large, variegated, brightly coloured or otherwise ornamental leaves, planted in informal groups in which the picturesque effect of the individual plants was more important than the pattern of the bed. In contrast, with carpet bedding the pattern was all-important. Dwarf or creeping foliage plants were trained into a surface as uniform as a carpet, dwarf succulents and plants with unimportant flowers such as sedums sometimes being added for special effects. Early carpet beds were laid out in geometric patterns but the success of butterfly-shaped beds at Crystal Palace in 1875 started a brief fashion for zoomorphic and emblematic shapes. Public parks maintained bedding systems of all kinds long after their decline

in private gardens – for example, on private estates the fashion for carpet bedding faded by the mid-1880s but the style remained a staple of public park practice until well after the First World War.

William Robinson

The reaction against formal bedding out was most energetically expressed by William Robinson, whose life as gardener and writer was a horticultural version of the classic Victorian pattern of diligence and energy leading to success. He started his gardening career in Ireland and it was only after moving to London and joining the staff of the Royal Botanic Garden at Regent's Park that he began the writing that led to an independent career as a prolific journalist and author. His influence still flourishes in the current taste for informality, with bulbs massed among grass, mixed borders of native and exotic plants, and a soft and more subtle use of colour and plant associations. In *The Wild Garden*, first published in 1870, he encouraged 'the

placing of perfectly hardy exotic plants under conditions where they will thrive without further care'. His most important work, *The English Flower Garden*, which was first published in 1883 and ran to fifteen editions during the author's lifetime and several more later, catalogued and illustrated the numerous plants available to the gardener, many of them introduced during the 19th century. There was also advice on planning small or large gardens, with lists of appropriate plants for particular situations and purposes and encouragement for a more natural style of design. At Gravetye Manor in West Sussex, which Robinson bought in 1885, he made the surroundings of the Elizabethan house an example of the kind of gardening he preferred. Largely through Robinson's influence, the herbaceous border, which initially had been an attempt to revive 17th-century garden practice with the planting devoted to 'old-fashioned' flowers, developed independently of its presumed historical associations.

In 1885 William Robinson, the enormously influential exponent of informal gardening, bought the estate of Gravetye Manor in Sussex, where he made the surroundings of the

Elizabethan house an example of the kind of gardening he preferred. After Robinson's death the garden suffered periods of neglect but restoration began in 1958.

OTHER EUROPEAN COUNTRIES

Bernardo Bellotto's view (1760) from the Upper Belvedere, Vienna, with the cityscape as background shows the full glory of Austrian baroque landscape design.

GERMANY

Influences from Italy, the Netherlands, France and England have played an important part in the design of German gardens since the 16th century. While no style of uniquely German character has evolved, these influences have been absorbed and modified in such a way that the most notable gardens of the last four or five hundred years are far from straight translations of foreign ideas and generally show great originality in the adaptation of styles to particular circumstances.

Renaissance garden design

In the 16th and early 17th centuries German gardens were particularly influenced by developments in Italy. A strong interest in botany found expression in numerous written works and in private plant collections, often laid out after the Italian model by doctors and botanists on their return from studying in Italy. The interest spread later to merchants and princes, the grand tour becoming a necessary part of classical education and culture. Between the 16th and 18th centuries every one of the numerous princely gardens in Germany had a pleasure-garden, and patricians and burghers created many only slightly less grand. Among the botanic gardens, which in the main belonged to universities, that of the Bishop of Eichstätt on the Willibaldsburg was outstanding. The plants it contained have been recorded in one of the great monuments of botanical illustration, Basil Besler's *Hortus Eystettensis*, published in 1613.

Hortus Palatinus

The most important German garden of the Renaissance was the Hortus Palatinus, attached to the Schloss at Heidelberg. Elizabeth Stuart, daughter of the English king James I, who was married to the Elector Friedrich V of the Palatinate in 1613, employed her former drawing-master, Salomon de Caus, to design and construct a new garden around the castle. From 1615 five superimposed narrow terraces were laid out, with high retaining walls built up from the Neckar valley to support the lowest terrace. The east terrace, at right angles to the rest of the garden and extending northward towards the river, affords a splendid view over the valley.

The individual terraces were divided by hedges and pergolas and were embellished with typical Renaissance elements such as a maze, gazebos, ponds, statuary and pots of plants. However, much of the garden's reputation – at the time it was hailed as 'the eighth wonder of the world' – derived from its innumerable waterworks and grottoes. These were designed by Caus and, a unique occurrence in German garden design, were musical. The Renaissance terraces survive and in addition a number of grottoes and the ruins of the bathing grottoes and heating chambers. However, the musical water mechanisms have proved less enduring.

Versailles and the baroque

The Thirty Years' War devastated large areas of Germany, where garden-making stagnated in the period from 1618 to 1648. In the second half of the 17th century the new baroque style of garden design was imported from France. German princes summoned French gardeners and fountain designers to their courts or sent their own gardeners to France to be trained. Of the baroque princes, the seven Electors, who elected the Emperor, played the most important part in the creation of gardens. There were four temporal Electors – Brandenburg, Saxony, Palatinate, and Bohemia (later also Bavaria and Hanover) – and three spiritual Electors – Mainz, Cologne and Trier. Of the second group, the Counts of Schönborn, Electors of Mainz, were outstanding patrons of the arts, closely following artistic developments in Vienna.

Although Versailles became the model for the whole of Europe, in Germany there was no attempt to imitate it in every detail.

The gardens of this period reveal great individuality in their ground-plans and decoration. For example, in the design of the Favorite in Mainz, the Archbishop and Elector of Mainz, Lothar Franz Count Schönborn, departed radically from the ideal by laying out the garden mainly with transverse axes. A similar design was used at Veitshöchheim in Bavaria. In some instances the house or castle was set in the middle of the garden, as in the Grosser Garten in Dresden. A number of gardens were laid out in a star shape, as was the case with the Belvedere of Duke E. A. von Sachsen-Weimar at Weimar, where the sections contained animal enclosures.

Karlsruhe

The Schlossgarten at Karlsruhe, Baden-Württemberg, also designed in the shape of a star, is one of the most original German baroque gardens. In keeping with the spirit of absolutism of the time, when the town was founded in 1715 it was made to conform to the same strict geometrical star design as the castle. Thirty-two avenues were designed to radiate from the high central hunting-tower built by Margrave Carl Wilhelm of Baden-Durlach. The boundary of the garden was established by a circle running round the tower at a distance of 440 m (480 yd). The segment of the circle between the two wings of the castle contained a pleasure-garden with a parterre and a *bosquet*, while the main area around the tower was left as a hunting park.

Weikersheim

In Germany the orangery assumed a completely new significance, not only providing winter protection for exotics but also being used to stage musical and theatrical entertainments. Much thought was given to its design and position in the park. In the Favorite in Mainz, for example, the Orangery is the principal building, flanked by three pavilions on each side. At Weikersheim, Baden-Württemberg, the ancestral

In its day the Hortus Palatinus in Heidelberg was hailed as 'the eighth wonder of the world' on account of its waterworks and grottoes. It was created by Salomon de Caus for Elizabeth Stuart, wife of the Elector Friedrich V of the Palatinate.

seat of the Counts of Hohenlohe, the Orangery was built as the termination of the middle axis of the garden, which was begun in 1708. This highly original building, constructed between 1719 and 1723 to a design by the architect Johann Christian Lüttich, consists of two wings extending across the whole width of the parterre. A semicircular recess in the middle, where originally there was an equestrian statue of Count Karl Ludwig of Hohenlohe, who had the garden and Orangery built, opens up to give a vista of the Tauber valley.

Schwetzingen

Many gardens were laid out to a circular plan, as was Schwetzingen, Baden-Württemberg, the summer residence of the Palatine court in the 18th century. Karl Theodor, who became Elector of the Palatinate in 1743, commissioned the famous theatre architect Alessandro Galli da Bibiena to redesign the castle. The two circular buildings that he and the architect Nicolas de Pigage built inspired the court gardener, J. Ludwig Petri, to create a circular parterre. The cross-shaped arrangement of the avenue of limes, beyond which lay *bosquets*, emphasized the garden's highly original circular design. Later additions to the gardens, which contained many statues and fountains, were the Orangery and the rococo theatre of 1752, both designed by Pigage. The parterre was reconstructed to Petri's original design in 1974.

Pillnitz

In many cases the layouts of gardens exploited riverside settings. This was so at Pillnitz, Dresden, where the Indianisches Lustschloss, a water palace, is joined to the landing stage on the Elbe by a flight of steps with two sphinxes. Many of the designs drawn up for August the Strong, who acquired the estate in 1718, were not realized. However, in 1723, the Bergpalais was built to match the Indianisches Lust-schloss 120 m (131 yd) to the north of it. The two buildings were linked by a magnificent parterre formed by 12 compartments arranged around four ponds. To the west the garden consisted of individual hedged gardens, known as Charmillen, where members of the court played garden games. On

the other side of a ha-ha a wide avenue led to Dresden. Other parts of the garden north of the Bergpark laid out between lime and chestnut *allées* (still preserved) or within hedged compartments were devoted to sport, games and entertainment.

Herrenhausen

Although the French baroque garden was the model most generally followed, Dutch gardens also exerted an influence, which was particularly evident in the use of canals to enclose all or parts of the garden. The Grosser Garten at Herrenhausen, Hanover,

The redesigning of the Schloss and garden at Schwetzingen, in Baden-Württemberg, was largely the work of Karl Theodor, who became Elector of the Palatinate in 1743. The highly original garden, circular in design, contained a great deal of statuary and many fountains.

was the creation of Sophie, wife of Ernst August, who had spent her childhood in the Netherlands. Her gardener, Martin Charbonnier, was sent there to study garden design. Sophie began planning her garden in 1680 and extended it in 1692 to its present size of 50 hectares (124 acres). The rectangular layout, enclosed by a canal, is extremely regular, with a middle axis dividing the whole area. The half of the garden nearest the castle (destroyed in 1943) has as its central element a large parterre, richly furnished with sculpture, with a round pond in the middle. High hedges at both sides of the parterre separate it from two large garden rooms – on one side a hedge theatre and on the other a maze. Hedge theatres were popular in German gardens and that at Herrenhausen is an important feature. The stage, decorated with gilt-lead figures from the Netherlands, is in the shape of a trapezium, while the auditorium is constructed in the form of an amphitheatre. There is a small orchestra-pit in front of the

stage, where beech hedges form the wings. Sandstone statues once stood around the sides of the auditorium. The theatre is again being used for performances.

Four ponds and a number of small hedged garden rooms separate the parterre from the other half of the Grosser Garten. This was laid out as a star-shaped *bosquet*, in the middle of which, on the main garden axis, stands the principal fountain. Its jet now reaches a height of 82 m (269 ft), although it was originally only 35 m (115 ft). Ponds with fountains stand at the intersections of the paths in the hedged lateral *bosquets*. Wide avenues lead around the whole garden and terminate at two pavilions at the southern corners.

Schleissheim

Schleissheim in Bavaria is another example of a garden showing Dutch influence and, never having been turned into an English landscape park, it now ranks next to Herrenhausen as the best preserved baroque garden in the German Federal Republic. Max Emmanuel, Elector of Bavaria, as Governor of the Spanish Netherlands in the 1690s had lived in the province and there became acquainted with canal building. Canals play a dominant part in the layout of the baroque gardens that lie between the two castles Max Emmanuel had built, the Lustheim, begun in 1684, and the Neues Schloss, started in 1701. Not only is the garden bounded by canals but the middle

The celebrated baroque garden at Herrenhausen, the summer residence of the Dukes and later Electors of Hanover as early as 1666, reflects Dutch influence, with the extremely regular rectangular layout enclosed by a canal. High hedges bound the parterre.

At Nymphenburg, the summer residence of the Electors of Bavaria, the lavish castle garden was constructed under Max Emmanuel. The long central canal extends the whole length of the garden behind the Schloss and also for some distance in front of it in the direction of the town.

axis is formed by a canal which terminates in a cascade at the end of the parterre nearest the Neues Schloss. Water was used in a particularly original way in the garden around the Lustheim: a circular canal gives the impression that the Schloss and its parterre are on an island. *Bosquets* containing garden rooms linked by hedged paths were placed on either side of the central canal. The parterre is slightly sunk and at each end of the two long beds that flank the central axis stands a round pond with a fountain.

Nymphenburg

Dominique Girard, who had been engaged from Versailles to design Max Emmanuel's garden at Schleissheim, also worked at Augustusburg, Brühl and at Nymphenburg, the summer residence of the Electors of Bavaria. At Augustusburg Girard proposed a similar arrangement for the parterre to that laid out at Schleissheim. A series of French-trained or French gardeners worked at Nymphenburg yet here, too, Dutch

influence is evident. The long central canal not only flows through the whole length of the garden behind the castle, originally terminating in a great cascade, but extends in front of it in the direction of the town. Owing to the arrangement of the side canals, the parterre and the castle seem to stand on an island. *Bosquets* lay each side of the parterre, which was originally laid out with an elaborately embroidered pattern, the pool in the middle being decorated with gilded statues. A *patte-d'oie* arrangement provided three vistas to distant church towers, the boundaries of the park being concealed by the use of ha-has. When the gardens were redesigned as a landscape park by F. L. Sckell, the parterre, central canal and side canals in front of the castle remained unaltered.

Wilhelmshöhe

Wilhelmshöhe in Hessen represents a unique example in Germany of a garden laid out in the Italian baroque style. Landgrave Karl of Hesse-Kassel chose the slopes of the

Habichtswald outside Kassel as the site for the lavish garden, which he ordered to be laid out around the hunting-lodge of Weissenstein. Work began in 1701 to plans by the Italian architect Giovanni Guerniero. The focal point and central axis was a series of cascades, the idea coming from the villas at Frascati, which the Landgrave had seen while visiting Italy in 1699-1700. However, at Weissenstein the idea was translated into gigantic proportions: the difference in height between the octagonal Wasserschloss at the head of the cascades and the Schloss itself is more than 200 m (650 ft) over a distance of more than 1,000 m (3,250 ft). A bronze copy of the Farnese *Hercules*, the emblem of Kassel, was set on a pinnacle rising from the octagonal reservoir, forming the culminating point of the central axis. The waterworks are still operative but only the upper third of the fantastic plan for grottoes and cascades was ever completed, changes in taste contributing to the work being stopped.

From the rococo to the landscape style

In the mid-18th century, while in England the landscape style was already beginning to develop, German garden design underwent a further change from the baroque to the rococo. The gardens attached to princely residences no longer had a merely representative function but served to promote social intimacy: they were divided into numerous small rooms, usually enclosed by hedges, gazebos, or trellises. The layout of these gardens seems deliberately confusing, sometimes even labyrinthine.

Hofgarten, Veitshöchheim

One of the most original of all surviving rococo gardens is the Hofgarten in Veitshöchheim, Bavaria. It served first as a pheasantry, fruit, and kitchen garden, and also as a flower garden around the summerhouse of the prince bishops of Würzburg. After being redesigned at the beginning of the 18th century and undergoing numerous alterations, the final rococo garden was

Work on the lavish gardens in the Italian baroque style created by Landgrave Karl of Hesse-Kassel at Wilhelmshöhe began in 1701. Only the upper third of this fantastic plan of grottoes and cascades was completed.

The Residenz of the prince bishops of Würzburg presented a small and difficult site for the Hofgarten. The design by J.P. Mayer makes ingenious use of embankments, supporting walls, landings, ramps and stairways.

begun in 1763 for Prince Bishop Adam Friedrich of Seinsheim, probably with the assistance of the master gardener, J. Prokop Mayer. The house stands on a slightly raised terrace within a small parterre and the walled garden lies to one side, not aligned on the building, as was almost invariably the case with baroque gardens in the French style. The Hofgarten could be described as a hedge garden, which is divided by longitudinal and transverse axes formed by hedged walks that meet at right angles; short diagonal walks make the garden appear confusing despite its very regular design. At a number of intersections small hedged

garden rooms of varied design were formed, some with small Chinese pavilions, hedge arbours and small fountains.

The most delightful feature of the garden is the rococo statuary, which includes gods, allegorical figures, musicians, and court figures – and even stone seats in fanciful rococo shapes. At the centre of the garden's focal point, a large, irregularly shaped pond known as the Grosser See, rises Mount Parnassus, surmounted by the winged horse Pegasus. A hidden glockenspiel provided a delightful accompaniment when the fountain played.

Residence, Würzburg

Mayer's design for the Prince Bishop's Hofgarten at the Residence in Würzburg was accepted after many other proposals for the difficult site had been considered. The Residence was situated directly by the fortifications of the town so that only a small area was available and its shape was already predetermined by the two triangular bastions standing in front of the building on the garden side. Work on Mayer's plan began in 1774. Stairways adorned with statues lead on to the rampart and enclose the garden, which is divided in a unique three-dimensional arrangement by supporting walls, landings, embankments, stairs and ramps. The garden is lavishly decorated with pergolas, balustrades and sculptures, but the plans for cascades were never executed.

Rheinsberg and Sanssouci

Other important examples of rococo gardens include Rheinsberg and Sanssouci, both in the district of Potsdam. At Rheinsberg Prince Heinrich carried out work from 1744 to 1778 on the former garden of his brother Friedrich II of Prussia. A short main axis and a long transverse axis had been laid to make the best use of the terrain, the transverse axis extending between a range of low hills and the Grienerick Lake. What makes Rheinsberg so impressive is the harmony achieved between the large expanse of lake and the detail of the rococo garden with its gentle undulations.

It was in the mid-18th century that Friedrich II gave the garden of Sanssouci its rococo character. He was responsible for the creation of the vineyard on six curving parabolic terraces, each terrace divided by 28 glazed windows and 16 yew pyramids. Above the vineyard stands the summer Schloss Sanssouci, built between 1745 and 1747 to plans by the architect G.W. Knobelsdorff. Vineyard and Schloss are situated on a hill and afford a splendid view of the countryside and it was this commanding position that was the starting point for

Friedrich II of Prussia was largely responsible for giving the gardens of Sanssouci in Potsdam their rococo character. The vineyard, on six curving parabolic terraces, was laid out in 1744. Glazed windows divided each terrace.

numerous extensions to the garden. Characteristic of this period was the Chinese tea-house, built between 1754 and 1757. This is situated in an area of the garden divided into *bosquets*, through which run two diagonal *allées* with fountains. The tea-house has its own garden, which later became the centre of several vistas.

The oriental style

The popularity of buildings in oriental style was more widespread than survivals might suggest. At Mosigkau in the district of Halle, for example, the old manor-house, which had been retained in a rococo layout, was demolished in 1774 and a Japanese garden was laid out, taking its name from a tea-house in the chinoiserie style. The rococo garden, created between 1752 and 1757, and the Japanese garden were lost when the estate was redesigned in the landscape style during the 19th century, but the 18th-century Schloss survives and houses a valuable art collection. At Oranienbaum, also near Halle, where the cultivation of oranges had been important since the park was created in the late 17th century, Prince Franz Anhalt-Dessau took his ideas from Kew in England. The unified baroque arrangement of parks, Schloss and

town was preserved when the island garden was redesigned in about 1795 as a Chinese garden with a tea-house, five-storeyed pagoda and several small Chinese bridges spanning the canals on which gondolas sailed. The baroque castle survives and the baroque parterre and Chinese garden were reconstructed earlier this century.

Eremitage

Just as buildings in oriental style came into vogue, so too did mock ruins. Eremitage near Bayreuth is an outstanding example of a garden incorporating a number of them within an informal layout in which no attempt was made to arrange them in an axial pattern. In 1735 Margrave Friedrich of Brandenburg-Bayreuth gave the hermitage to his wife, Wilhelmine, sister of Friedrich II of Prussia. The first Eremitage, the Altes Schloss, had been built in 1715 as a place of retreat where members of the court could live in simple seclusion. Scattered in the surrounding woods were other hermitages which could be reached by irregular paths. The Margravine extended the Altes Schloss and built beside it the Neues Schloss, which was originally used as a bird-house and orangery. Some distance from these two buildings is the Untere Grotte, with a large basin in which stands a group of nymphs. It is surrounded on two sides by ruined archways and is equipped with an intricate system of water-jets. Among the mock ruins is a Roman theatre, which was intended for open-air operatic performances.

Sanspareil

Very different in character to Eremitage is the Margravine Wilhelmine's other garden, Sanspareil, Bayreuth, which is regarded as probably the earliest example of a landscape garden on the Continent. The inspiration for the garden was partly the setting, a grove of birch trees with, alongside large masses of rock, strangely shaped isolated boulders. The design of the grove was based on literary allusions drawn from *Les Aventures de Télémaque*, the famous novel by Fénelon. Wilhelmine interpreted the centre of the grove as the magical island of Ogygia, on which Télémaque was shipwrecked during his search for his father Odysseus. The novel had a didactic purpose, and visitors to the grove were to relive Télémaque's experiences and thus undergo a process of purification. The garden was begun in 1744. Only a very few buildings were included in the design, one of the two surviving being a theatre built as a ruin set in a grotto.

Wörlitz

Forerunner though it may have been of the informal landscape, Sanspareil was essentially idiosyncratic. The prime mover in the development of the landscape style in Germany was Prince Franz of Anhalt-Dessau. Wörlitz, the park he laid out in the district of Halle between 1765 and 1817, is the crowning achievement of the so-called Dessau-Wörlitz cultural circle, which was responsible for the creation of an artistically arranged landscape extending for over 25 km (15 miles) from Kühnau near Dessau to the Rehsener Lake near Wörlitz. Classical fronted observation posts on the surrounding dike give the impression that the park extends even further.

Prince Franz played the major role in designing the landscape, but he had working with him gardeners of considerable talent. English gardens were an important influence, particularly those of Claremont, Stourhead, Stowe and The Leasowes. There were Italian influences, too, particularly in the so-called New Gardens of Wörlitz. These were laid out by Johann George Schoch in a sentimental-romantic style with

The Margravine Wilhelmine of Brandenburg-Bayreuth, a sister of Friedrich II (Frederick the Great) of Prussia, was given the Eremitage in 1735. In her development of the retreat the buildings, many of them constructed as ruins, were arranged with complete informality.

The idiosyncratic garden created by the Margravine Wilhelmine at Sanspareil, Bayreuth, was really in the landscape style. The design of the rocky grove was based on literary allusions to Fénelon's famous novel Les Aventures de Télémaque.

Prince Franz of Anhalt-Dessau was greatly influenced by English gardens in the creation of Wörlitz, the first landscape park in Germany. However, the Isle of Rousseau (1782) was directly inspired by the Ile des Peupliers at Ermenonville.

many elements reminiscent of southern Italy and the ancient world.

Prince Pückler-Muskau

Another German landowner whose ideas on landscaping were considerably influenced by the study of English gardens was Prince Hermann of Pückler-Muskau. Humphry Repton was the perceptible influence at Muskau, the park he began to lay out in 1816. A large portion of this now lies in Poland, but the essential part is in the German Democratic Republic. The picturesque quality of the landscape was enhanced by the skilful use of existing trees and by new plantations, and also by the addition of small buildings for purely decorative purposes.

Financial difficulties forced Pückler-Muskau to sell Muskau and at the family estate of Branitz, in the district of Cottbus, to which he moved, the influence of Repton is less obvious in his landscaping. Thanks to his social position, he was able to spread the picturesque style on the Continent. He carried out extensive work at Babelsberg, Potsdam, for the future Emperor Wilhelm I and advised on, and influenced the design of, various parks. Eduard Petzold is regarded as his disciple and, through his own work and writings – he wrote many influential textbooks – he made Pückler-Muskau's ideas more widely known.

Public parks

In the mid-19th century the formal gardens of Renaissance Italy inspired a number of gardens, including works by Peter Joseph Lenné. He was a highly imaginative gardener, whose influence has extended into the 20th century. It is particularly in the area around Postdam that he left his mark, for there he laid out several princely parks in the English landscape style linked by marvellous views across the lakes. In 1833 he drew up a 'Plan to Embellish the Isle of Potsdam' which determined the layout of the landscape for decades to come.

The Englischer Garten in Munich was laid out as a large public park in the new English style after 1789 on the orders of the Elector Karl Theodor.

Lenné made plans for three people's parks (*Volksparke*), beginning with Magdeburg in 1824. However, a much earlier public park, the Englischer Garten, had been created in Munich. In 1789 the Elector Karl Theodor ordered a large public park to be laid out in the new English style. Friedrich Ludwig Sckell worked in collaboration with an American, Benjamin Thompson, to create a typical landscape park which had no specific relationship with any building.

In designs of public gardens in the second half of the 19th century the ideal of social utility, involving the provision of playgrounds and areas for sunbathing, grew in importance, superseding the aesthetics of the landscape park. This can be seen in the work of Gustav Meyer, a disciple of Lenné who became Berlin's first Director of Gardens in 1870. He designed the first people's park in Berlin, Friedrichshain, in 1846, the Humboldthain in 1869 and prepared the final plan for the Treptower in 1874.

AUSTRIA

The raising of the siege of Vienna by the Ottoman Turks in 1688 created such emotion that for some 60 years Austrian baroque art and landscape was unsurpassed. In the field of garden design this is all the more remarkable given the previous 60 bleak years, during which the German states were thrown into chaos by the Thirty Years' War and subsequently by the wars with Louis XIV of France on the one side and the Turks on the other.

The influence of Italy

Hellbrunn, to the south of Salzburg, is the one Renaissance garden of distinction made in Austria and it bears clearly the mark of Italian influence. Markus Sittikus von Hohenems, Archbishop of Salzburg, who commissioned Santino Solari to design the palatial castle and gardens, was a humanist who had lived in Italy and was well acquainted with Italian gardens. The main work was carried out between 1613 and 1615, stone for the castle being quarried on the estate. The quarry itself was made into an amphitheatre, the Felsentheater, and it was here that the first open-air performance of opera north of the Alps was given, which included Monteverdi's *Orfeo*.

A menagerie had existed on the site from before 1424 and in 1613 Markus Sittikus had it rebuilt and enlarged. At the same time, in the immediate vicinity of the castle, he created a sequence of temples, alcoves and grottoes containing numerous hydraulic jokes and toys. Remarkably, many of these survive and are maintained and repaired with impressive fidelity. They were inspired by Italian *giochi d'acqua* and by a 1st-century technological work, the *Pneumatica* of Hero of Alexandria, that had been a source of ideas for Italian Renaissance hydraulic engineers. The Orpheus grotto contained singing birds and the Midas grotto a crown lifted up on a jet of water. In the Roman theatre was a stone table with a central water-channel for cooling wine (as at the Villa Lante in Italy) and with water-jets concealed in the surrounding stone seats.

Subsequent changes to the garden have included simplification in the 1730s and the addition of an 'English park' to one side in the late 18th century. In the mid-18th century a water-powered marionette theatre was added to the water toys.

The two Belvedere palaces in Vienna are linked by a rectangular garden consisting of two parts but so ingeniously blended as to form a whole. This view across the garden, with its fountains, parterres, stairways, sculpture and tall hedges, shows the Lower Belvedere, completed in 1716.

The flowering of the baroque

From the reign of Leopold I (1657–1705) to that of Maria Theresa ((1740–80) the Habsburg empire rose to be, superficially at least, the first power of Europe and, as confirmation of this, its principal palaces and gardens were built on a heroic scale. They were the creations of an elite aristocracy expressing, without hint of domesticity, the grandeur of their age. Architects and craftsmen were at first imported from Italy to deal with the rush of building immediately following the defeat of the Ottoman Turks. Later these were superseded by native architects, among whom Fischer von Erlach and Lukas von Hildebrandt were the dominating force. With the death of Hildebrandt in 1745 the great age of Austrian baroque came to an end.

The Belvedere Palaces

Its full glory is perhaps best appreciated at the Belvedere Palaces built for Prince Eugene of Savoy, the hero who had saved Austria from the Turks. They lie to the south-east and immediately outside the medieval city of Vienna on land made safe after the raising of the siege in 1688. The land slopes upwards from the city, providing a natural view over roofs and spires and giving a sense of space impossible within the old walls. The Lower Belvedere was completed in 1716 and the Upper in 1732, the architect being Lukas von Hildebrandt, who designed the gardens in collaboration with François Girard.

The palaces form a group of great gardens in the following order: the Botanical Gardens, the Salesian Nunnery, the Belvedere main garden and subsidiary, and the garden of the Schwarzenberg Palace, which was built for Prince Eugene's rival, Heinrich Mansfield, Count of Fondi. The main Belvedere garden is a rectangle joining the two palaces and is in fact two gardens (lower and upper) but so ingeniously blended as to form a whole. A meticulously detailed view from the Upper Belvedere painted by Bernardo Bellotto in the 18th century shows a scene which virtually still exists today. Pools, fountains, parterres, paths, stairways, sculpture and tall, immaculately clipped hedges are the foreground to a sky and cityscape that together form a single spectacle. There is a magni-

ficent forecourt to the Upper Belvedere and to one side there was once a menagerie, whose animals formed the nucleus of the one at Schönbrunn.

The gardens of the Schwarzenberg Palace are not quite so well preserved as those of the Belvedere and one side has been curtailed to widen the Prinz Eugen Strasse. It is a baroque shade garden with an open terrace on the higher ground, from where there is a view of the city similar to that from its neighbour, the Upper Belvedere.

The Mirabell Gardens

The Mirabell Gardens in Salzburg are another expression of the buoyant mood in Austria after the raising of the siege of Vienna. The new palace and gardens outside the city walls which were begun in 1689 for Count Thun were probably designed by Fischer von Erlach. Palace and gardens were remodelled by Lukas von Hildebrandt in 1721-7 and were partly rebuilt after a fire in 1818. The gardens were confined within existing ramparts and are ingeniously planned to lead the eye to the spectacular Hohensalzburg, the 12th-century fortress on the opposite bank of the Salzach. There are four baroque groups of sculpture of remarkable quality in the centre of the original parterre and a garden

Schönbrunn, the Viennese palace of the Habsburg dynasty, was intended to rival Versailles in magnificence. Although technically not as mature as any of the designs of Le Nôtre, the gardens are impressive in scale, the principal parterre extending as an open and richly ornamented rectangle apparently carved out of a forest.

theatre in hornbeam is cleverly accommodated on a rampart.

Schönbrunn

The imperial palace of Schönbrunn, beyond the suburbs of Vienna, resembles Versailles in its relation to the capital and the designs commissioned for it from Fischer von Erlach by Emperor Leopold I in the 1690s were for a rival to Louis XIV's palace. The first designs were prodigious. The site, where a Habsburg hunting-lodge had been destroyed by the Turks in 1683, was level to the north, with a sudden short rise to the south. Von Erlach placed the palace on the rising land to the south, with a great architectural garden and a cascade of seven streams leading towards the plains, with the distant city as background. The cost was prohibitive and these plans were abandoned, the palace being placed at the lower level facing the hill.

In general the present palace and park

are as designed by von Erlach and his assistants. Later additions, which did not substantially alter the composition, were made by Maria Theresa in 1744. The menagerie was added in 1752, reflecting an interest of Maria Theresa's husband. The dramatic Gloriette, which occupies the site originally planned for the palace, was built in 1775, and a few years later the first of the garden's sham Roman ruins was erected.

Like those of Versailles, the gardens seem carved out of a forest. The vast park is divided by avenues with spectacular clipped walks of trees into squares and rectangles, with occasional diagonals centring on architectural features. Among the woods there are hidden *bosquets*. In the same intimate vein is the *giardino segreto* fashioned out of trellis that adjoins the palace. The principal parterre garden extends as an open rectangle approximately the same width as the façade. The first view from the palace of this long, simple rectangle, enriched with sculpture and water, and the distant hill crowned with the

Fischer von Erlach's first plans for Schönbrunn were too costly and had to be abandoned. The dramatic Gloriette, built in 1775, occupies the site originally planned for the palace. Its spectacular silhouette crowns the view across the parterre from the palace.

Gloriette set against the sky is spectacular. However, for all its impressive scale and dramatic impact, Schönbrunn is not the equal of the gardens by Le Nôtre that it sought to emulate.

Schlosshof and Schönborn

Two baroque country gardens have fared less well than these magnificent survivals. The palace of Schlosshof was acquired in 1725 by Prince Eugene of Savoy, who employed the architect Fischer von Erlach to rebuild it and possibly Lukas von Hildebrandt to remake the gardens. Alterations were carried out by Maria Theresa in 1755. A view painted by Bernardo Bellotto in 1758 shows that the gardens, extending from the ramparts of what had been a semi-fortified manor, were in grandeur second only to those of the Belvedere and Schönbrunn.

At Schönborn, built by Lukas von Hildebrandt for Friedrich von Schönborn and completed in 1717, the palace, the orangery and most of the avenues still exist. The latter run out on all sides but for no purpose, suggesting how small a part the countryside plays in the Austrian garden. Although features have been altered or removed and the park has been partially landscaped, vestiges of a distinguished and interesting baroque garden still remain.

RUSSIA AND THE SOVIET UNION

In the territories of the Soviet Union there is a long tradition of garden-making going back to the 11th century at least, when it is known that monastic and princely gardens in Kiev were laid out by Greek gardeners. By the end of the 15th century there were extensive gardens in Moscow, and an early 17th-century plan of the city (published in Amsterdam) suggests that the gardens were numerous. They included the Tsar's apothecary's garden, shown with an avenue of trees, and the large imperial garden, which dated from 1495. This riverside garden opposite the Kremlin was rectilinear in layout.

Utility was an important element in early gardens and this is also true for the numerous estates established around Moscow during the reign of Ivan IV in the mid-16th century. A great deal of fruit was grown, as at Ivan's estate of Kolomenskoye, and also some cereals. Birch and cedar were planted for timber and fuel and there were fishponds and beehives. At Ismailovo, a Tsarist summer residence near Moscow, elaborate gardens were laid out in the second half of the 17th century. Although scattered randomly on the estate, a dammed river serving as an informal and picturesque axis, these gardens were formal in style with ingenious flowerbeds, arbours and fountains and reflected the influence of the western European Renaissance garden. However, a wide range of fruit and cereals (including melons and grapes) was grown within the formal layout and interesting experiments were undertaken in the acclimatization of plants.

The great advances made in the art of garden design in the early 18th century owed much to Peter the Great. His genuine interest in the subject had been broadened by visits to gardens in England, the Netherlands, France and Berlin during his travels. He had taken back with him books on gardening and engravings of gardens and had arranged for others to be purchased and sent to him. Furthermore, he engaged foreigners, including the architect and garden designer Jean-Baptiste Le Blond (a pupil of André le Nôtre) and the gardener Jan Roosen, to create new gardens in Russia and to train Russians in their skills.

Dutch influence: Peterhof

The first gardens created by Peter the Great show the influence of Dutch models. This is true of the Summer Garden at St Petersburg (Leningrad), begun in 1703, and the Monplaisir garden at Peterhof (Petrodvorets), the summer palace and park on the Gulf of Finland, 30 km (19 miles) from Leningrad. However, the major influence was the French formal garden and the inspiration of Versailles is evident in the later work at Peterhof and in other gardens.

Peter himself chose the site of Peterhof, where the palace is imposingly situated on a natural terrace. He probably also conceived the overall plan. Much of the existing layout dates from the period 1716-19, when Le Blond was in charge, although there have been numerous subsequent additions. Many of these were carried out by Niccolo Michetti, Le Blond's successor, and later by Bartolomeo Rastrelli, who extended the palace for the Empress Elizabeth in the mid-18th century.

The double cascades on the sea-facing north façade are among the most impressive in the world. The water tumbles down the marble steps into a large basin in which a gilded fountain depicting Samson prising open the jaws of the lion sends up a jet 20 m (66 ft) high. This fountain, and indeed all of Peterhof, celebrates Russia's recovery of the Baltic lands from the Swedes. The triumphant note is sustained by numerous gilded fountains and statues of mythological figures gracing the cascades and basin and the fountain-flanked canal that carries the water to the sea, Russia's vitally important new access to Europe. Peterhof owes much of its special character to the presence of the sea, as background, as foreground, and as a symbol.

Peterhof, Peter the Great's summer palace and park on the Gulf of Finland, celebrates Russia's recovery of the Baltic lands from the Swedes. The spectacular double cascade descends to the Samson fountain, the water flowing to the sea by a fountain-flanked canal.

On both sides of the canal the Lower Park is formally laid out with *allées, bosquets*, a great variety of fountains, including some good trick fountains, and two cascades. There are also three small palaces, including Monplaisir. The original Upper Park, on the south front of the main palace, was widened in the 1750s to take account of the extensions to the palace. The large formal parterre, between the palace and the entrance gates, with *allées*, grass plots, basins, fountains, and statues, is bounded on each side by covered galleries and lines of clipped trees.

French influence

At Ekaterintal in Estonia and at Oranienbaum (Lomonosov) and Strelna, two other residences of Peter the Great on the Gulf of Finland, French influence was dominant. A Polish visitor to Strelna in 1720 wrote: 'After dinner we went to the Versailles garden, which is quite large and extends to the sea-shore. There are a number of canals flowing into the sea, a covered walk planted with limes, labyrinths, many fountains and many beautiful features. By the shore a grove, surrounded by canals, is reserved for wild animals.' Some Russian features were, however, retained in the new gardens, particularly the planting of fruit bushes in formal areas and the use of native trees, including clipped fir trees and junipers.

In the middle of the 18th century, during the reign of the Empress Elizabeth, palaces became more magnificent and gardens more elaborate. Rastrelli rebuilt the Yekaterininsky palace at Tsarskoye Selo (Pushkin) for her and designed superb baroque pavilions for the remodelled gardens. The formal gardens at Kuskovo, the country estate of the Sheremetyevs, 10 km (6 miles) from Moscow, also date from this period. This great parade garden, frequently the setting for receptions, theatrical performances, concerts, fêtes and firework displays, was planned by the architect F.S. Argunov, a serf.

'Anglomania'

The shift away from formal gardens in the French style during the latter part of the 18th century owed much to the example of Catherine the Great. 'I now love to distraction gardens in the English style,' she wrote to Voltaire in 1772, 'the curving lines, the gentle slopes, the ponds in the form of lakes, the archipelagos on dry land, and I scorn straight lines and twin allées. I hate fountains which torture water in order to make it follow a course contrary to its nature; statues are relegated to galleries, halls etc: in a word, anglomania rules my plantomania.' This enthusiasm was reflected in the table and dessert service depicting views of Great Britain, including many of landscape parks, which Catherine ordered from Wedgwood and Bentley.

At Tsarskoye Selo she employed the architect Vasily Neyelov (who had earlier been sent to England to study gardens), John Busch (or Bush), a native of Hanover who had established a nursery in Hackney, London, before moving to St Petersburg and Charles Cameron, an architect and landscape gardener of Scottish descent, to redesign large areas of the park. The 'natural' landscape that was formed was embellished with a range of new garden structures in the styles then fashionable in western Europe. Neyelov's Palladian Bridge owes much to an English model, the bridge at Wilton, though its setting recalls Stowe. Many of the buildings designed by him, his son, and by Charles Cameron are in the Chinese style; the Chinese Village in what is now the Alexandrovsky Park was the largest group of Chinese buildings in Europe. However, the most important contribution Cameron made was the neo-classical covered promenade – Catherine allowed it to be called the Cameron Gallery – adjoining the palace and forming a boundary between the formal garden and the newly planned landscape. It served as a viewing point for both and was the focal point of the whole visible landscape, which at the end of the 18th century also included the model town of Sofia, itself designed by Cameron.

Pavlovsk

The greatest of Russia's landscaped parks is at Pavlovsk on the banks of the Slavyanka, 25 km (15 miles) from Leningrad and 3 km (2 miles) from Tsarskoye Selo. The palace, subsequently much altered, was designed by Charles Cameron for Paul and Maria Fedorovna when Paul was Grand Duke. Cameron also laid out rather formal gardens near the house and designed the 'natural' landscape along the wooded slopes of the river. For the park he designed a number of fine buildings, an important focal point being his Temple of Friendship, a large domed rotunda with Doric columns. Among Cameron's other classical buildings are the Apollo Colonnade (the allusion to the protector of valleys and groves and patron of the arts underlined the role of the park as a sanctuary), the Aviary and the Temple of the Three Graces. Less prominently situated rustic buildings – a thatched dairy, a hermit's cell, and a charcoal-burner's hut – reflected the sentimental tastes of the Grand Duchess and the changing fashions of western Europe.

The park was given a more ceremonial character by Vincenzo Brenna when Pavlovsk became an imperial residence on the

At Tsarskoye Selo Catherine the Great adopted the English style of landscape design with passionate enthusiasm. Much of the work was carried out for her by Charles Cameron, an architect and landscape gardener of Scottish descent who went to Russia in about 1779.

accession of Paul I in 1796. The principal addition was Old Sylvia, a central clearing from which radiate twelve paths. A statue of Apollo stands in the clearing and at its edge, between the paths, are statues of Mercury, Venus, Flora and the nine Muses. Pietro Gonzaga, an Italian painter with wide experience in stage design, made the last major changes to the Pavlovsk landscape in the early 19th century, transforming the former parade-ground of Paul I into a landscape of meadows, water and wooded islands with particularly striking tree combinations. Even more interesting is his work at the area known as the White Birches, where he took the scenery of northern Russia as his model, creating a landscape of meadow and forest, using birch, pine and other trees. He grouped clumps of trees like side-screens in stage scenery and was able to achieve a remarkable feeling of depth in landscape.

The growth of landscape parks
Well before these changes at Pavlovsk, landscape gardens were enjoying a wide following among landowners. The favourite of Catherine the Great, Prince Potemkin, shared the Empress's enthusiasm for the English style. It is said that when he travelled to the Crimea with several hundred serfs to lay out the grounds of his residence there, a garden in the English manner was made around his travelling pavilion wherever he stopped. Peter III's decision to release the nobility from compulsory service and the Charter of the Nobility of 1785 encouraged landowners to settle on their estates and to develop industry and agriculture there. When they turned to gardening, the landscape style, emblematic of freedom, was a natural choice. Apart from their sentimental appeal, landscape parks also made better economic sense.

An influential writer on agricultural improvements was A.T. Bolotov, who advocated landscaping in the English style, though favouring the retention of some formality near the house. He also advised allowing a place for the fruit trees and bushes that were traditional in Russian gardens. The formality that Bolotov recommended in the vicinity of the house and the frequent planting of straight avenues, usually of lime or birch, helped to give Russian

parks their own particular character. Other factors contributing to this were the choice of site, generally elevated with a wide grass slope descending to a river or a lake, and the preference for meadows rather than lawns. Cameron's Temple of Friendship at Pavlovsk inspired many similar structures, although the Russian Gothic style was also used for garden buildings.

Among the best-known estates near Moscow are Sukhanovo, containing the impressive mausoleum of the Volkonskys; Marfino, with a formal and landscape park; Seredniko, associated with the poet Lermontov; and Kuzminki, with its many garden buildings and striking cast-iron ornaments. Notable parks in the Ukraine are Aleksandria near Belaya Tserkov and Sophievka near Uman. Of the many Cri-

The Temple of Friendship at Pavlovsk, designed by Charles Cameron and the forerunner of many similar temples in Russia, is an important focal point in the landscape park. Statues honour the presiding deity, Apollo, protector of valleys and groves and patron of the arts.

mean estates, Kiskov, Gurzov and Alupka are among the most important.

The French invasion of 1812 checked the building of country seats and in the following decades other pressures, culminating with the abolition of serfdom in 1861, prevented a revival. The social and economic base of the country estates was crumbling so that the few new parks that continued to be made, such as Palanga on the Baltic, designed by Edouard André, were the indulgence of the very rich.

SCANDINAVIA

In the sphere of garden and landscape design the Scandinavian countries have much in common. There are, of course, important differences of climate and topography in such a large area. In the west and south-west the Gulf Stream tempers the climate but cold air streams can cause hard winters. The humid continental climate of the centre gives way to the harsh sub-Arctic conditions of the north. The countryside of Denmark is low and undulating and in eastern Sweden the land slopes gently, but Norway and parts of western Sweden are mountainous and the coastline is indented with fiords.

In addition to climate and topography, there are political, social and economic developments that have contributed to certain national characteristics being evident in the gardens of each country.

Sweden

The oldest known Swedish garden plan, of a small parterre for a courtyard in Uppsala Castle, reflects inadequately the passion for buildings and gardens of the Renaissance kings of the Vasa dynasty. In the 16th century, foreigners such as the Frenchman Jean Allard and the German Hans Friese played an important role in introducing new ideas of gardening. In 1563, for example, Allard was ordered to modernize

the Royal Garden (Kungsträdgården) in Stockholm, previously laid out by Friese. He introduced a more architectural layout and created a genuine pleasure-garden that included an orangery, the first in Sweden. The elaboration of some pleasure-gardens in the early 17th century may show the influence of the famous Hortus Palatinus at Heidelberg, a garden that had impressed the Swedish king Gustavus II Adolphus. As a rule, though, even well into the century gardens seem to have been very simple and in an older tradition in which garden and architecture rarely form a coherent whole.

Sweden's elevation to the status of a great power in the mid-17th century, after the Thirty Years' War, gave an impetus to the

The botanic garden at Uppsala was established as early as 1665. It is particularly associated with the great Swedish botanist Carl Linnaeus, who devised the binomial system that remains the basis of modern plant classification.

The royal palace and garden of Drottningholm in Stockholm is the finest example of the baroque style in Sweden. The plan adopted from 1681 was by Tessin the younger. The Turkish Tent represents the taste for the exotic of the second half of the 18th century.

building of palaces and gardens on a grand scale. The art-loving Queen Christina summoned foreign architects and gardeners, the foremost being two Frenchmen, Simon de la Vallée and André Mollet, who had already co-operated with each other in the Netherlands on royal palaces and gardens. Mollet's first commission was to modernize the Royal Garden in Stockholm, where he laid out an impressive *parterre de broderie*, imported plants and built orangeries. Mollet's influence was not only through his commissions but also as a result of the publication in Stockholm in 1651 of his work setting out the principles of classic French garden design, *Le Jardin de plaisir*. These were further developed by the architects Nicodemus Tessin the elder and Jean de la Vallée, son of Simon. After studying in France both made numerous projects for great houses and gardens, many of which were carried out. Count M. G. de la Gardie, a grand potentate with original ideas on gardening, was one of La Vallée's chief employers and among the works commissioned by him was the Franco-Italian terraced garden at Venngarn Castle.

Tessin the elder is closely associated with the royal palace and garden of Drottningholm in Stockholm, dubbed the 'Versailles of the North', which was completed between 1680 and 1700 for the dowager Queen Hedvig Eleonora. However, the plan adopted for the gardens from 1681 is by Tessin the elder's son, also Nicodemus. The garden now reflects its evolution over 300 years but its main composition is totally that of Tessin the younger. Completely enclosed by a double avenue of limes, the garden includes a *parterre de broderie* (now grass), *bosquets* and a water parterre on a lower level. The sculptural adornments are of very high quality, many of them war trophies from Denmark and Prague. Many of the garden's details were borrowed from Italian and French gardens: the *parterre de broderie* was after a pattern from Vaux-le-Vicomte and the design of the water

The garden of the unpretentious manor-house of Sandemar, south-east of Stockholm, is among the best preserved baroque examples in Sweden. The manor was built in about 1670 and the garden is probably of the same date.

parterre from Chantilly. Nonetheless, Drottningholm is evidence of Tessin the younger's own original talent.

Johann Hårleman, who often co-operated with Tessin the younger, designed some of the finest gardens in the French style. However, the best preserved 18th-century baroque garden in Sweden is at

Sandemar, south-east of Stockholm. The wooden manor-house on the coast of the Baltic, dating from about 1670, is representative of the more unpretentious architecture of the period and the garden gives a vivid impression of gardens of the time, which were adapted to modest means as well as to the hard climate. The original parterres have been simplified, but the clipped globes of lilac, the hedges, the pyramids of fir (now, it is true, somewhat out of scale), and the white-painted wooden sculptures – the whole surrounded by clipped lime trees in six rows – are practically unchanged.

Another well-preserved manor-house and garden is Sturefors in Östergötland. The garden, laid out by Tessin the younger for a house he had built in 1704, includes a *parterre de broderie* (now grass), a long central axis, arbours and a maze. This part of the garden is framed by avenues of lime. A cross-axis at right angles leads to the kitchen garden and an orangery. Later in the century an elongated pond and a classical temple on the top of a hill were added at the end of the central axis. A small-scale landscape garden, distinctively continental in character, was laid out about the same time. A flower meadow with a Chinese pavilion and an imitation of the Ile des Peupliers at Ermenonville (celebrated as the site of Jean-Jacques Rousseau's tomb) are famous features.

The era of great mansions and gardens ended with the wars at the beginning of the 18th century. The wealthy bourgeoisie did not aspire to rival royalty and their gardens assumed a more intimate character; the main principles were still those of the baroque but were applied with less formality. Good examples are Övedskloster and Osterby. Gunnebo, near Gothenberg, has a well-preserved, slightly Italianate, terraced garden dating from the end of the century that is unique.

By then the fully developed English landscape garden had been introduced to Sweden. In this the principal figure was Fredrik Magnus Piper, who had studied in England and been much impressed by the English landscape garden. After returning home he was commissioned by Gustavus III to lay out parks in the English style at Drottningholm and at Haga in Stockholm. Although it was never completed and much has changed, the Haga park still shows Piper's command of landscape design in a grand style.

Throughout the 19th century, and even into the 20th, the landscape style remained important. Adelsnäs in Östergötland, laid out after 1900, is considered one of the finest modern examples of the English landscape park. During the 19th century there were, however, other trends too. German influence increased considerably and developments in horticulture provided the material for gardens that included carpet bedding, shrubberies, foreign trees and winding paths. The designer K. Forsberg was the leading exponent of a kind of gardening in which irregularity was combined with symmetry.

Denmark

On a visit to France King Frederik IV, who established an absolute monarchy in Denmark in the late 17th century, had been overwhelmed by his impressions of the gardens of Le Nôtre. Frederiksberg Castle in Copenhagen, begun in 1699, was an expression of the monarch's new status, as was its garden in the French baroque style. An initial design by the Swedish architect Tessin the younger was not carried out; a formal terraced layout begun by Hans Henrik Scheel was later taken over by Johan Cornelius Krieger. This baroque design was lost later in the 18th century, when the gardens were naturalized in the English style.

Two other royal residences have gardens laid out in the French baroque manner. Fredensborg Castle in Sjælland, the summer residence of the Danish royal family which was built by Frederik IV in 1717, lies at the centre of a *patte-d'oie* pattern of radiating *allées*, with a *tapis vert* falling towards the lake. The original *bosquets* between the *allées*, laid by Krieger, have now grown into mature beechwoods.

The finest of these royal gardens are those of Frederiksborg Castle in Sjælland, laid out in 1720, also by Krieger. The terraces, cut out of the hillside opposite the main north façade of the castle, with interconnecting ramps, are emphasized by clipped box and pleached limes. On the top terrace an oval *bassin* enclosed by limes supplied a series of cascades which fell eventually into the lake at the foot of the hillside. The strength of the design is still evident in the interplay between the lime-tree avenues and the oval pool.

In laying out their own estates the nobility were greatly influenced by the new garden ideals, as can be seen in a number of manor-houses. An early example, probably designed by Tessin the younger in 1722, is Clausholm in Jutland. Probably the best-known gardens in Denmark, those of the 16th-century manor-house of Egeskov in Fyn, contain parts in very different styles. As well as a traditional farmhouse garden, a French Renaissance garden and an English garden, there is a baroque formal layout of 1730. In many instances there were not the resources to build terraces and cascades in marble. Instead, grassed and planted earth

The manor-house of Sturefors in Östergötland was built in 1704 to a design by Nicodemus Tessin the younger. The formal gardens he laid out were in the French manner but later additions included an English landscape garden.

ramparts and excavated ponds edged with timber and glacial boulders gave a distinctively Danish expression to formal gardens in the French style.

The late 18th-century rococo garden at Liselund in Møn is evidence of a marked shift in aesthetics. Its design, influenced by the ideas of the French writer Jean-Jacques Rousseau, incorporates a stream dammed to form pools, a waterfall and a lake; the paths that wind through the beechwoods give sudden glimpses of the sea below. Artificial graves, mounds, and dark leafy pathways were combined with the wild natural scenery of rocks and waterfalls to give alternating feelings of sorrow and happiness.

In the 19th century many landscaped parks in the English style were laid out in the grounds of castles and manor-houses, sometimes, as at Frederiksberg in Copenhagen, involving the loss of fine baroque gardens. Glorup, in Fyn, is a classic example of evolution in garden design over a period of 400 years, with parts of all phases being visible. Conceived on a grand scale as a baroque garden, with the passage of time it has gradually changed into a romantic garden, with part of the grounds laid out in the landscape style by

H. A. Flindt in the second half of the 19th century. Flindt and his predecessor as Chief Inspector of the Danish royal gardens, Rudolf Rothe, can be regarded as the founders of the Danish landscape architecture tradition. Another fine country-house park, Gisselfeld in Sjælland, was laid out in the late 19th century by the English garden designer H. E. Milner as a setting for the moated red-brick house situated on an isthmus between two lakes.

Norway

Gardening in Norway was inevitably affected by the general economic and cultural depression that seized the country in the late Middle Ages. A new era dawned with the introduction of the Renaissance garden by the first Lutheran bishop of Bergen in the mid-16th century. The Bishop's Garden, designed by a skilled Flemish gardener specially brought in for the purpose, provided a model for many other gardens. Rosendal Barony in Hardanger has a formal garden dating back to 1660-70 that retains some of the spirit of these early gardens. This is most obvious in the geometric pattern that has been preserved in the rose parterre. A remarkable survival that still

reflects the basic design pattern of the Renaissance is Lurøy Garden in Nordland, situated on the Atlantic coast just below the Arctic Circle. The garden, which dates from about 1750, is partially enclosed by a rough stone wall and contains a symmetrically placed wooden pavilion and a geometric parterre with perennial flowers.

After 1725 a number of more representative formal gardens were created, mainly in south-eastern Norway. Typical of these are Linderud in Oslo and Rød in Halden. Attempts were usually made to arrange the composition on a main axis in a layout featuring regular terraces and reflecting pools. The influence of the French baroque garden can be detected, but Norway had no wealthy and powerful aristocracy who could carry out a full-scale design in this style and no important master of garden design was employed there. There are, though, several estates, such as Jarlsberg and Hafslund in the south-east, where monumental avenues were planted, and similar layouts exist in the vicinity of Trondheim in the north.

The new upper class that developed towards the end of the 18th century kept close international relations, especially with England, and they soon became acquainted with the new vogue for landscape gardens. The first example in Norway of a park in the English manner is at Bogstad Manor outside Oslo. This landscape, developed in about 1780 in a scenic lakeside setting, still survives but very few of the romantic parks created after it remain intact.

Introductions in the 19th century greatly extended the range of plants grown, particularly in the more favourable maritime climate of the south-west coast. The little seaside town of Molde became famous for its lush plant growth and colourful gardens.

Several public parks were made in this period, notable among them the Nygård Park in Bergen with its collection of exotic trees, and the Ravnedalen Park in Kristiansand where steep granite cliffs and majestic trees create a strongly romantic effect.

SPAIN AND PORTUGAL

The best-known gardens of the Iberian peninsula are those that were created by the Moorish conquerors of Spain (see section 'Gardens of Islam', page 115). It is easily forgotten, however, that those of the Alhambra and the Generalife, although inevitably somewhat altered since they were made, date from the 13th and 14th centuries and are the only surviving gardens in Europe of this period. Subsequent developments in western Europe have led to the creation of gardens quite distinct from the Moorish tradition, although it has continued as an influence and contributed especially to the particular character of the gardens of Portugal.

Spain

The first of the Habsburg kings, the Emperor Charles V, built a new palace entirely Italian in character but neither he nor any other Spanish monarch created any large-scale gardens in the Italian style. Indeed, garden design was not of great importance under the Spanish Habsburgs. This is

perhaps partly explained by the way court life centred on the monastery-palace, where devout exercises alternated with formal ceremonial occasions. Philip II's Escorial Monastery and Palace, built between 1563 and 1584, has numerous inner courtyards but they do little to alleviate the bleak spaces of this gloomy building.

Aranjuez

At Aranjuez, the shooting-box he converted into a permanent summer residence, Philip made interesting alterations to the garden. He had had a Flemish upbringing and always employed Dutch gardeners, preferring the Dutch style of small compartments with clipped hedges. Following Arab practice, he had a reservoir created first and then, in about 1562, the gardens were laid out in squares and rectangles. In the original layout, which no longer survives, there were low fountains and also tall ones with basins one above the other. Whether any of the existing fountains belonged to the original layout is not clear. The only Italian features were statues of mythological heroes.

In the early 1580s the king thought of joining the Tagus Island (separated from the palace by the river of that name) and the Ria Canal to the main layout. The character of the original Jardin de la Isla, as it is now called, is not clear. The major transformation occurred in the mid-17th century, when Cosimo Lotti, who had worked at the Boboli Gardens in Florence, created the Hercules Fountain in the centre of a large pool, clearly reminiscent of the Isolotto.

In 1660 the gardens were given a new and rather austere design in which, 17th-century travellers agreed, the fountains were the most interesting feature. A further transformation took place in the first half of the 18th century under the first Bourbon king, Philip V. Some elements of the French style were used, innovations including long avenues of lime trees and hedges of hornbeam.

Buen Retiro (Parque de Madrid)

The Florentine Cosimo Lotti also worked on the last of the Spanish Habsburg gardens, at Buen Retiro, now the Parque de Madrid. The work was carried out in stages from 1628, which perhaps accounts for its lack of unity and perspective. The great square pool, for example, is out of line with, and invisible from, the palace. The great lake, which used to have square pavilions in the corners, has an oval island, which was the scene of lavish entertainments. A canal, navigable by gondola, led out of its south-eastern corner to other *bassins*.

La Granja

At La Granja, on the north slope of the Guadarrama mountains near Segovia, Philip V created a new palace as a summer retreat. The gardens, laid out in the first half of the 18th century, were made to remind him of the gardens of his grandfather, Louis XIV of France. However, the effect is very different to that achieved at, for example, Versailles, because of the mountainside setting and the lack of a dominant axial relationship between house and garden.

By 1661 an Italian, Cosimo Lotti, who had worked at the Boboli Gardens in Florence, had created the Hercules Fountain in the Jardin de la Isla, Aranjuez. The arrangement is clearly a reminiscence of the Isolotto in the Boboli Gardens.

The fountains were the outstanding feature of the gardens, water being readily available from the nearby mountains. The cascade of marble and coloured jasper, at the head of which stands a pavilion of pink stone in the Régence style, centred on the king's private apartments to one side of the palace. The avenues flanking the cascade are bordered alternately by statues and vases. The cascade was a present from Isabella Farnese to her husband Philip V, who commented sadly: 'It has cost me three millions and amused me three minutes.' No new royal gardens were created after the death of Philip V, although Isabella Farnese's son Charles III was inspired by La Granja to create the gardens of Palazzo Reale at Caserta in Italy.

El Laberinto
At the end of the 18th century numerous neo-classical gardens were created on the outskirts of Barcelona. El Laberinto, so-called on account of the giant cypress labyrinth occupying the principal terrace, is the only surviving example. The new layout, on a higher level, was not centred on the previous garden, the labyrinth providing the focus for the cascades, pools, grottoes and stairways. An avenue flanked by cypresses leads to the great reservoir surrounded by a white balustrade, with a beautiful neo-classical pavilion on the water's edge. The transition is masked by a semicircular cypress hedge strengthened by tall stone posts. The terraces beyond the hedge merge into the woodlands.

Although small courtyard gardens of great charm were then, as now, a feature of many fine Spanish houses, there were no significant developments in garden style during the 19th century. Landscaping in the English manner had little influence here, unlike most other areas of Europe, except for some additions to Aranjuez.

Portugal
Ideas borrowed from east and west but blended and given a distinctive national stamp have produced the highly individual gardens of Portugal. Most of the country's

Philip V, the first Bourbon king of Spain, created La Granja as a summer retreat, with gardens to remind him of those of his grandfather, Louis XIV of France. The elaborate waterworks, the garden's outstanding feature, took advantage of the copious supply of water.

finest buildings date from the 15th to the 17th centuries, paid for by the fortunes made in Brazil and the East Indies. The Manueline style, a specifically Portuguese variant of late Gothic, was to give way to an exuberantly imaginative baroque. Gardens often provide a setting that enhances the unique qualities of these buildings.

The *azulejo*
The main ingredients of many Portuguese gardens may seem conventional: terracing (for the landscape is often hilly), box parterres, hedged compartments, clipped trees of various kinds, fountains and stone ornaments. The Portuguese garden is, however, special in having incorporated into this setting the *azulejo*, the glazed tile of Moorish origin. Until the mid-15th century

The garden of the Palace of Fronteira in Lisbon remains an exceedingly fine example of 17th-century design and details. Its water-tank (above) is one of the loveliest in Portugal and the azulejos (right) are of exceptional quality.

medieval knights on prancing horses reflected in the water.

Another famous water-tank is at the Quinta da Bacalhoa near Setubal. The house, which was built in 1480, and the gardens have been skilfully restored this century. A long flowery terrace links the water-tank to the formal garden, which is surrounded on two sides by the house. On the south side of the huge square of water is an enchanting pavilion consisting of three little lodges joined by an arcaded, roofed loggia. Doorways in the lodges lead into the water and the interior of the pavilion, a series of tiny rooms, is lined with green, blue and yellow azulejos.

Portugal's hilly terrain lends itself to other water features. Moorish influence can be seen again in the use of water-stairways and cascades. Monasteries frequently displayed water-stairways, using the platforms at each level as the Stations of the Cross. The mixture of religious devotion and love of watery devices is very individual to Portugal.

Castelo Branco

The special qualities of Portuguese gardens can be fully appreciated at Castelo Branco in Beira Baixa. The palace and its remarkable garden were laid out by the Bishop of Guarda in 1598. Two staircases, facing each other, are noteworthy for a procession of statues of crowned kings descending the balustrades. The combination of formal elements arranged in a series of terraces, with hedges, pleached trees and topiary, ingenious displays of water and, on the topmost terrace, a splendid tank, draws on many garden traditions and yet forms a coherent whole.

English influence

In the 19th century one or two gardens were laid out in the Romantic English fashion, such as Pena Palace and Monserrate, both in the Sintra hills of Estremadura and both containing rich collections of trees and shrubs. This concept of gardening never caught on however. Plant introductions from China and the New World, especially camellias and rhododendrons, have flourished in the temperate climate of central and northern Portugal, creating magnificent woodland effects.

the designs were geometrical, showing their Islamic ancestry, but thereafter the Italian taste for figurative decoration took over and the Portuguese made the azulejo their own. Pavilions, grottoes, niches, basins, fountains, inserted panels, the walls of loggias – all were embellished with tiles treated as frescoes, depicting with great creative vitality classical and biblical stories or tales of medieval chivalry. The details obtainable and the exquisite range of colours achieved made the azulejo particularly suited to express the baroque spirit. Later again, in the 18th century, the azulejo was adapted to designs of rococo flamboyance.

The most lavish 18th-century example of the use of azulejos is at the Palace of Queluz in Estremadura, now maintained by the state as a residence for foreign guests. A beautiful staircase leads down to a lower garden that is cut across by a Dutch canal, now dry. The sides are lined with blue and white azulejo panels of shipping scenes and the rococo bridges that straddle it are decorated with polychrome tiles and statuary.

Water features

Another Moorish feature that has been adapted to the Portuguese garden is the water-tank. Indeed, no garden is complete without a water-tank backed by a panel of azulejos. One of the most beautiful is at the Palace of Fronteira in Lisbon. Statuary and azulejos animate this fine example of a 17th-century garden. It is on two levels, the upper boasting the Gallery of the Kings, rich in lustred azulejos, and the lower featuring the Tank, backed with panels in cerulean-and-white azulejos, depicting

During the 18th century Colonial Williamsburg, Virginia, preserved the Dutch-English tradition of parterre gardens and geometric topiary.

GARDENS OF THE EARLY SETTLERS

Explorers of the New World had reported upon the fertility of the soil, the prevalence of springs, the overwhelming plenty of wild fruits, the availability of timber for building and burning and the quantities of fish. But, being quite honest, they had also mentioned the extremes of climate, the hordes of insects and the dearth of gold. The 'gardens' seen by the early explorers on the shores of North America were the work of Indian tribes who populated, however sparsely, those coastal cliffs and meadows. That the settlers referred to these areas of cultivated ground as 'gardens' reveals both the skill of the natives and the inclinations of the settlers. For, in early 17th-century colonial America, gardens were symbols of survival.

In making their gardens the settlers of the New World began with the standard practice of their native countries. The first accounts of New England gardens show that these were ornamental as well as providing food plants and herbs for flavouring and medicine. Their design, however, had to depend upon convenience and efficient management. With stock allowed to roam, fencing was regulated by law. Houses built along main streets are recorded as having gardens on one side and orchards on the other, the arrangement sometimes extending over miles. Where houses were built around a green, gardens and orchards extended to the rear.

In the New Netherland (New York) colony established by the Dutch West India

Company in 1624 the gardens created were similar to the small city or farm gardens of the Netherlands. Although essentially utilitarian in nature, these gardens sometimes included intricate flower parterres of the kind popularized in northern Europe at the end of the 16th century by the pattern book of Hans Vredeman de Vries. The most ambitious of these gardens were those laid out by the Company and by Peter Stuyvesant, Director-General from 1646 to 1664. The garden at his mansion on the Battery in Manhattan was laid out in about 1658 and shows similarities to a simple Dutch plan, with compartments of parterres and orchards either side of a main axis.

During the 18th century, Williamsburg, capital of Virginia from 1699 to 1781, preserved the Dutch-English tradition of parterre gardens and geometric (rather than figurative) topiary. Restoration of the architecture and gardens of Williamsburg

began in 1926, only those plants known to have been originally used in Virginian gardens being included. Another representation of the earliest sort of garden prevalent in New England is at Whipple House Garden, Ipswich, Massachusetts.

Governor's Palace, Williamsburg

At Williamsburg the largest gardens are those of the Governor's Palace, Palace Green. The upper garden, directly behind the ballroom and symmetrically arranged about a central axis running northward from the house, consists of 16 diamond-shaped parterres enclosing 12 topiary cylinders and a dense growth of periwinkle and English ivy. The topiary is not of box but of yaupon (*Ilex vomitoria*). The ballroom garden on both sides of the house is of the same simple geometric type. The lower garden, separated from the upper by a broad east-west cross-axis, has a

In the restoration of Colonial Williamsburg, begun in 1926, only those plants known to have been originally used in Virginian gardens were included. In the largest of the gardens, those of the Governor's Palace, Palace Green, a tunnel of American beech (Fagus grandifolia) forms a cross-axis.

similar layout, but is more brightly planted, with red tulips in April and large beds of perennials in the summer. The final cross-axis is marked by a tunnel of American beech (*Fagus grandifolia*), with gazebos at each end. Beyond the north gate is a maze, modelled after that at Hampton Court but planted in American holly (*Ilex opaca*), not yew. There is also an elaborate mound, which insulated the ice-house, and further to the west a canal. The ornamental part of the citizens' gardens followed the style of the Palace gardens but a large part of these was devoted to vegetables and herbs.

John Bartram

Settlers were progressive in adding the beautiful plants and trees of their new countryside to the garden standbys then familiar in Europe. One of the most active of American plant-collectors, praised by Linnaeus as one of the greatest of field botanists, was John Bartram, who between 1736 and 1766 made a series of expeditions to explore the country's flora. He introduced about 200 new species into cultivation and, through the consignments he sent regularly to Peter Collinson and others in England, he was responsible for many of these species becoming known in Europe. The nurseries he established on the family farm became, under the management of his sons, the leading suppliers of what George Washington called the 'clever' sorts of trees and shrubs. Even earlier established, however, were the Prince Nurseries on Long Island, which were founded by Robert Prince in 1737. For a time this nursery was the leading exporter of American plants to Europe, as well as a major importer from all regions.

THE DEVELOPMENT OF AN AMERICAN STYLE

The development of a distinctive American style owes much to two leading Americans who, during the Revolutionary War, played key roles in the subsequent forming of the United States. Both Thomas Jefferson and George Washington were men of wide interests that included all aspects of agriculture, architecture and gardens. Jefferson in particular showed his interest in horticulture at an early age and in later life developed a particular involvement in growing American specialities. As architect and garden designer, he designed his own home, Monticello, in Virginia, the University of Virginia, which Monticello overlooks, and numerous residences and their surroundings for his friends. To accommodate the small classical mansion he had designed for Monticello he had the hilltop site levelled, allowing views around three-quarters of the horizon. Terraces for vegetables and fruit fell gradually from a truncated oval lawn, which was surrounded by a path curving between four great oval beds for shrubberies. As Jefferson's letters reveal,

The orderly gardens of Colonial Williamsburg are a happy match for buildings of unpretentious domestic scale.

The plant-collector John Bartram had what George Washington referred to as a 'Botanical Garden' on the family farm at Kingsessing, near Philadelphia. Under Bartram's sons this became a leading nursery of trees and shrubs. Replanning and replanting have restored the garden to a condition worthy of its importance.

it was intended that the path should be bordered by garden flowers. Small oval beds cut into the lawn behind the house were also filled with a profusion of flowers. The family burial-ground, also designed by Jefferson, lay in a grove on the slope at the back of the hill. The gardens at Monticello were planned to suit Jefferson's own tastes; those of the University of Virginia clearly draw some of their inspiration from Louis XIV's Marly.

George Washington was equally remarkable as an amateur designer. At Mount Vernon, on a bluff above the River Potomac, he was responsible for the layout and the planting scheme. The enlarged plantation house looks over the river while behind it there is a bell-shaped terrace, its outline defined by sinuous entrance drives on either side. The terrace is flanked on one side by a flower garden and on the other by a vegetable garden; the flower garden lies on the side of the house with the drawing-room addition and the greenhouse, both designed by Washington. The fruit-trees in both gardens and the flowering evergreen

trees and shrubs in the serpentine drives and in the ovals of shrubbery are individually recorded as planted by him.

A distinctively American development during the 18th century were the planters' gardens along the coast and on tidal rivers from Maryland to South Carolina. At the James River Plantation in Virginia, for example, the houses and their impressive gardens were situated to preside over the river frontage. Stately terraces (or 'falls', as they were called near Charleston, South Carolina) serve as mountings for the house as viewed from the river. The falls were architectural features, lofty perches to catch the breezes and command views for miles. They were not cluttered with planting but great trees graced the inland drives towards the houses and framed the houses as seen from the river. The garden was usually walled high on one side, the enclosed area containing square beds of flowers and shrubs divided by wide grass walks.

The Louisiana Purchase of 1803, by which the whole of the Mississippi Valley up to the Rocky Mountains was acquired from France (doubling in the process the size of the United States), excited the interest of American and European gardeners and botanists. The houses and gardens of the traders along the Mississippi are quite different from the planters' houses of the east coast, where the owners lived beside their wharves and among their tobacco fields. At Natchez, for example, the owners of the vast cotton and sugar-cane plantations congregated in congenial and prosperous groups, Similarly grand town houses were surrounded by well-tended formal urban gardens, which, though greatly simplified, retain their affluent air.

André Parmentier

Though they created their gardens to their own geography, needs and tastes for many years, Americans were not closed to new ideas from outside. By a curious twist the definition and example of natural landscape design in what came to be considered the English school was brought to America by a Belgian, André Parmentier. When this member of a distinguished European gardening family arrived in New York to start a nursery in 1824, he created an elaborate layout upon an unpromising stony

Like George Washington, Thomas Jefferson had a consuming interest in growing American plants, many of which were included in the garden he designed for himself at Monticello, Virginia. The small classical mansion is set on a levelled hilltop, giving a distant view of the University of Virginia, which Jefferson also designed. Below the house there are terraces for growing vegetables and fruit.

headland in Brooklyn, overlooking New York harbour. In no time he had laid out an artistic garden, a nursery and a vineyard and, as a result of an article he wrote on the new style he had employed, he was considered responsible for introducing natural landscape gardening to the new World. Visitors who flocked to see the ornamental section of his nursery were reportedly charmed by the 'picturesque' style, which produced 'an agreeable effect'

by its 'natural appearance . . . in harmony with the scenery'. Rustic seats and arbours of contorted tree-limbs were later immortalized in cast-iron replicas.

The natural landscape that Parmentier defined was not so far from the early landscape design of rural cemeteries. From the earliest years of settlement, it was general practice in rural communities for a choice spot to be selected, usually a hilltop, as a burying-ground. At Mount Vernon,

Handsome plantation houses in the surrounding countryside and town houses in the small South Carolina city of Charleston frequently have gardens that retain much of their early 19th-century charm. The planting typically includes the use of exotic trees, shrubs and vines.

Monticello and General Jackson's home, the Hermitage, at Nashville, Tennessee, the family burial sites featured as part of the landscaped gardens. The laying out of

Manhattan's Central Park was designed by the father of American landscape architecture, Frederick Law Olmsted, and Calvert Vaux. Olmsted thought of a public park as a democratic institution that would have a great influence on the moral health of citizens.

Mount Auburn Cemetery in Boston, Massachusetts, in the 1820s by Dr Jacob Bigelow, landscaped according to the contours of the land and including an 'experimental garden' planted with indigenous and exotic trees, began the deliberate creation of 'rural cemeteries'. They were to become accepted examples in the United States of the 'English style' of gardening.

Andrew Jackson Downing

The rural cemetery as realized at Mount Auburn led to the idea of American public parks, which was first put forward towards the middle of the 19th century by Andrew Jackson Downing. Downing's influence on the development of American gardens is incalculable. He was an ex-nurseryman and expert gardener who, by the time he had laid out his own garden, Newburgh Garden, for his house on the Hudson River, was widely read in the literature of gardening and architecture. He was particularly influential in adapting to American conditions the ideas of the leading English writer on gardening in the first half of the 19th century, John Claudius Loudon. Downing defined beautiful and picturesque gardens in terms that were comprehensible to American readers and reduced his ideas so that they were within reach of the smallest householder.

In advancing for the first time the idea of American public parks, Downing recognized the popular appeal of rural cemeteries as places of recreation. At the time of his premature death in 1852 his ideas had not been developed in a practical way but Calvert Vaux, the assistant he had taken on when visiting England in 1850, and who helped him lay out the grounds of the Capitol, the White House and the new Smithsonian Institution, later played a part in the development of New York's Central Park.

Following Downing's early death there was a spate of small books by avowed disciples of his offering guidance in landscape design. The assumption behind all of them was that every American man could and should have his own home, for which he would lay out his own garden and grounds in a suitable way. In a book published in 1870 and dedicated to Downing, Frank J. Scott offered a view of the ideal American suburban garden that has become ingrained in the designing of landscape and gardens in small American towns. According to this view the owners of adjoining properties should maintain front lawns so that the length of a town or city block presents an uninterrupted expanse of groomed greenery. The owners of individual houses can enjoy privacy and practise their own styles of gardening only at the rear of their property. 'It is', Scott says, 'unchristian to hedge from the sight of others the beauties of nature which it has been our good fortune to create and secure.'

The ideas on public parks first outlined by Downing were eventually developed in the plan for Central Park by Frederick Olmsted and his partner Calvert Vaux, formerly Downing's assistant. Olmsted was greatly influenced by Downing's ideas but was also inspired by his visit in 1850 to Birkenhead Park in England. He recognized that 'in democratic America, there was nothing to be thought of as comparable with the People's Garden'.

Biltmore House in North Carolina, built for George W. Vanderbilt, is a fanciful François I château surrounded by a garden modelled in part on Le Nôtre's Vaux-le-Vicomte. It is, in fact, a remarkable example of several styles combined to create a lavish effect.

Although Central Park owes something to the English picturesque garden tradition, Olmsted's overriding purpose and his major innovation (the system of sunken transverse roads) were directed towards creating a public park as part of large-scale town planning. He was, therefore, a pioneer in landscape architecture rather than a garden designer, and most of his subsequent career went in this direction.

THE COUNTRY PLACE ERA

One garden design project Olmsted took up was at Biltmore House in North Carolina. The owner, George W. Vanderbilt, was among the very wealthy elite who, between the 1880s and 1920s, spent part of their vast fortunes building mansions in the country and laying out lavish gardens, generally inspired by European models. Olmsted, engaged to assist in the acquisition of land for the estate in the 1880s, was deeply interested in Vanderbilt's ·pioneer efforts with scientific forestry in the spectacular mountain setting of Biltmore. The mansion, built between 1891 and 1895, is in the style of a François I château but, typical of the eclecticism of the Country Place era, the gardens reflect several European styles: there is a large formal area modelled after Vaux-le-Vicomte in France, an espaliered walled English garden, an Italian garden with pools, a rose-garden and a greenhouse with an orchid display.

The Italian villa rather than the French château was a more frequent source of inspiration for later houses and gardens of the Country Place era. Charles A. Platt, who was one of several American visitors to Italy to write enthusiastically about the happy relation between architecture and site so typical of its villas, was a leading exponent of designs in the Italian manner. A more literal version of the Italian Renaissance villa than Platt would have designed is Vizcaya, Florida, built as a winter home between 1912 and 1916 by James Deering. The formal gardens surrounding the creamy-yellow *palazzo* overlook Biscayne Bay, Florida. Like all true Italian gardens, these are not flamboyantly colourful; the effect is achieved by delicacy of design emphasized by the neatly clipped plants.

Other great properties of the Country

The grandiose layout of Old Westbury Gardens in New York, constructed for John S. Phipps in 1906, like other gardens of the Country Place era draws on a wide range of European models.

Longwood, the Pennsylvanian estate bought by Pierre S. du Pont in 1906, covers 400 hectares (990 acres) of hills. The garden occupies nearly a quarter of the estate.

Place era dating from before the First World War include Old Westbury Gardens, New York, and Longwood Gardens, Pennsylvania. At Old Westbury Gardens, constructed in 1906 for John S. Phipps and designed by George Crawley, monumental wrought-iron gates and an *allée* of European beech, originally consisting of 286 trees, herald an extensive composite of gardens drawing on· several traditions. Broad steps flanked by great banks of rhododendrons lead down to a small lake, a boxwood garden on the far side and, beyond, a walled Italian garden. Adjacent to this is the Ghost Walk, a tunnel of hemlock copied after the one at Battle Abbey in Sussex, England, with a pinetum nearby. Then there is the English rose-garden and a Primrose Walk, which leads to the Children's Cottage Garden with its four play-

houses. Further on is the great South Lawn, with its grand *allée* of European lindens followed, in turn, by the swimming-pool and the large lake, its woodland walk bordered by wild flowers.

Longwood Gardens were bought in 1906 by Pierre S. du Pont, primarily to save the notable arboretum that was begun in 1798. The gardens proper occupy under one-third of the wooded property set in rolling hills. The gardens have become a major horticultural showplace and the vast conservatory is a leading attraction. Facing the conservatory is the Fountain Garden and the open-air theatre. In addition to these features there is an Italian water-garden, formal and informal gardens of bulbs, annuals and perennials, a rose-garden, a gigantic rock-garden, waterlily pools, a vegetable garden and woodland walks.

GARDENS OF ISLAM

The Koran, the sacred book of Islam, promises believers who perform righteous acts that 'the Gardens of Paradise shall be their hospitality, therein to dwell forever, desiring no removal from them'. In the monotheistic religion founded by Muhammad in the 7th century AD the notion of paradise owes much to the image of the desert oasis. The Koran makes reference to 'spreading shade', 'fruits and fountains and pomegranates', 'fountains and running water' and 'cool pavilions'. At the heart of this imagery is water, a source of life in a hot climate and barren landscape, refreshing both body and spirit. It is not surprising that the imagery of the paradise garden was translated into earthly gardens, granting a foretaste of the reward promised to the faithful.

The royal hunting grounds and pleasure-gardens of Persia were a major influence in the development of the Islamic idea of the paradise garden. (The English word 'paradise' is derived originally from the Old Persian *pairidaēza*, meaning an 'enclosure' or 'park'.) Their influence was not simply as a model of lush seclusion. The Persians shared with other peoples a recognition of the symbolic value of the number four and in their tradition, dating back to 2000 BC, the garden was a square enclosure divided into four equal parts by intersecting water channels. The image of a central spring of life branching into four rivers can be found both in Buddhist iconography and in the biblical book of Genesis, which recounts that 'a river went out of Eden to water the garden; and from thence it was parted, and became four heads'. The *chahar bagh* (literally 'fourfold garden') of Islam is, however, in direct descent from the quadripartite gardens of Persia. The Persian tradition was particularly important in what is now Iran and in Mogul India. At Samarkand, in Uzbekistan, USSR, from the late 14th to the early 16th centuries the Timurids, descendants of Tamerlane the Great (Timūr Leng), built many well-watered gardens modelled on the Persian tradition which were to inspire the first Mogul Emperor, Bābur.

The ordained conversion of all non-believers led to the spread of Islam, holy wars taking the religion to North Africa, southern Europe, and southern Asia. The Islamic garden travelled with the religion. Although each site was unique, there was a remarkable unity of concept that was reflected in gardens from southern Spain to north-west India, over a time span of a thousand years.

The first Mogul Emperor, Bābur, was a great garden builder, his gardens in Kabul and Agra drawing on the Persian tradition, as this miniature of c. 1625 suggests.

The shape was nearly always rectangular, with a surrounding wall pierced by a gateway giving on to the main axis. This was often formed by a watercourse, with one or more subsidiary axes at right angles. Channels and pools were flanked by paths and terraces, always straight, often bordered by defined areas planted with flowers and shrubs and taller trees for shade, the use of plants softening the man-made geometry. A pavilion was a common central feature, all vistas being precisely terminated by a further pavilion, gateway or vaulted recess. The pattern of water channels was determined principally by irrigation techniques. On flat sites, channels were given a slight gradient to ensure a flow. On sloping sites, where the garden was arranged in terraces, water was carried from one level to the next by *chadars*, water-chutes tilted at an angle and with a patterned surface to increase the sparkle and sound of the water. Water in pools and channels was always contained in a precise way.

Among the earliest Islamic gardens were those built in the new capital of the Abbasid dynasty, Baghdad, founded in 762 AD and now the capital of Iraq. The city was built on the fertile ground beside the River Tigris, water being obtained from the river and also from underground canals or *qanats*. Palaces with magnificent terraced gardens overlooked the river; in some there were trees of silver and mechanical birds.

As a leading centre for education and science, including horticulture, and lying on a major trade route, Baghdad exercised considerable influence, though it had declined in power long before it fell to the Mongols in 1258, when it was laid waste.

Islamic gardens in North Africa first appeared in 9th-century Tunis. Cairo, founded in the latter half of the 10th century, had several garden palaces and many courtyards and it is the courtyard tradition in several older private houses that remains to this day. Earlier in the same century the Moors entered Sicily, where they established new irrigation techniques, built public baths, and introduced water in many forms to garden and courtyard.

In Turkey, converted to Islam in the 10th century, an early distinctive feature in the Ottoman period, beginning in the late 13th century, was the kiosk. Some 10 kiosks survive at Topkapi Saray, Istanbul, the great palace of the Osmani Sultans, the building of which began in the 15th century and continued to the 19th on the site of the old Acropolis of Byzantium. Since rainfall was more abundant in Turkey than in many parts of the Islamic world, the design of Islamic gardens there, although ordered, was less determined by irrigation channels and formal axes than elsewhere.

In contrast, on the Arabian peninsula rain is very scarce. However, there is an irregular fall in the south and west, and the early cultivation of gardens in that area was possible. The city of Riyadh's name implies the presence of gardens, although there is little trace of early Islamic gardens there today. Gardens and orchards surrounded the early Umayyad capital of Damascus, in modern Syria, a city that itself was regarded as an earthly paradise.

Although remarkably consistent in its general outlines, the Islamic garden was adapted to various needs. It might be a place of privileged retreat or the setting for ceremonial occasions. On a more modest scale, the walled courtyard was a feature not only of palaces and private residences but also of bazaars and caravan hostels. It was also adapted to the needs of mosques and theological colleges. In these, water, regarded as a symbol of purity, was necessary for ritual ablutions and, since paradise overflowed with water, tanks were filled to the brim.

In Islam the garden was yet another expression of the religious principle of unity and order, its design reflecting the rational and spiritual nature of man. For all the sensuous appeal of their calm seclusion, cool shade, fragrant and colourful flowers, shimmering pools and murmuring fountains, it is the spiritual dimension of these gardens that gives them their unique character. The following sections deal more fully with some of the finest gardens of the Islamic tradition.

The paradise garden as a setting for court life or as a private retreat is a constant theme in Mogul art, as in this tile panel dating from the reign of Shāh Abbās.

THE MOORISH GARDENS OF SPAIN

The Court of the Myrtles, also known as the Court of the Pool, in the Alhambra is one of the strongest images of Moorish Spain.

The Islamic culture of the Moors who became established in Spain in the 8th century AD was far more sophisticated than the Visigothic culture it replaced. It left an imprint that endured long after the Moors themselves lost the last vestiges of their political control of the country in the late 15th century. The Moors brought with them advanced scientific and architectural skills and horticultural techniques that continued to develop throughout their rule in Spain. In the 9th century a major source of knowledge and new ideas was Baghdad, in modern Iraq, which, as the capital of the Abbasid dynasty, had become a leading centre for education and science. In the 10th century Córdoba itself became a major centre of botanical studies. The application of this knowledge to gardens was subsequently set out in treatises by, among others, Ibn al-'Awwam (the *Book of Agriculture*, late 12th century) and Ibn Luyun (*Treatise of Agriculture*, 1348). By the 10th century the Córdoba countryside had an extensive irrigation network supplying vineyards, orchards and gardens.

In their order and geometry and in the way water is used as the focus of a cool and private enclosure, the Moorish gardens of Spain show a strong family resemblance to other gardens of the Islamic tradition. They have, nonetheless, their own distinctive character, although it is difficult to form a general view from the small number that survive. Many were small and urban but even when they were large they were

To the side of the mosque begun by Yusuf II in 1171 and now the cathedral of Seville lies the Patio de los Naranjos, best viewed from the Giralda, the minaret of the adjacent mosque. Irrigation channels feed the individual orange trees.

divided into small linked enclosures. Large pools of water rarely featured. Paths were often raised, resulting in the impression of walking at the level of the tops of flowers. Enclosing walls were of stuccoed masonry and tiles were used as facings on seats, pools, paths and steps. The great use made of accessories such as benches and pots may be of relatively recent vintage. Evergreens, especially citrus fruits, were widely planted and fragrant flowers were highly prized.

CÓRDOBA AND SEVILLE

One of the outstanding gardens in the region of Córdoba was at Medina Azahara, built by the first of the rulers of the Western Omayyad Caliphate of Córdoba. The palace city of 'Abd-er-Raham III, built in terraces on the high slopes of the Sierra Morena, was designed by architects from Constantinople and much of the work was carried out under the supervision of Byzantine and possibly also Egyptian craftsmen. The garden, for which reportedly 10,000 labourers were employed for over 40 years, consisted of canals and fountains spread out below a marble terrace. Under a dome a porphyry basin filled with quicksilver dazzled the eye. The garden is now an overgrown and picturesque ruin but partial excavation has revealed simple divisions into four, with the intersection of the axes marked by a pavilion. A very large pool reflected the palace.

Patio de los Naranjos, Córdoba
A surviving though somewhat altered example of the first Omayad gardens in Córdoba

is the Patio de los Naranjos. An 11th-century text describes it as a beautiful courtyard of white marble with a channel bordered by trees. The patio, with little decoration other than horeshoe-shaped arches at the sides, measures 120 × 60 m (394 × 197 ft) and is divided into three rectangles. It is planted with rows of orange trees, which continue the lines of columns inside the building, of which it is an outdoor extension. All the trees are connected at their bases to narrow irrigation channels, which are fed by the overflow from fountain basins. The spaces under the arches were filled in with masonry after the Christian conquest of Córdoba in 1256.

Patio de los Naranjos, Seville
Seville, which eventually became the Moorish capital, also had beautiful gardens, although little is known of their appearance before the 12th century. Recent excavations have apparently revealed that in the palace of Qasr al-Mubarak the sides of the sunken flowerbeds were stuccoed and painted, a type of decoration that does not seem to have become as important as tile decoration, which gave rise to the *azulejos* of Portugal. The Patio de los Naranjos adjoining the mosque, begun in 1171 by Yusuf II, has a similar arrangement to its namesake in Córdoba, with irrigation channels supplying water to each tree.

Alcazar Palace
The garden of the Alcazar palace in Seville is the largest surviving garden in Spain that preserves the Moorish tradition. Even after

the fall of Córdoba and Seville in the 13th century Moorish influence continued, amalgamated with Spanish-Christian forms in the Mudéjar style. The original 12th-century building was destroyed but the palace of the kings of Seville was rebuilt in the 14th century by Moorish architects. The garden consists of several arcaded courtyards with a low pool in the centre, and a large central area, having eight sections divided by clipped hedges. There have been many alterations and additions, including a pavilion built by Charles V in the 16th century and features such as joke fountains (*burladores*), influenced by the gardens of the Italian Renaissance. Nonetheless, the Moorish character of the garden survives, showing in the enclosed geometrical arrangement, raised paths, fountain basins and glazed tiles. Low benches, recessed window seats, glittering water, paving of brick and unglazed terracotta, trees such as cypress, orange and lemon, and many intimately scaled views, add to the garden's overall attraction.

GRANADA

Until its conquest in 1492, Granada remained the last corner of Muslim Spain.

Although the planting of the Alhambra's Patio de Daraxa (also known as the Patio de Lindaraja) is of later date, the basin is Arab and the courtyard still retains its early Moorish character.

Here gardens were set on the hillsides, giving views of the nearby town from open terraces or through pierced walls. The gardens of the Alhambra and Generalife survive and, although much altered, are still essentially Islamic in character.

The Alhambra

The Alhambra or Red Castle was established in the mid-13th century as a royal residence by Mohammed ben Al-Ahmar. The fortress complex, with the gardens forming part of the total enclosure, stands on a plateau east of the city above the River Darro, which supplies its water. Within the Alhambra there are three main courtyard gardens. The Patio de la Alberca (Court of the Pool), now more commonly known as the Patio de los Arrayanes (Court of the Myrtles), built by Yusuf I in the mid-14th century, comes as a sunlit surprise after the small courts by which it is approached from the main entrance. The surface of the long central rectangular pond, only slightly below the level of the surrounding paving,

reflects the battlemented mass of the Torre de Comares at the north end. Below this tower is a graceful arcade, with carved plaster filigree above the arches and a rear wall faced with coloured tiles. At the south end of the pool is a matching arcade, while to the east and west the court is bounded by two-storeyed wings of the palace, unadorned except for an occasional elaborately carved stucco panel over a door or window. The clipped myrtle hedges either side of the pool are of more recent date.

The Patio de los Leones (Court of the Lions), which is entered from the south-east corner of the Patio de la Alberca, was begun in 1377 by Mohammed V. This courtyard takes its name from the central fountain, a 12-sided basin supported by 12 simply carved lions, through whose mouths water pours in thin jets. Contrasting with the simplicity of the lion figures is the richly decorated surrounding architecture. At the points of the compass behind an arcade of slender clustered alabaster columns are four rooms with gilded stalactite ceilings. Within

The pools and fountains of the Alhambra and the Generalife are fed by the waters of the Darro, which flows in the valley below the Red Castle and the summer palace of the sultans. Their setting is completed by the backdrop of the snow-covered Sierra Nevada. Shown here are the gardens of the Partal in the Alhambra.

the rooms to the north and south and in front of those to east and west water bubbles up from small fountains at ground level and flows along narrow channels that divide the courtyard into four, meeting at the hexagonal base of the central fountain. The edge of the basin is inscribed with an ode by Ibn Zamrak acknowledging the beauties of the Alhambra and its abundant supply of water. There is little planting in this courtyard but it is probable that its level was once a metre lower and then shrubs and flowers would not have obscured its architecture.

Leading from the Patio de los Leones is the last of the major courts, the Patio de Daraxa, sometimes known as the Patio de

Lindaraja. This still retains an early Moorish flavour; the raised fluted basin of its centrally placed fountain is Arabic. The planting of box hedges, cypresses and orange trees is of a later date. Nearby is another small courtyard, the Patio de la Reja or de los Cipreses, containing a fountain and four tall cypress trees.

Despite repairs and some considerable

The Alhambra's Court of the Lions takes its name from the beasts of the central fountain. The richly ornamented rooms on the east and the west are linked to the open courtyard by narrow water channels.

The main approach to the Generalife leads to the Court of the Long Pond. Although in its present form much is of fairly recent date, it still recalls the early Islamic concept of the paradise garden.

alterations to the buildings and gardens, the Alhambra's presence, the proportion of its patios, and the imagination, assurance and skill with which water was introduced, have all enabled it to remain as a remarkable Moorish achievement. The total effect of the warm-coloured buildings on their plateau encompassing some of the most beautiful gardens in the Islamic tradition,

with rocky tree-covered slopes below and the snow-covered Sierra Nevada behind, presents a strong and justifiably famous image.

The Generalife

The buildings and gardens of the Generalife, once the summer palace of the sultans, lie on a steep slope of the Cerro del Sol, overlooking the Alhambra and the city of Granada to the west. The original palace in this location dates from the mid-13th century. The restored buildings have been much altered and their decorations have suffered through neglect, but the gardens retain their attraction. The sight and sound of water, obtained from the upper reaches of the Darro, is present everywhere, and there is a lush growth of flowers, trimmed hedges, and orange and cypress trees that contrasts with the surrounding landscape.

The chief focus of the garden is the Patio de la Acequia (Court of the Long Pond). This is a little under 50 m (164 ft) long and is set between a pair of three-storeyed porticoed pavilions. Water bubbling from lotus-shaped basins feeds the central long canal, which is bordered by a loose arrangement of flowers, trimmed hedges of myrtle, and orange and cypress trees. Fine jets arch over the canal, but these are relatively recent additions. The original garden was half a metre lower than the present one.

On the west of this garden is an arcaded gallery from which there are views of the Alhambra and the city, with the north mirador giving views of the Albaicin and Sacromonte hills. On the east side, beyond a narrow service wing, is the upper garden, probably created after 1319. The first compartment, the Patio de los Cipreses, enclosed by cypress trees and bounded on the north by a two-storeyed gallery dating from the 16th century, contains a U-shaped pool with fountain jets. The cascade in the Camino de los Cascades, at a higher level, flows down a channel in the balustrades of rough masonry. Small basins with tiny jets animate each landing of the staircase, while overhead there is an arch of dense foliage.

Despite the views from the periphery of the Generalife, the gardens are intimate in scale and, set as they are in a relatively harsh environment, their lushness recalls the Islamic concept of the paradise garden.

INDIA AND PAKISTAN

The refinement of Mogul gardens is often beautifully represented in miniatures, such as this late 17th-century example.

Long before the establishment of the Mogul Empire in India there were well-established traditions of garden-making in the sub-continent. Central to Buddhism is the idea of a garden as a place of retreat and meditation. This is reflected in the number of gardens attached to Buddhist monasteries and seminaries, as well as to the dwellings of the nobility. Layouts divided into four already existed in Hindu temple gardens, and gardens in the south used running water extensively in their design.

Muslim forms were, in fact, introduced before the Moguls were established politically, but it was under their rule that gardens developed in their full splendour. The great period of the Islamic garden in India began in the first half of the 16th century with Bābur, the first emperor, and continued until the early 18th century. Although the dynasty was not extinguished until 1857, the last emperor to create gardens of any merit was Aurangzīb, who died in 1707.

THE FIRST THREE MOGUL EMPERORS

The ancestors of the dynasty were the Mongols from Central Asia, directly descended from Genghis Khan and Tamerlane the Great. During the 13th and 14th centuries they conquered territory which had previously formed part of the Persian Empire for long periods and, having no sharply defined culture of their own, they adopted that of the Persians. This included the Persian tradition of symbolism and the fourfold garden or *chahar bagh*. The Mogul emperors were not, however, mere imitators. They adapted their gardens to the demands of climate and site, taking into account the differences between the high, dry Persian plateau, the lush well-watered valley of Kashmir, and the hot plains of northern India.

The first Mogul emperor, Bābur, was, throughout a lifetime of incessant and successful warfare, devoted to the making of gardens and the cultivation of the arts. At the age of 14, he briefly captured Samarkand, where he was deeply impressed by the city founded by his ancestor Tamerlane the Great. His first gardens were at Kabul in Afghanistan, the base for his invasions of India. After his decisive victory at Panipat, in 1526, he moved his capital from Delhi to Agra, where his court soon created a series of gardens along the bank of the River Jumna opposite Agra Fort. At least three great gardens in Agra are attributed to

Bābur, the first Mogul emperor, shown here in a garden, was a highly successful warrior but also a great lover of the arts and devoted to the making of gardens. He always regarded Kabul as his home but after his invasion of India he and his followers laid out a series of splendid sites, mainly on the banks of the River Jumna in Agra.

Bābur himself – Zahara Bagh, Dehra Bagh and Ram Bagh, of which only the last (also known as Nur Afshan) survives in recognizable form. This, although much changed, is almost certainly the oldest surviving Mogul garden, and exhibits many features to be found in later examples. The first elements built were a large well, an aqueduct and irrigation channels. The classic layout included geometrical walks and terraces, which here are raised some 3 m (10 ft) above the ground so as to bring them level with the blossom of the surrounding fruit trees. These were irrigated by narrow channels running down the centre of the walks. At the corners are *chabutras*, small square daises, on which to rest and enjoy the view. Some fine pavilions overlooked the river, while provisions were also made for dwelling houses and hot baths. The original planting of fruit and flowers was later overgrown with forest trees.

Humāyūn, the second Mogul emperor, made comparatively little contribution to garden design but his tomb, in Delhi, is the earliest Mogul garden to have survived relatively unchanged. It was built by his widow and completed in 1573, although the surrounding layout was probably begun in his lifetime. If this is the case, it would be an early example of the Mogul tradition in which the tomb garden was treated as a pleasure-ground during the owner's lifetime, with the central pavilion becoming the mausoleum on the owner's death. The site is level and the design, a *chahar bagh* with an intricate pattern of squares arranged around an imposing central mausoleum, shows early Persian influences in the narrow watercourses and shallow pools.

The third and greatest of the emperors, Akbar, who reigned from 1556 to 1605, was comparatively uninterested in gardens but his annexation of Kashmir in 1586 – which he once called his private garden – was of the greatest significance to later garden design, for its ample water, brilliant sunshine, fertile soil and dramatic scenery provided his successors with superb opportunities.

The tolerant policies he pursued in matters of religion and race – he married Rajput princesses and employed Rajput craftsmen – encouraged the development of new concepts of design, resulting in a fusion of

At Amber, capital of the powerful Rajput state of Jaipur, a garden in the women's quarters of the old palace contains complicated stone parterres, in detail more Rajput than Mogul.

Hindu and Muslim traditions. In terms of garden design this Rajput style can be seen at its most brilliant at Amber, from 1037 to 1728 the capital of the powerful Rajput state of Jaipur. Two gardens, one adjoining the women's quarters in the old palace and the other a lake garden, display complicated stone parterres with an underlying star pattern. The details are more Rajput than Mogul.

THE GOLDEN AGE OF MOGUL GARDENS

The outstanding gardens of Mogul India, and some of the world's finest gardens, were created in the first half of the 17th century by Akbar's son and grandson, Jahāngīr and Shāh Jahān. Jahāngīr, who was emperor from 1605 to 1627, developed a lifetime's attachment to Kashmir, which he first visited to accompany his father. Late in life he married the Persian Nūr Jahān and together they became the leading figures in

designing the gardens of Kashmir. Their example was followed by members of the court; it is said that in Jahāngīr's time there were no less than 777 gardens laid out around the shores of Lake Dal in the centre of the Vale of Kashmir.

Vernag

At least three of Jahāngīr's Kashmir gardens have survived: Achabal and Vernag, both near Islamabad, and Shalamar Bagh, near the capital, Srinagar. The favourite garden of the emperor and his wife was Vernag. Serene and remote, this was where he had chosen to be buried. He died, however, at a resting place on the road from Kashmir and his body was taken to Lahore for burial. The garden is on the site of an ancient spring with a tradition of snake worship. An inscription records a date of 1609 and Jahāngīr's employment of Haidar Malik, known for his skill in the management of water. The design now comprises an octagonal pool, surrounded by arcaded reces-

ses, from which a canal, nearly 300 m (984 ft) long, extends to the river. A smaller canal forms a cross-axis. There is hardly a trace of the palace built by Jahāngīr or of other buildings added by Shāh Jahān, but the setting, and especially the contrast between the level garden and the steeply rising hills behind, give the garden its enduring romantic quality.

Achabal

Achabal lies near the point where the Vale of Kashmir dies out against the mountains. This, too, is the site of an ancient spring, Akshavala, which pours out with great force at the foot of the hills. No other Mogul garden retains a water feature of such power and volume and its abundance has helped preserve Achabal's original character to a remarkable degree. The design, attributed primarily to the Empress Nūr Jahān, dates from about 1620.

The great waterfall at the top of the garden, once lit from behind by lamps,

widely in India between 1658 and 1664 and who visited Kashmir, the garden was once full of fruit trees: 'Apples, Pears, Prunes, Apricocks and Cherries'.

Shalamar Bagh, Srinagar

The name Shalamar, meaning Abode of Love, was given to three great Mogul gardens, of which that laid out by Jahāngīr on Lake Dal is outstanding for the perfection of its proportions and the exquisite refinement of its detail. A stream at the head of the garden was diverted to form the central canal, which originally flowed through the three terraces of the garden before reaching the lake. A modern road now severs the original magnificent approach by way of a long canal from the lake, which took one to the Diwan-i-Am, the Hall of Public Audience. Here the emperor sat on his black marble throne to show himself to the people. The emperor's private garden and the zenana, or ladies' garden, lay beyond this. Each was a square of approximately equal size, with water, fountains and pavilions set centrally. Of the Diwan-i-Khas or Hall of Private Audience, built across a cascade in the emperor's garden, only the base remains but the stone throne in front of the cascade is intact. The zenana garden, its entrance guarded by two small pavilions, contains the Black Pavilion by Shāh Jahān. Completely surrounded by water and fountains, this domed marble structure (the dome now replaced by a three-tiered roof) was the garden's climax. The cascade behind it included rows of niches, called *chini-kanas*, in which lights were set to glow through the falling water. The causeways to the pavilions were arcaded to allow the water to move more freely, creating an illusion of great depth, although the water was comparatively shallow.

This garden was animated by many gravity-fed fountains which sent up great plumes of water rather than the sprays which are familiar today. On either side of

broadens out below in a succession of pools filled with fountains. An island pavilion, reached by causeways, is set in the first pool. Beyond, the water passes under the main pavilion, continues down two water-chutes or *chadars* to yet another level and so to the river. On either side of the garden two more canals carry a rushing flow of water cascading down tall water-chutes and

then running nearly level with the ground. Great plane trees surround the heart of the garden and among them, set at intervals, are solid stone platforms (*chabutras*) for sitting out to catch the breeze and for viewing the garden. To one side is a *hummum* or bath. The existing pavilions are of later date, set on the old Mogul bases. According to a European, François Bernier, who travelled

the central canal tall plane trees separate the centre of the garden from the orchards of Persian tradition, which are at a lower level. The outside world could be viewed from two-storeyed gazebos at the corners of the garden.

Nishat Bagh

The only other surviving Kashmir garden of this period is Nishat Bagh, neighbouring Shalamar on Lake Dal. It is generally attributed to Asa Khan IV, a brother of the Empress Nūr Jahān. The drama of this garden lay in the series of 12 terraces, one for each sign of the zodiac, rising from the lake against a background of mountains and the approach by boat from an inner lake. The same road that truncates Shalamar Bagh has cut off the lowest terrace and the main pavilion now faces the road.

As it was not a royal garden, Nishat Bagh did not have to accommodate elaborate ceremonial. It consisted of only two sections, the terraced pleasure-garden and, at the topmost level, the zenana garden, flanked by handsome three-storeyed gazebos giving superb views of the rice fields and Lake Dal, below. The main feature of the garden was the central canal filled with fountains. Formerly the water flowed through the pavilion to discharge directly into the lake. Changes of level on the canal were firmly modelled and marked by broad pools, by flights of steps, or by water thrones – great slabs of stone placed so that the view and the freshness from cool water flowing below could be enjoyed together. The overall design of the garden is contained by great plane trees and orchards.

Chasma Shahi

The luxury of the court of Shāh Jahān, emperor from 1628 until deposed by his son Aurangzīb in 1658, was served by designers and craftsmen of outstanding calibre from Europe and Asia. In buildings and gardens there was a marked reassertion of Persian influence and an emphasis on design and craftsmanship of superb quality. While the greatest of Shāh Jahān's projects were on level sites on the Indian plains, he made his own contribution to the gardens at Shalamar and it is likely that he was responsible for the creation in 1632 of Chasma Shahi at Srinagar. A small, enclosed garden, the

Garden of the Royal Spring as it was called, made dramatic use of levels on a steep site high above Lake Dal. Water from the powerful spring that gave the garden its name rose up into a fine lotus basin, now lost, in the upper pavilion, before flowing through a small cascade and canal to a wide rectangular pool, in which was reflected the main pavilion. This was set on a high retaining wall and the water was discharged down a steep cascade to fill another water garden below. Much has been altered but the outward views of Lake Dal, its islands and background hills are still superb, especially when seen catching late afternoon sunlight.

Shalamar Bagh, Lahore

One of the most grandiose of Mogul gardens was Shalamar Bagh at Lahore, the jumping-off point for the emperor's journeys to Kashmir. The garden, completed about 1642, celebrated the construction of a canal that alleviated the city's water problems. It was built on three levels, with, on the middle terrace, an enormous reservoir over 70 m (230 ft) broad, sparkling with the jets of over 100 fountains and with a marble platform at its centre. The garden was originally a place of great luxury, with marble and agate pavilions, fine brickwork, and the cascades decorated with lights at night and golden vases filled with flowers during the day. The rich planting included many fruit trees, flowers and aromatic

plants. The garden was provided with baths and both Shāh Jahān and Aurangzīb used it as a royal camping ground. Although the garden is still maintained in good condition, little survives of the original buildings. The present entry to the gardens means that the levels are viewed in the opposite direction from that originally intended.

Red Fort

At Shāh Jahān's new city of Delhi, the Red Fort, surrounded on three sides by a moat, consisted of a complex of houses, palaces and gardens, all irrigated by running water. Two gardens – the Hayat Baksh, or Life-giving Garden, and the Mahtab Bagh, or Moonlight Garden – were combined in one grand design. They were planted in contrasting colours, the Hayat Baksh glowing in reds and purples, the Moonlight Garden in pale colours only. The Mahtab Bagh is lost but the Hayat Baksh remains in part. It was designed as a water garden with a great central tank for bathing; a red sandstone pavilion was added to it in the 19th century. Like other parts of the complex, the qualities of this garden are difficult to appreciate without the presence of water.

Taj Mahal

During the last years of his life Shāh Jahān was held in captivity in the Red Fort at Agra, from where he could see, across the River Jumna, his greatest architectural achievement and the ultimate expression of

The Shalamar Bagh at Lahore, here somewhat naïvely depicted, was built to celebrate the completion of a canal bringing water to Lahore from the River Ravi. The luxurious gardens were ceremonially opened by the Emperor Shāh Jahān in about 1642.

Mogul garden art, the Taj Mahal. The tomb and its surrounding garden were a memorial to Shāh Jahān's favourite wife, Mumtaz Mahal, who died in 1631 after the birth of her fourteenth child. The layout followed the classical fourfold division of the paradise garden but instead of the tomb being placed centrally it stands as a climax in white marble at the end of the garden on a raised terrace overlooking the River Jumna. Red sandstone has been used for other buildings belonging to the complex – the gatehouse, the surrounding walls, the mosque and assembly hall flanking the tomb and two pavilions marking each end of the cross-axis. At the centre lies a raised marble reflecting pool. The garden was formerly divided into an intricate pattern of squares and a 17th-century description refers to parterres filled with flowers. The tree planting would almost certainly have been of

fruit, with taller shade trees along the walks. The causeways are slightly raised to allow irrigation of the garden. The quality of the craftsmanship is still evident but the character of the garden has been much altered, particularly by the informal planting of large trees, giving the garden a European rather than a Mogul appearance. The star patterns of the parterres along the canals can still be seen but the flowers and fruit have disappeared. The tomb and its garden were built over a period of 22 years and at his death Shāh Jahān was buried there beside his wife.

Rabi 'a-ud-Daurāni

The long reign of Aurangzīb, which began with the deposition of his father, was marked by almost incessant war and religious controversy. A complete contrast to his predecessors, deeply religous and with

little interest in the arts, Aurangzīb's achievements in this field were in building. He set up his southern kingdom in Aurangabad, where the mausoleum of Rabi 'a-ud-Daurāni was erected in memory of his first wife. The design and layout echo those of the Taj Mahal but lack the perfect balance of Shāh Jahān's masterpiece, a clear indication that a decline in quality had begun. Aurangzīb's policies of repression led to tensions within his empire, which contributed to its decline under his successors and its eventual disappearance under British rule.

The best-known tomb garden of Mogul India is that surrounding the Taj Mahal, built by the Emperor Shāh Jahān for his favourite wife, Mumtaz Mahal. The planting shown in this 19th-century view has given the garden a European character.

IRAN

The Madrassa Mader-i Shah at Isfahan, built in the early 18th century, is a fine example of a courtyard garden contained within a theological college.

Although the Persian tradition played such an important part in the development of the Islamic garden, no Iranian garden today dates back substantially more than 500 years. The Arab invaders who brought Islam to the Iranian plateau in the 7th century AD were among many who have fought over territory that for the greater part is so harsh that the creation of gardens in it seems little short of miraculous. Except for the Caspian coast, with its mild temperatures, heavy rainfall and intensive culti-

vation, Iran has little surface water and endures summers of searing heat followed by often bitterly cold winters. The natural vegetation of this apparently inhospitable environment is very sparse. Much of the irrigation on the plateau has been through *qanats*, the underground tunnels aired by vertical shafts at regular intervals that take water from a mountain source of melted snow.

The physical evidence of early gardens is scanty and yet engraved and written rec-

ords, miniatures and garden carpets speak powerfully of a delight in gardens that can be traced through the long history of Persia. Irrigation was indispensable for the creation of tree-shaded cool retreats from the hot and dusty world outside. Fruits, flowers, birds, animals and fish gave these a gaiety and animation that Persian artists have captured in ravishing detail. It is perhaps the patterns of irrigation necessary to bring to life a corner of the desert and create the image of an earthly paradise that are the

most important legacies of the ancient Persian gardens.

SHAH ABBAS AND THE GARDENS OF ISFAHAN

Isfahan, one of the oldest cities of the Iranian plateau, benefited from major public works carried out by the Safavid ruler Shah Abbas I (1587–1628), who made the city his capital. The principal elements of the town plan still survive, though their original character has been much altered. The Maydan (Garden of the Plain), one of the largest public squares in the world, links some of the greatest monuments of the Safavid architecture. To the north is the entrance to Isfahan's great bazaar, to the south the Royal Mosque, on the east the blue-tiled Lutfullah Mosque and on the west the Ali Qapu or Gate of Ali. The vast complex of royal buildings surrounded by trees, ponds, fountains and channels of flowing water to which this monumental gateway led is now largely built over. However, the six-storeyed building, which had richly decorated private and public apartments, survives. Beneath a large porch supported by 18 slender wood columns is a lead-lined marble basin, which once contained three fountains fed by water drawn to an upper level by oxen.

From this porch the Shah could look down on the varied activities of the Maydan below. A two-storeyed frontage with a unifying series of niches completely surrounds the square. Although its upper level is mostly façade, the lower bays once sheltered a great variety of merchants, whose wares spilled out into the Maydan on market days. Some commercial activity is still to be found along the square's periphery and its grand scale and monumental buildings remain. Municipal planting has, however, completely altered the original surface treatment of the square itself which, in the time of Shah Abbas, was used to display horsemanship and marksmanship, and for the playing of polo.

The major axis of Shah Abbas's plan for Isfahan was the Chahar Bagh Avenue, running north to south, west of the Maydan, and terminating at the 17th-century Allahverdikhan Bridge crossing the Zayandeh-Rud River. In this area near the

river there were formerly other royal gardens. The Chahar Bagh was itself built as a leafy promenade, and was bordered by palatial buildings and handsome kiosks, with shady gardens beyond. Originally it was 75 m (246 ft) wide, with a stone-edged canal bordered by poplar and plane trees flowing down its centre. The slight gradient allowed for cascades and there were many pools and fountains along its length. The central canal has since disappeared, along with many of the plane trees. Although the central strip remains popular with pedestrians, it is now bounded on both sides by shopping streets that are busy with traffic.

The northern terminus of the Chahar Bagh Avenue, the Hazar Jerib, was a point where three avenues running east-west crossed 12 running north-south. There were pavilions, variously shaped pools, water-jets, and many flowers. The Hazar Jerib no longer exists but a description by a 17th-century traveller, Sir John Chardin, gives a vivid impression: 'One was surprised by so many fountains appearing on every side as far as one could see, and was charmed by the beauty of the scene, the odour of the flowers, and the flight of the birds, some in aviaries and some among the trees.'

At the end of the 16th century a royal pavilion, Chehel Sutun (Forty Columns), was built to the north-west of the Maydan. This was subsequently extended by Shah Abbas II and repaired after fire at the beginning of the 18th century. This is a remarkable example of a building wholly interrelated with its adjacent garden. The

The Chehel Sutun at Isfahan owes its name, meaning Forty Columns, to the 20 columns supporting the great porch that are reflected in the long pool lying in front of the pavilion. This is set in a garden containing geometrically subdivided parterres.

roof of the partially enclosed great porch is supported by 20 fluted cedar columns. Doubled by reflection in the long pool which the porch overlooks, they have given the pavilion its name. At the terrace floor level is a white marble basin into which four carved lions once spouted water, in turn reflected in tiny panels of mirror contained in the painted wood mosaic ceiling above. The garden in which the pavilion is set contains geometrically subdivided parterres and there are many trees. Originally there was more than one pool with several fountains and entry pavilions; apart from the central reflecting pool, these have all but disappeared.

Later in date than the work of Shah Abbas I is a fine example of a courtyard garden attached to a theological college. The Madrassa Mader-i Shah, which was built in the early 18th century, is entered from Chahar Bagh Avenue through a marble and tiled entry porch decorated with gilt medallions and intricate arabesques. The courtyard garden contained within the college is surrounded by a two-storeyed arcade, behind which are the students' rooms. Down the centre of the garden is a long step-lined canal that links the entry portal with a vaulted recess at the east end;

in the centre of the south side is a sanctuary. The ablution pool is filled to the brim with dark water and there is shade from several old plane trees.

OTHER GARDENS OF IRAN

Most of the other gardens that survive in Iran date from the 18th and 19th centuries and are to be found in or near such cities as Shiraz, Tabriz and Tehran. Six km (3½ miles) from Kashan, however, the Bagh-i-Fin is to be found. In the 16th century Shah Abbas I erected buildings round the perennial spring of this oasis in the desert but these have now all disappeared. The present garden, also known as the Bagh-i Shah (King's Garden), dates from the early 19th century. The spring of Fin provides a continuous flow of water to various channels lined with green tiles, and feeds a large pool lying in front of a centrally placed pavilion. There are many fountains and, in the flowery garden, plane and cypress trees border paths to give shade.

Bagh-i Takht

An early garden of Shiraz, the Bagh-i Takht (Garden of the Throne), survived into this century, albeit in a poor state, but the site has now been devoted to housing. The garden was established by a local ruler early in the 11th century; it was only in the second half of the 19th century that it acquired its present name. A European traveller of the 17th century described the garden as 'belonging to the ancient kings of Persia, called Bagh-i Firdaus. It is full of fruit trees and rose trees in abundance. At the end of the Garden upon a descent of a Hill stands a great piece of Building and below a large Pool affords it water'. The water which supplied the hillside garden and filled the artificial lake on which small boats plied originated from a spring in the rock. Its pressure was also sufficient to maintain jets of water that could be opened and closed.

Haft Tan and Chehel Tan

Two small Shiraz gardens, both probably dating from the late 18th century, almost certainly owe their preservation to the fact that they contain graves. The Haft Tan (Seven Bodies) and Chehel Tan (Forty Bodies) are both enclosed by high walls and each has a pavilion running the full width of the garden. Chehel Tan contains many tall trees, while at Haft Tan there is a central rectangular pool on the terrace in front of the pavilion.

Bagh-i Eram

Typical of 19th-century Iranian garden art and architecture is Bagh-i Eram (Garden of Paradise), laid out at the foot of a mountain range in north-west Shiraz. A path leads from an entry on the north to a pavilion set on the garden's central axis. A water channel runs through a tiled room at a lower level of the pavilion and in front is a large reflecting tank, from which runs a narrow channel with several off-shoots. These, with tall trees and straight paths, provide long internal vistas. There are many shrubs and flowers and a rose garden.

Narenjestan-i Qavam

A very much smaller garden, the Narenjestan-i Qavam (Qavam Orange Grove), is situated off a busy artery in the east part of the city of Shiraz. The rectangular garden, flanked by arcaded walls, is entered through a vestibule which forms part of a set of small rooms protecting it from the noise and activity outside. A narrow canal lined with blue tiles runs down the centre of the garden, widening at intervals into pools of various geometrical shapes. The principal rooms of a two-storeyed house, which extends across the full width of the property, face south over the garden. In front of the house is a raised terrace with a central rectangular pool. The garden is well planted and palm trees line the sides.

Qasr-i Qajar

The expansion of modern Tehran has transformed large areas of what was once a typically oriental city. Qasr-i Qajar (Castle of the Qajars), built by Fath Ali Shah at the beginning of the 19th century, had gardens that survived until the mid-20th century. Most of its area was on level ground divided by straight paths with regular rectangular sections. A much smaller walled-in area, with a pool at its foot, rose in terraces up the adjacent hillside. An early description refers to poplars, willows, fruit trees and many roses, as well as to the royal castle itself, with rich finishes of ebony, ivory, mosaic and painting, pools and canals.

Gulistan Palace

Fath Ali Shah also built Gulistan Palace, the Palace of Roses. Both traditional and recent features can be found here. A shallow tiled fountain pool reflects the carved front to the platform of a deep porch that overlooks the garden. Adjacent to the palace are courtyards, some paved in marble. The main garden, which now serves as a city park, has further pools, which are faced with blue faience. There are extensive grassed areas with flowers such as anemones and carnations and tall cypress and pine trees. In quality, like other surviving gardens in Iran, this garden hardly conveys the glory of the Persian Islamic tradition in its prime.

The Narenjestan-i Qavam at Shiraz, built in the 19th century, retains its Islamic character despite planting influenced by European practices.

ORIENTAL GARDENS

No culture, eastern or western, has produced a longer continuous tradition of garden design than that of the Chinese. We know from hieroglyphs on oracle bones dating back to the second millenium BC that the ancient princes of China set aside vast tracts of land for hunting and military exercises. Legend suggests that this land was later embellished with artificial lakes and terraces. By the end of the 4th century BC a royal garden described in a collection of Southern poems has the scarlet balconies, latticed pavilions, winding waterways and views of distant mountains of a kind still to be seen, some fifteen centuries later, in the Yi He Yuan, the Summer Palace, a few miles north-west of Beijing.

In the turbulent years of the late 19th and early 20th centuries, when the Yi He Yuan was destroyed twice by European forces and rebuilt after both lamentable episodes, China's principal influence on the gardens of the West was a source of new plant material. The introductions by such collectors as the French missionary Père David and the Englishman Ernest Wilson from the country's exceptionally rich natural flora included many plants of outstanding horticultural merit that have become mainstays of Western gardens. Westerners are therefore sometimes puzzled that, with such a wealth of material to choose from, the Chinese have in general used a very limited repertoire of plants in their gardens.

Two factors help to explain this. Firstly, as we shall see, plants are not the most essential components of the Chinese garden. What count above all are rocks and water, then architecture and only then trees, shrubs and flowers. Secondly, the appreciation of plants is based more on their accumulated symbolic and literary associations than on their rarity.

The lotus, which in summer makes a new, swaying, blue-green surface above the level of garden pools, symbolizes the Buddhist soul rising, in the words of the 11th-century Zhou Tunyi, 'without contamination from the mud, reposing modestly above the clear water, hollow inside and straight without'. Bamboo, which bends with the wind but does not break, suggests an honourable man, and the orchid a true gentleman because it scents a room so subtly that nobody notices it until he leaves. The peach still promises fecundity and immortality; the peony wealth and elegance. The chrysanthemum, probably the oldest cultivated flower in China, symbolizes autumn. A classic association which recurs again and again in Chinese gardens consists of the 'Three Friends of Winter' – pine, plum and bamboo.

China's long tradition of garden-making has been most extravagantly expressed at numerous imperial residences, including the Yuan Ming Yuan, of which this is an 18th-century view.

The significance attached to particular plants is symptomatic of the resonances with which the components of a Chinese garden are charged. The garden is not only a place 'to refresh the heart' by contact with nature; it also has to engage the intellect and in this expresses a profound and serious view of the world and man's place in it. In the remarkably homogeneous culture shared by educated Chinese for centuries the garden is a place where all arts come together – it needs a painter to design it and to appreciate it, a poet to immortalize it and a calligrapher to record its qualities. In each garden visitor these accomplishments should ideally be combined. The tributes of past visitors that we still see today, the poems engraved on stone tablets let into garden walls, draw on that fund of shared culture and add yet further layers of significance to gardens already rich in allusions for those steeped in the Chinese classics.

The West has been slow to appreciate the distinctive character of Chinese gardens and the culture of which they form an important part. When, in the late 17th century, the Englishman Sir William Temple, who is sometimes credited with originating the English landscape movement, used the word 'sharawadgi' to define the beauty of the Chinese garden, 'without any order or disposition of parts', the vision that ostensibly served as a model for successful irregularity of design was, like the word he had coined, more European invention than Chinese reality. The same fancifulness typifies the charming but inauthentic buildings 'in the Chinese taste' that were fashionable embellishments of Western gardens in the 18th and 19th centuries. The vogue for chinoiserie was not unimportant, but it bore only a superficial resemblance to the forms and spirit of Chinese gardens and architecture.

In Japan the appreciation of Chinese culture has been altogether more profound and enduring in its influence. Since the 7th century AD at least there have been recurrent phases in which cultivated Japanese have deliberately adopted China's culture and, even in less active phases, there has been a steady movement of ideas from the Middle Kingdom to the Japanese islands. The towering significance of the adopted culture is reflected in garden design, as in all other branches of the arts and crafts, sometimes almost nostalgically. There is, however, no mistaking the uniquely Japanese character of the country's garden tradition. In their extraordinary level of accomplishment and refinement Japanese gardens rank among the supreme expressions of the national culture.

Fortunately, a number of Japan's finest traditional gardens, including imperial parks and austere Zen gardens of contemplation, survive in reasonably good condition. In China the process of rehabilitating gardens that have often been long neglected has begun, and perhaps in the near future yet more of the country's impressive heritage will be accessible to the public.

The garden was often the setting for gatherings of Chinese scholars and connoisseurs. In this detail from a handscroll of the late 16th or early 17th century the scene is dominated by a fantastic Taihu rock.

CHINA

The Wang Shi Yuan – informal, intricate, sparkling and lively – is one of the smallest of the famous gardens restored in Suzhou, the 'Venice of the East'.

The Chinese approach to the design of gardens – in comparison with that of the West, remarkably consistent over its long history – has been profoundly influenced by traditional concepts and by the two main indigenous philosophies, Confucianism and Daoism (Taoism).

The choice of a site for a building or garden was – and still is in some Chinese communities – determined by the ancient geomantic art of *feng shui*. The basic principle of *feng shui* is that streams of currents of 'vital spirit' or 'cosmic breath' *(ch'i)* run through the earth according to its topography. These currents forcefully influence the fortunes of individuals and their descendants, depending on how they place their houses and – most importantly – their graves in relation to the winds *(feng)*, waters *(shui)*, hills *(kan)* and valleys *(yu)* of the landscape in which they live. Since the traditional view is that changes to the landscape affect the flow of *ch'i*, a complex set of rules and principles was developed to guide men's building activities. Although different schools developed, there is general agreement that the ideal dwelling should stand facing south, two-thirds the way up a hill on dry ground, with lower, protective hills to east and west. Water should gather in a pool below the dwelling, forming a reservoir of benevolent influences, which might be carried away should there be a stream flowing too swiftly past the property. Since evil influences *(sha)* were thought to travel in straight lines, winding walls and roads which seem to follow the patterns of the landscape were preferred to straight ones. The masonry screens or 'spirit walls' built just inside Chinese courtyard entrances not only give privacy to those inside, but were also intended to deflect the straight 'arrows' of evil and protect the good fortunes of the family.

Before a garden could be designed a *feng shui* practitioner checked the site, its surroundings, the flow and availability of water and advised on the garden's orientation. An important factor to be taken into account was the balance of *yin* and *yang* forces. The traditional Chinese view is that these two elemental forces lie behind all creation. They are opposites: *yang*, active, bright and strong, is represented, for instance, by the male; *yin*, dark, tranquil and weak, by the female. This simplification, however, cannot convey the subtlety of the pairing of opposites that is the expression of these two forces. In a favourable site these elements would be in a state of balance and the designing of a garden called for a conscious patterning of opposites, high places leading to low, open to closed, shady to sunny and wide to narrow.

In the traditional view the most important opposition in the garden is between the rocks, representing 'the bony structure of the earth', the hard, rough and unmoving *yang* element, and the soft reflective *yin* of water. The 'false mountains' (*jia shan*), piled mounds of rocks, that have been an integral part of Chinese gardens since the Han dynasty (206 BC–AD 220) represent the *yang* and they are always sited near water. Although an expression of untamed nature, in form artificial hills have been much influenced by Chinese landscape paintings. Rather than repeat the forms of nature in miniature, they aim to inspire in the viewer a succession of emotions similar to those he might expect to experience while walking among mountains, or following the small painted figures through a landscape scroll. The unique Chinese passion for displaying unusual single stones (*shi feng*), both big and small, seems to have taken hold from the Tang dynasty (618–907).

According to the principles of *feng shui* gardens ideally should be at the back or to the east of a house; if the site was so limited that its garden had to lie on the west (considered the most harmful location), a gate was always opened in the east wall of main residence to make another courtyard, even a corridor, to the east.

Walls were essential to preserve the peace of a garden and to hold the good influences

SIMPLIFIED CHINESE DYNASTIES

Shang c. 1600–1027 BC
Zhou 1027–256 BC
Qin 221–206 BC
Han 206 BC–AD 220
Northern and Southern Dynasties 317–580
Sui 589–618
Tang 618–907
Five Dynasties 907–960
Northern Song 960–1127
Southern Song 1127–1279
Yuan (Mongol) 1279–1368
Ming 1368–1644
Qing (Manchu) 1644–1911
Republic 1911–1949
People's Republic 1949–

of the site. These walls, it was thought, should not be pierced by large doors or low window-openings (*lou chuang*), otherwise the accumulated vitality might leak away. Winding walls within the enclosure not only add to the intricate charm and seclusion of a garden but, it was believed, also concentrated good influences. Old trees were valued and preserved not simply for their picturesque quality but because they were repositories of *ch'i*. In some gardens certain plants were grown – among them crab-apples, magnolias and peonies – with names and features associated with happiness and wealth. Water also symbolized wealth and for that reason after it had been led quietly through the garden landscape and gathered in pools in front of the main pavilion its exit was made as inconspicuous as possible, often hidden by rockwork mountains. In the late Qing period few caves were made in these artificial 'mountains' for fear that any evil influences overlooked in the garden's planning might accumulate in their open mouths.

Confucianism and Daoism

Attitudes to nature and gardens belonging to Confucianism and Daoism, both philosophies dating from the 5th century BC, went hand in hand with traditional beliefs. While Confucianism concentrated on man's relationship to man, Daoism sought to discover how man could best fit into the

great universe in which he lived. The 'Dao' was the 'totality of all things' – past, present and future – in its constant state of transformation through time. And Daoists, seeing man as inescapably part of this pattern, aimed to become so finely tuned to its changing currents that they would become one with the forces that produced them. Daoists often opted out of organized society but their philosophy, apparently so opposed to the Confucian emphasis on rites and duties, proved in time to be its necessary complement. Daoism provided a release from the constraints of being a 'superior man', as prescribed by Confucian principles. The eminently practical Chinese found both philosophies valuable. The Daoist's love of nature and Confucius's encouragement of self-cultivation both lie behind the planning and design of the Chinese garden. The formality and order of the classic Chinese house, with its symmetrical progression of rectangular courtyards, may be seen as a reflection of the Confucian desire to regulate human relationships, while the apparent disorder of the Chinese garden, with its irregular winding waterways, its rocky hills and pavilions tucked into trees, mirrors the Daoist principle of harmony with nature. This is true of both main types of Chinese garden – the great parks of the emperors, and the private gardens, made sometimes by merchants but traditionally by scholar-officials, who were the élite of old China. Both are ultimately based on the idea of nature enhanced by harmonious contact with man. Almost equally important, however, were two ancient themes, which early came to be represented in Chinese gardens; one was the idea of the garden as a microcosm; the other was the representation of the magical islands of the Immortals.

The garden as microcosm

In 221 BC Qin Shi Huang of the short-lived Qin dynasty unified, for the first time, the ancient Chinese states. In the Shanglin Park, beyond his capital, he began to collect rare animals and vegetation as tribute from all corners of the conquered empire. These were accepted as a potent symbol of imperial power and the Han emperors who followed him (206 BC–AD 220) continued this collection. It is in descriptions of their

Similar features recur in Chinese gardens over many centuries but with infinite variations in the detail.

Below: *Pebble flooring* (luan shi pu di) *sometimes includes broken porcelain, bricks and tiles set on edge as well as pebbles. The designs may be geometric or derived from animal or plant forms.*

Right: *Open-sided galleries* (lang) *link different parts of the garden and, particularly in the south, often take a zigzag course.*

Bottom left: *An opening* (lou chuang, meaning leaking window) *in a garden wall can be an open frame, simply geometric or of fantastic shape, to frame a view. Sometimes the view is half-hidden by elaborate latticework.*

Bottom right: *Chinese bonsai* (peng jing) *are often displayed in special collections or are used to decorate tables and stands in garden settings.*

parks in the great prose poems of that dynasty, where myth and fact are mixed to produce a magic portrait of the empire in miniature, that we have the first flowering of the idea that the garden is not simply a particular landscape of nature embellished, but a microcosm symbolizing all the riches and variety of the universe; it is an idea that still – in the close-packing of many effects in small spaces – affects gardens in China today.

The islands of the Immortals

It was the Han emperor Wudi who first gave form, in gardens, to the search for immortality. The legendary Chinese Immortals were thought to live partly in the Western Mountains and partly on movable islands in the Eastern Sea. These islands – Penglai, Fangzhang and Yingzhou – like the Immortals themselves, dissolved into mist as human travellers approached. Qin Shi Huang had already sent an unsuccessful expedition to find them; Han Wudi instead built replicas of their magical islands in the great lake of his park thinking thereby to encourage them, flying by on the backs of storks, to descend and reveal to him their secrets.

Though the Emperor lived a not unusually extended life, the fame of the hunting parks of Han, which also contained palace complexes, farms, and orchards, set a pattern for imperial gardening, embodying lakes and islands, which was enthusiastically followed right up to modern times.

IMPERIAL PLEASURE GROUNDS

Imperial and private gardens in China share conventions and characteristics. They have in common architectural forms such as the pavilion (ting) for viewing or repose and the open-sided gallery (lang); architectural details such as decorative moon-shaped doorways (di xue); and the ingenious incorporation in a composition of 'borrowed' views (jie jing) from outside the garden boundary. In imperial estates this common ground is most clearly evident in the detail of gardens-within-gardens, often enough directly inspired by celebrated examples of private gardens. However, the scale of imperial pleasure grounds sets them apart and justifies considering them as a group.

Hangzhou's West Lake, Xi Hu, surrounded by gentle hills, epitomizes the Chinese ideal of 'hills and water'. It is divided into three unequal parts by dikes planted with willows.

Luoyang

The great park at Luoyang of Emperor Yangdi, the second emperor of the Sui dynasty (589–618), contained three great themes that run through all imperial gardens : the natural landscape embellished; the riches of the empire symbolized; and the isles of the Immortals recreated. But to these were added extravagant devices for entertaining imperial guests. These included a unique collection of sumptuously dressed mechanical figures, which sailed in boats along specially constructed channels to perform 72 scenes from Chinese history. A report describes the park's bare trees in winter decked out with silk flowers; in summer its real lotus flowers were increased by artificial flowers 'constantly renewed'. A 'million' people reportedly worked to create this park, of which one in five were said to have died in the process. The philosopher Mencius (372–289 BC), the first Chinese philosopher to advocate 'humane government', had already recorded the excesses of the emperors, such as the legendary King Qieh of Hsia (2000–1600 BC), who 'extended their parks and terraces without limit' until their empires dissolved in chaos. He had contrasted the dissoluteness of such rulers with the model conduct of King Wen of the Zhou dynasty (c. 1027–256 BC) whose imperial lakes and terraces were open to the public and used for religious rituals. Yandi's park, destroyed in the rebellion that finished both emperor and dynasty, encouraged the idea of gardens as symbols of imperial indulgence, but did little to curb the landscaping ambitions of later emperors.

Hua Qing Gong

Xuan Zhong (712–55), a cultivated and powerful ruler of the Tang, developed an elaborate garden-palace, Hua Qing Gong, 20km (12 miles) east of the city of Xian in Shaanxi province. There he spent each winter with his favourite concubine, Guifei, whose legendary beauty is supposed to have so bewitched him that he lost interest in affairs of state. There had been a short-stay royal villa on the site, famous for its hot springs, as far back as the 3rd century BC, which the earlier Tang emperor Tai Zhong had already developed as a palace. Xuan Zhong's lavish complex, covering a whole hillside, included bathing pools, pavilions and hidden retreats. An ingenious arrangement in one pavilion made water rise inside the four corner pillars and fall as cooling screens in place of the walls. The garden was famous above all for the effects of its huge bluish-green firs and jade-green pines in the evening twilight. The Emperor's dissoluteness eventually led to an uprising, and the palace was greatly damaged. What today is still called the Hua Qing Spring, which includes a bathing pool said to be that of Guifei, is in fact only a very small part of what was then the palace. Its buildings, rebuilt and opened to the public in 1956, nevertheless still preserve names like the 'Hall of Dancing Frost' and the 'Crab-apple Flower Bathing Pool' given them in Tang times.

Gen Yue

Among the most famous of all imperial gardens was Gen Yue, a vast man-made landscape built between 1117 and 1123 by the Emperor Zhao Ji (Hua Tsung) of the Northern Song dynasty. It lay north-east of the capital Bian Liang, now the city of Kaifeng. The name given to it suggests that the park had some geomantic purpose beyond that of the Emperor's own personal pleasure: *yue* means 'high mountain' and *gen*, one of the Eight Trigrams in the ancient book of philosophy *Yi Jing*, usually signifies mountain and the orientation north-east.

The Emperor, a painter of considerable merit, was, it seems, personally involved in planning the park but it was supervised by Liang Shi Cheng with several commissioners working under him. One, a merchant, Zhu Mian, became notorious for his pursuit of rare plants and rocks around Suzhou; another, Ling Bi, collected for the park 1,500 km (940 miles) away in South China.

The park, with a perimeter of nearly 5 km (3 miles), had water in the west and hills and rocky peaks in the east. Collections of bizarre and fantastic rocks spiralled out of these ridges, which rose at their highest point to the Peak of Ten Thousand Years' Longevity, with a pavilion at its top. From here the Emperor beheld what seemed a microcosm of the universe, with city and park spread out 'as if lying on the palm of the hand'. All around 'peaks, caverns, mature trees and grasses' blended with nature 'as if it had all been here since creation', while islands embellished with palatial halls and gazebos lay along the waterways. Among innumerable buildings

were the Red Sky Chamber, the Hall of the Flower with Green Sepals, a library, and a circular Pavilion for the Immortals. Unfortunately, the expense of building Gen Yue weakened an already tottering dynasty. Today nothing remains of it except two great monolithic rocks, one in Shanghai and one in Suzhou, supposedly chosen for the mountain of Gen Yue.

The gardens of Hangzhou

After 1126 the imperial survivors of the Northern Song fled south, the court establishing its capital at the prosperous city of Hangzhou (formerly Hangchow) in Zhejiang province. Its West Lake, Xi Hu, and the amphitheatre of gentle hills that surrounds it epitomize the Chinese ideal of 'hills and waters'. Since flooding was always a danger to the city, willow-planted dikes divide the lake, forming three unequal parts. Members of the court built palaces and gardens along the willow-fringed shores. Rulers often abdicated and, surrounded by painters and poets, spent the rest of their days boating and giving parties. When Kublai Khan finally conquered the Southern Song in 1276 the palaces and gardens were left to crumble: their ruins were described by Marco Polo. Little remains even of a subsequent phase of villa building in the 17th and 18th centuries, encouraged by long visits paid to Hangzhou by two Qing dynasty emperors, Kang Xi and Qian Long.

Beijing as capital of the empire

Kublai Khan made his Great Capital (Da Du) in what is now Beijing. The site, Beihei Park, which literally translated means North Sea, is the oldest and largest park in the Chinese capital. It was first recorded under the Liao dynasty in the 10th century as the site of the Precious Islet Imperial Lodge. In 1179, under the Jin dynasty (on the outskirts of whose capital Zhongdu it then lay), the land was dredged and an artificial hill called Qionghua (the Isle of Fine Jade) was made from the earth. On it was built the Guanhan dian or Hall in the Moon Palace, and the whole became part of a great villa – the Daning Gong – which was used for short royal visits.

When Zhongdu was destroyed in the early 13th century, Daning Gong was left

Beihei Park, lying north-east of the Forbidden City in the centre of Beijing, is the oldest and largest park in the Chinese capital. Most of the buildings that survive, including the elegant double-storeyed walkway, date from the reign of the Emperor Qian Long in the 18th century.

undamaged. The new city begun by Kublai Khan in 1260 had at its centre Qionghua Islet. This was reshaped, renamed the Ten Thousand Year Hill and planted with evergreens and rocks of lapis lazuli. Marco Polo describes its 'trees and rocks alike . . . as green as green can be . . . no other colour to be seen'. Under Kublai, the lake was renamed Tai Yi, Pool of Heavenly Water, and further palaces – later destroyed by the first Ming emperor – were built on its east and west banks. When the Ming moved their court from Nanjing to Beijing in 1408, they enlarged this lake and built their great palace, the Forbidden City, next to it. Under the Ming emperors and their successors, the Qing, still more buildings were added and since the middle of the 17th century the White Dagoba, a Tibetan-style tower shaped like a flat-bellied bottle, has stood at the top of the island. Today nearly all the buildings below it, including the elegant double-storeyed walkway that runs along the north shore of the island, date from the 18th century.

Beihai, which once provided a necessary release from the oppressive conservatism of the Ming court and the symmetrical, recti-linear grandeur of the imperial city, is now a large public park much used by the people of Beijing. The two great water-gardens that form its southern extension, Zhonghai and Nanhai (generally run together as Zhong Nan Hai), the Central and Southern Seas, are only partly accessible. Zhonghai was excavated in the late 12th and early 13th centuries and was formerly part of the Tai Yi. Nanhai was built under the Ming. The significance of this complex of water-gardens today lies in the delicate play of contrast between the open areas of park and lake and the enclosed and more intensely landscaped 'little sceneries' scattered along the shores. An old courtyard garden on the shores of Beihai, the Limpid Mirror Studio or Jing Qing Zhou, renovated in 1982, is considered among the best examples of its kind in Beijing.

Jin Shan

Yet another imperial park, Jin Shan, the Hill of Scenic Beauty, overlooks the Three Seas and gives panoramic views over the capital and the Forbidden City. Also known as Mei Shan or Coal Hill, it was, until tall buildings were put up in the 1950s, the highest point in the capital. The hill itself is man-made, built up from earth and sludge dug up to create Tai Yi and from material dredged in the 15th century from the river surrounding the Forbidden City. From being a dumping ground, the area became an imperial garden that included enclosures for deer and cranes, symbols of longevity. Most of the buildings on Jin Shan date from the 18th century, erected during the reign of the Emperor Qian Long. Wan Chun Ting, the Pavilion of Everlasting Spring, a square structure with double eaves, makes a dramatic silhouette on the horizon at the end of many vistas in the imperial palace.

Yu Hua Yuan

The dusty red walls of the Forbidden City itself enclose several gardens. The Yu Hua Yuan is the last in the vast processional sequence of gates, halls and courtyards that lead north from Tien An Men Square to Jin Shan. Coming after the triple halls of state and their marble terraces, it is a deliberate anticlimax, a place where the emperors could relax after the awesome formalities of court ceremony. The plan is, however, meticulously symmetrical, the trees in rows, the flowers (peonies in late spring, chrysan-themums in autumn) in beds, and the ground paved. Although the garden now owes much to Qing rebuilding, it was originally laid out during the 15th century and its most extraordinary feature, vener-able junipers (*Juniperus chinensis*), were planted in the Ming period. Their ancient trunks are patterned with swirls and knots and their twisted branches are braced with huge wooden props above the enclosing walls and imperial yellow roofs.

Qian Long Garden

The Qian Long Garden, located near the north-east corner of the Imperial Palace, and built for the Qing emperor of that name, consist of five parts or courses arranged consecutively along a north-south axis. In form it is somewhat like a courtyard house with a garden or courtyard separating each of its halls. Between the buildings the courtyards are laid out in the style of south-east China, freer and more lyrical in design than the other parts of the palace. Pavilions, open-sided galleries, rockeries and artificial hills seem to be arranged spontaneously but are in fact carefully placed in relation to each other and create a subtle balance of high and low, foreground and background, solid and void. One pavilion, Xi Shang Ting, which commem-orates an ancient ceremony for dispelling bad influences, contains an allusion to a famous garden, Lan Ting, where, on the third of the third lunar month AD 353 the great calligraphist Wang Xi Zhi composed his *Preface for the Anthology on Orchid Pavilion*. Wang and his cultivated friends floated their wine bowls down a winding brook while they recited the poems and prose later collected in the *Anthology*. For the next fifteen centuries their literary game, in which each had to compose a poem by the time the floating cup passed in front of him, was a standard entertainment of gentlemen poets. The floor of the Xi Shang Ting is engraved with the pattern of a running brook.

The conservatism of the Ming court is expressed in the symmetrical grandeur of the Forbidden City. Behind its dusty walls there are, however, small gardens and pavilions, such as the Fu Pi Ting, that are in marked contrast to the areas devoted to formal court ceremonies.

Chang Chun Yuan

The rulers of the Manchu Qing dynasty continued enthusiastically the tradition of building imperial palaces and gardens. 'Every Emperor', wrote one of its most cultivated emperors, Qian Long, 'when he has retired from audience and finished his public duties, must have a garden in which he may . . . refresh his heart. If he has a suitable place to do this, it will regulate his emotions and relax his mind. If not, he will become engrossed in sensual pleasures and lose his will power.'

One of the first Qing gardens for an 'imperial short-stay villa' was Chang Chun Yuan, the Garden of the Exuberant Spring. It was built on the site of a ruined Ming dynasty estate on the outskirts of the capital, near the present Beijing University, after Emperor Kang Xi's two southern tours in the 1680s. It was planned, designed and supervised by Ye Tao, a southern artist who specialized in landscape painting. The rockeries were executed by Zhang Ran, the best-known rock master of the time. After the villa's completion, Kang Xi spent most of his time there, and the Emperor Qian Long lived and studied in it from his childhood until he came to the throne.

The garden, severely damaged in 1860 by French and British troops, included, in the eastern part, the palace, court and imperial lodge. Behind them, to the north, much of the large park was occupied by a lake, which narrowed and widened along its course and was divided by islets and dikes. The buildings, some in groups and some scattered at random, were arranged to accord with the natural contours of the land. The western parts also included sheets of water and contained two building complexes used by the young princes.

Yuan Ming Yuan

The Chang Chun Yuan was once joined to two other imperial gardens that collectively were called the Yuan Ming Yuan, the Garden of Perfect Brightness. The same name is used for one of these, which is also known as the Old Summer Palace. This garden, once a private estate owned by a relative of the Ming emperors, was expanded into an imperial garden by the Emperor Yong Zhen when he came to the throne in 1723 and subsequent additions

The Yuan Ming Yuan, the Old Summer Palace, was destroyed and looted in October 1860 by the combined forces of Britain and France. Its fame rested on the many small gardens of individual character contained within it.

were made by Qian Long. The terrain was naturally flat, all the hills and mounds that were subsequently part of it being man-made. Water flowed through it from the Jade Fountain of the Western Hills and nearly a third of the total area was covered with water. Sometimes this was in large sheets, as the Fu Hai, Sea of Felicity, in the centre of the three gardens, sometimes irregularly shaped, and sometimes in tortuous brooks or wide canals.

The Yuan Ming Yuan is celebrated for the many smaller gardens, each with its own characteristic features, contained within it, so that it has long been called the garden of ten thousand gardens. There were some 150 specific scenes, among them 40 dominant ones celebrated in poems by the Qing emperors and painted by many artists. In most of these architecture played an important role. Many of the scenes were modelled after famous sites south of the Chiangjiang, the Yangtze River: Sunset Behind the Thunder-Peak Pagoda from Hangzhou; Shi Zi Lin, the Lion Grove Temple, from Suzhou, and from Hainin the garden known as An Lan Yuan are but a few of the examples. As well as a great library there were temples for worshipping the Buddha and commemorating the sages, halls for

attending ceremonies and for stage performances, mountain villages and mock-up shopping streets, and facsimiles of the mythical island homes of the Chinese Immortals. The ruins of this masterpiece of classic Chinese gardening, destroyed and looted by English and French forces in 1860, have been extensively planted with trees since 1956 and draw an increasing number of visitors.

The Yuan Ming Yuan included a unique group of structures built for Qian Long that were designed in Western style under the supervision of a Jesuit priest, Père Giuseppe Castiglione, and his colleagues, who were serving in the imperial court. The ruins and contemporary etchings show that it was baroque in style, though many of its details were distinctively Chinese.

Bi Shu Shan Zhuang

The largest imperial garden remaining in China today, Bi Shu Shan Zhuang, Mountain Resort to Escape the Heat, was also

begun by the Emperor Kang Xi. The Rehe (formerly spelt Jehol) Xing Gong, Hot River Summer Palace, as it is also known, is located beyond the Great Wall in Chengde, Hebei province, 260 km (160 miles) north-east of Beijing. When touring the region early in his reign, Kang Xi had been impressed by the genial climate and the borrowed views offered by the foothills of the surrounding rim of mountains. One particularly impressive feature is a strange geological formation, Club Peak, shaped like a gigantic pestle standing on the horizon. Work on the park began in 1703 and continued on a large scale for 87 years. From 1711, the Qing emperors regularly moved their courts there in summer to escape the heat and dust of the capital so that it became an important political centre.

Hills cover four-fifths of the vast park; the rest is low-lying, and includes lakes drawn from the hot springs. The palace area near the main entrance is formally planned, with straight covered walkways linking a succession of finely proportioned halls and courtyards enclosed by walls and planted with old pine trees. The effect, calm and ageless, is unique in China; the simplicity and elegance of the architecture harmonize agreeably with the natural landscape.

The lakes lie in the south-east of the park but north of the palace. Dotted here and there with small islands, they are crossed by willow-planted dikes and surrounded by embankments and low hills. Towers and pavilions for viewing embellish the lake. Two, called Moon White and Water Tunes, on a central island were used by the imperial families to celebrate the serenity of the lake on moonlit nights. A tall building, Misty Rain on the Heliotrope Islet, was modelled after its namesake in the South Lake of Jiaxing, Zhejiang province, and used for viewing the lake on misty days.

The grassy plain of the lowland, the Garden of Ten Thousand Trees, was once a deer-park. Here the Emperor Qian Long entertained Mongolian princes and the Banchan Lama VI of Tibet to imperial picnics and it was here, too, that he received Lord Macartney, Britain's first envoy to China. On this lowland stand also the

The Qing emperor Kang Xi was responsible for the creation of the largest surviving imperial garden in China, the Bi Shu Shan Zhuang, beyond the Great Wall in Chengde. The lakes, with their islands, dikes, pavilions and surrounding hills, reflect the southern landscape tradition.

Library Weng jin Ge and the Pagoda of Buddha's Remains.

The natural hills of the western part covering most of the Resort contained over forty garden structures, a few of which have recently been restored. Their siting often exploited the 'borrowed scenery' of the surrounding hills and also of the eight great Outer Temples built in Mongolian, Tibetan and traditional Chinese styles.

Yi He Yuan

Qian Long's garden-making activities included the relandscaping of another imperial retreat which is commonly known as the Summer Palace. The name Yi He Yuan, the Garden of Happy Harmony, was given to this great park about 10 km (6 miles) north-west of Beijing by the Empress

Dowager Ci Xi, who reconstructed it – diverting funds allocated for establishing a national navy – six years after it had been burnt down by British and French forces in 1860. In 1900 it was destroyed yet again after the Boxer rebellion and then renovated in 1903. In 1961 it was restored once more and listed as a Key National Place of Historic and Cultural Importance.

Weng Shan, the Jar Hill, was a natural prominence in this landscape with a number of springs converging to feed the small Weng Shan lake. During the Ming dynasty the building of dikes and the cultivation of plants such as rice and lotus made the landscape resemble the favoured and well-watered region known in China as Chiang-nan, 'South of the [Yangtze] river'. Its charm had appealed to the Emperor Kang Xi, who had occasionally resided there.

Qian Long's relandscaping, begun in 1750 and lasting fourteen years, was on a grand scale, involving the transformation of the major features. The lake was dredged and enlarged, new dikes were built to divide it and the hill was remade. Two years after work began it was renamed Qing Yi Yuan, the Garden of Clear Ripples. Weng Shan became Wan Shou Shan, Longevity Hill, and the lake, Kunming Hu. Of all the pleasure-grounds Qian Long built in and around the Western Hills, this became the Emperor's favourite: 'Where in all Yan Shan is the mind so free?' he wrote in a poem, 'Peerless sight, the wind and the moon over Lake Kunming.'

The complex of palace courts at the main entrance in the east initially masks the two-fold division of the estate. Kunming Lake lies to the south and in front of Wan Shou Shan, which is dominated by the massive octagonal Tower of the Fragrance of the Buddha and the Hall of Dispelling the Cloud. To the north, Wan Shou Shan falls steeply to the irregular ribbon of the narrow 'back lake'. This is actually a long watercourse winding along the narrow foot of the hill. The north bank was piled up with mud dug from this excavation, creating the expectation of a contrasting expanse of open land beyond. The middle part is relatively narrow and in Qian Long's time rows of make-believe shops simulating a riverside street in Suzhou were lined up along the bank. North-east of this is the Xie

Qu Yuan, a garden-within-a-garden, planned and built after the style of Ji Chang, a celebrated garden in Hui Shan, Wuxi, which had pleased Qian Long on his southern tours. It is a garden of pavilions and open walkways centred on an irregular reflecting pool.

What makes the landscape of the Yi He Yuan is not, however, the winding course of the back lake but the great shimmering expanse of the front lake lying below Wan Shou Shan. Here the monotony of the surface is broken by the flowing lines and pavilion-bridges of Xidi, the West Dike, which divides it into three unequal parts, the largest of which is the eastern lake. Weeping willows lining the water's edge complete the association of the Xidi with a famous dike built by the poet Su Dongpo in Hangzhou. A 17-arch marble bridge draws the eye across the water to the rocky South Lake Island, on which stands Dragon King Temple. The islands forming a small group beyond take their names from the legendary home of the Immortals.

The panorama of the lake from Wan Shou Shan 'borrows' scenes of the Jade Mountain Hill and the whole sweep of the Western Hills beyond the park. Bordering the length of the shore is an unbroken white

balustrade, which curves out into the lake to emphasize the central axis. Running along the narrow space between it and the steep rise of the hill is the famous covered gallery, its numerous bays brilliantly coloured with little vignettes of garden scenes and flowers painted beneath the eaves. On the south side of the Wan Shou Shan there are still many buildings, their yellow roof-tiles gleaming against the hillside. On the north side, however, most have been reduced to broken walls and ruins.

PRIVATE GARDENS

Before the beginning of the Han dynasty in 206 BC literary records of private gardens are scarce and, so far, archaeological evidence is non-existent. From the 400 years of the Han dynasty, however, records survive giving the names of owners of large artificial ponds and constructed scenery which already included, even allowing for exag-

At the Yi He Yuan, the Summer Palace northwest of Beijing, the great panorama of the front lake and the 'borrowed' views beyond make the garden. The white marble balustrade runs the whole length of the shoreline, which curves out into the lake to emphasize the central axis.

geration, remarkable rockeries. One was said to be 30 m (98 ft) high and another, Cao Wei's Fragrant Grove Garden, to include 'eight gullies and nine streams'. But these were northern gardens, near the Han capitals along the Yellow River (Huang He), and their large halls, connected by open walkways, and collections of rare oxen, birds and trees mimicked the style of imperial parks.

With Confucianism adopted as the state orthodoxy, however, gardens even as early as the Han dynasty were increasingly likely to be made not by hereditary aristocrats but by the new élite appointed to run the civil service. Since Confucius required an ethical man to render service to the state, such appointments became the only socially acceptable route to success in China for almost 2,000 years. And since they were awarded only to those who were successful in stringent examinations on the classics, anyone wealthy enough to own a garden was also highly intelligent and exhaustively educated. Confucius himself had spent most of his life out of office, so his ethics included an ideal of 'recreation through the arts' both to replenish an official's energy and to make the best use of his time when out of favour. Gardens thus developed as places for self-cultivation, often, as time went on, sited in cities where, with the right attitude, a man could find 'peace in the heart of town' and still fulfil his duties to the state and his family.

The cultivated scholar's retreat

When the long collapse of the Han dynasty led to a loss of faith in the values that had once supported it, men of culture escaped from a disintegrating society into nature and metaphysics. The 3rd-century Seven Sages of the Bamboo Grove provide the classic example. A famous garden of this period, the Jin Gu Yuan, north-east of the city of Luoyang, was described by its owner, Shi Chong, as a 'simple pastoral retreat'. It was, though, the extravagant expression of great wealth, its 'many thousands' of cypresses, numerous buildings, and a private orchestra helping to make it for succeeding generations a symbol of luxurious living.

Many survivors of the Han fled south to regions hitherto scarcely colonized and, in the rich well-watered lands south of the

Chiangjiang (Yangtze) River, they found ideal conditions in which to develop a love of natural scenery. The ideal of a cultivated scholar's retreat was first given poetic form by Dao Yuanming (378–422): 'I had rescued from wilderness a patch of the southern moor/And, still rustic, came back to field and garden. . . . Long I lived checked by the bars of a cage;/Now I have returned again to nature and to freedom.'

From the 5th century the introduction of Buddhism, gradually spreading into China from the West, also began to affect attitudes, Buddhist monasteries set among hills enhancing the association of nature and spirituality. The example in Buddhism of a householder achieving Buddhahood by 'remaining unmoved in the midst of movement' reinforced the indigenous Confucian tradition (so unlike that of Europe's celibate priests) of a married élite – whose gardens were there for family parties as well as for contemplation.

Wang Chuan Villa

The perfect and lasting expression of the garden as the tranquil retreat of the cultivated scholar is represented in the Tang dynasty by one of the most famous private domains in Chinese history, the Wang Chuan Villa. Wang Wei (699–759), poet, painter, calligrapher and musician, and himself a devout Buddhist, retired to this country retreat south-west of Lan Tian county in Shaanxi province, recording it in poetry and painting on a long, and frequently copied, handscroll.

The valley of Wang Chuan was what the Chinese call a 'suddenly-opened-up space', with partially flat, partially undulating ground, a stream, a lake, and an island surrounded by layers of steeply folded hills. Along the rocky shore Wang Wei described 20 views, usually focusing on or seen from a different lodge or summer-house. Some of these were double-storeyed halls, with upturned eaves above open balconies. Others, like the Cottage in Bamboo Forest or Apricot-Veined Cottage reflected an ideal of rustic simplicity. Flowering fruit trees, willows, and *wu-tung* trees (*Firmiana simplex*) grew around them, making each a little green cell of its own, while stiff pine trees grew thickly on the hills behind. The villa itself lay to the south near the Lu Yuan,

or Deer-Park Temple, a rambling series of rooms, pavilions and halls connected by bridges, winding paths, and covered open-sided walkways. Wang Wei's great scroll made sure of his garden's continuing fame, but it was his own character and culture that ensure its place in Chinese history.

Lu Shan Cao Tang

Another Tang garden that has acquired classic status is Lu Shan Cao Tang, literally the Thatched Cottage on Mount Lu, where the famous poet Bei Juyi lived for two years from 817. Located to the north of Censer Peak on Mount Lu in Jiangxi province, the cottage was simply built of undercoated wattle and adobe. In front of it lay a terrace and a square-shaped pool planted with white lotus and stocked with red carp, overlooking to the south the Stone Gate Ravine with huge old pine trees standing both sides. There were waterfalls and springs to the east and west, and a rocky precipice, in which grew rare wild-flowers and trees, rose steeply up behind. In his *On Lu Shan Cao Tang*, the poet describes how he could 'lift his eyes to watch the mountains, bend his head to listen to the spring and turn to the sides to see the bamboo, the trees, the clouds and the rockeries; from dawn to dusk there are ever-changing views'. The place Lu Shan Cao Tang enjoys in Chinese gardening tradition owes much to the 'borrowed views', rich in seasonal and daily variations, made possible by the inspired exploitation of the cottage's natural site.

Ping Quan Villa

A retreat on a much grander scale was that of the celebrated Tang-dynasty Prime Minister Li De Yu (787–850). Ping Quan or Plain Spring Villa was situated in Henan province near the Yellow River, somewhere south of the present city of Luoyang. It was said to have been surrounded by a wall 20 km (12 miles) long. 'More than a hundred' halls and terraces, as well as pavilions of several storeys embellished its bamboo groves and streams. The garden's fame, however, rests largely on the elegant literary record Li has left in 'On Trees and Rockeries at Ping Chuan Villa' of his assiduous collecting of rare plants, brought back from various postings, and unusual rocks.

Taihu rock

The scholar's appreciation of rocks and stones that developed in a marked way during the Tang dynasty has remained a distinctive feature of Chinese connoisseurship. The garden, as well as the scholar's studio, has provided a setting for the display of prized specimens. Particularly valued in later periods were rocks from Dong Ting Shan, an island in Lake Tai (Taihu), near Suzhou. They are grey limestone boulders, excavated from beneath the water, that have been eroded into peculiar shapes and textures by the action of waves working on harder stones embedded in the rock. Those that are wrinkled, emaciated, and full of jagged holes are considered the best. In the Song dynasty they were some of the most expensive objects in the empire and from this period onwards, no garden was complete without specimen rocks and in Suzhou people would 'move houses and rebuild walls to display them'.

Song gardens

It is the Song dynasty that is often nostalgically seen as China's golden age of gardens, perhaps because so many were in cities and open to the public on festivals and holidays. But perhaps also it is because under the Song the standard of achievement in all the arts is so extraordinarily high. This is especially true in the field of landscape painting, which in China bears such a close relationship to garden design. Just as the connoisseur of painting unwinds a landscape scroll from left to right, and sees the hills and valleys rise and fall around the little figures travelling through it, so a gardener should unfold a series of linked views around the visitor as he strolls along its three-dimensional paths. But the scrolls are linear and the gardens enclosed, and to make the most of each successive vista the garden-maker creates a labyrinth, in which available space is layered by gateways and sub-divided by walls that wind among the

The fame of the Wang Chuan Villa has been secured by the long (and often copied) handscroll on which the Tang-dynasty poet and painter Wang Wei recorded it. He described 20 views, usually focusing on or seen from a different lodge or summerhouse, some of which reflect an ideal of rustic simplicity.

trees and rocks with the regular undulations of sea snakes or dragons. Each garden is a composition of courtyards, some large, some small, some disappearing round corners, some open-ended, some cul-de-sacs, some fitted together like pieces of a puzzle. And the visitor is led on through them, not only by pebble-patterned pathways and open doorways, but by the constant suggestion of something new and delightful half-revealed through the latticed windows or above the walls of the next enclosure.

The refinements of Song-dynasty gardens can now be appreciated only through descriptions of them. The *Luo Yang Ming*

The Ji Chang Yuan, west of Wuxi in Jiangsu province, became the country villa of a Minister of Revenue in the early Ming dynasty. The garden, which was destroyed in 1860 but has since been reconstructed, is small but its many subdivisions allow for very different effects.

Yuan Ji ('The Famous Gardens of Luoyang'), a 12th-century work written by Li Ge Fei, which describes the layout and histories of 18 gardens and one market-place in the capital of his day, was once known to every educated Chinese.

The fame of one 11th-century garden in Luoyang, the Du Le Yuan, rests on a collection of poems written about it by its maker, the great historian of the Northern Song dynasty, Sima Guang. A former Prime Minister and leader of a conservative faction, he later suffered such setbacks that he retired to the old capital city in Henan province and devoted himself to the study of history and his garden. Compared to other gardens of the time described in the *Luo Yang Ming Yuan Ji*, it was a modest retreat with beds of herbs, wooden fences, and thatched pavilions, lying in the southern part of the city and separate from his house. A 'fisherman's hut', was made of tree bamboos planted in a ring then bent over and tied together at the tips. However, the historian also collected a library of some five thousand volumes in the Book Reading

Hall, where, he says in his preface, he took 'the sages as his teachers and the many virtuous men [of antiquity] as his friends: if his resolve was weary and his body exhausted, he took a rod and caught fish, held up his sleeves and picked herbs ... His eyes, lungs, feelings were all his own. What enjoyment could be greater than this?' His words inspired many later gardeners and artists, especially the 16th-century painter Qiu Ying, whose long and exceptionally beautiful handscroll follows the historian's description of his garden.

Ming and Qing gardens

In the 13th and 14th centuries, during the Yuan dynasty, private gardens continued to flourish because old families, loyal to the conquered Song, refused to take active political part in the new Mongol government. By the time the Ming dynasty returned a Chinese emperor to the throne in 1368 the Confucian ideal of the retired scholar-without-portfolio had acquired new strength. Since the Ming was a repressive dynasty, it continued to be acceptable for a

gentleman to devote his time, with like-minded friends, to the cultivation of his spiritual, literary and artistic life in the elegant setting of an urban garden. From the mid-16th century private garden-making flourished in Beijing and many towns and cities of the south, with successful merchants as well as gentlemen scholars commissioning gardens. Though the gardens of the capital seem more stiff and formal than the typically graceful southern gardens of Suzhou, the similarity in design of gardens as far apart as Beijing and Taipei is more remarkable than the differences. A development that can be detected in some gardens is a tendency towards a rather vulgar interpretation of the tradition, lavish general effect counting for more than the refinement of detail that gave the cultivated garden owner personal pleasure.

Ming dynasty gardens, if they survive, have almost invariably undergone changes but a treatise on gardening, *Yuan Ye*, 'Garden Tempering', published in 1634, gives a remarkably comprehensive view of Ming practice. The author states firmly that 'in garden design there are principles but no fixed formulae' and his work aims to teach through suggestion rather than by rules.

Ji Chang Yuan

A masterpiece of Ming garden design that was destroyed in 1860 has fortunately been reconstructed in a way that, it seems, accurately follows the original plan. The Ji Chang Yuan, the Garden of Ecstasy, which was the inspiration of the Xie Qu Yuan in the Summer Palace, was built in the early 16th century at the foot of Hui Shan, a hill to the west of Wuxi in Jiangsu province. Though small, the garden has 'borrowed views' of the hills around and of the Dragon Light pagoda nearby to extend its views and the garden's many subdivisions allow it to contain very different effects. A great artificial mountain, credited to the rock-work artist Zhang Yue, takes up all of the north-west part of the garden but is so skilfully made that it seems to be part of the Hui hill beyond the trees planted on its crest. From it the musical sounds of the Stream of the Octave bubble down a rocky gully leading to the long and narrow pool which takes up the eastern side of the garden. This pool also manipulates the available space to create an illusion of depth and distance: its rocky edges curl out of sight into small coves, and a tiny peninsula, jutting out on the west bank at the Beach of a Crane's Stride, draws the eye to the opposite shore, where a swoop-eaved open pavilion with balustrades leans out over the water. Though this is, in fact, very near the garden's eastern boundary, a whitewashed wall and roofed open-sided corridor cut the remaining space down to a sliver, its trees and rocks only half visible and enticing behind and above the open windows. At the far end of the pond the Bridge of Seven Stars cuts diagonally across the water and the small space beyond it is again divided by pavilions, trees and open corridors so that the nearby wall no longer seems a barrier.

Yu Yuan

Another famous Ming garden, the Yu Yuan in Shanghai, although badly damaged in the 19th century, retains some of its original elements. Restoration has taken place since 1956 but, even with the inclusion of the neighbouring Nei Yuan, an early 18th-century garden, it occupies today only about half of its original site. A provisional governor of Sichuan, Pan Yun Duan built the complex garden in his home city between 1559 and 1577 for his father, Pan En: its name means 'to please the old parent'. During the first half of the 19th century the garden was used by some craft and merchant guilds and it is from this period that date the spirited dragon heads capping several of the garden's walls and a number of other sculpted figures. One of the main early features to survive is a large artificial hill with the elegant Ming-dynasty Cui Xiu Tang, or Hall of the Assemblage of Grace, below it to the east and, on its top,

the Wang Jiang or Viewing the River pavilion, which 'borrows views' of the Huang Po River from beyond the eastern wall. This hill, composed of the yellow rock known as *huang shi* and the largest of its kind to have survived in China, was the work of a Ming-dynasty master of rockery, Zhang Nan Yang. The garden also contains a magnificent standing rock 5 metres (16 feet) high named Exquisite Jade, which is said to have been earmarked, during the Song dynasty, for Gen Yue. A tea-house reached by a crudely designed zigzag bridge, now outside the garden, is supposed to have inspired the English 'willow-pattern' plate design of the 19th century.

One of the most celebrated gardens of Shanghai, the Yu Yuan, was built in the scholarly tradition by a Ming dynasty official for his father, hence the name meaning 'to please the old parent'. Damage and additions have coarsened the refined complexity of the original but some of its character survives, thanks in part to restoration work that began in 1956.

Lying in the south of the city of Suzhou the present Cang Lang Ting or Pavilion of the Dark Blue Waves represents Qing dynasty reconstructions of a 10th-century garden. Notable features of the garden are the artificial hill and the exploitation of 'borrowed' views.

The gardens of Suzhou

In the Ming and Qing dynasties gardens continued to be built in the ancient city of Suzhou, 'the Venice of the East', which already had a long history of garden-making. A garden belonging to He Lu was recorded in the area in the 14th century but the town was built up as a capital in the 6th century. In the following three or four centuries it suffered little from the turmoil affecting many other regions of China and became one of the richest provinces. One of its gardens, Cang Lang Ting, dates back to the 10th century, though what survives are the remains of successive reconstructions made during the Qing dynasty. The layout is unique in Suzhou in that a hill rather than a pond lies at its centre. The name Pavilion of the Dark Blue Waves was given to it by a noted poet, Su Zimei, who in 1044 built for himself a garden on the old site. The reference in the name is to an ancient saying which counsels acceptance of the vicissitudes of life: 'When times are good I wash my ribbons of office in the waters of the Cang Lang River – when times are bad, my feet.' In the 12th century the garden belonged to General Han Shizong, a national hero in the Southern Song dynasty.

During the Yuan period a number of officials who refused to serve under a foreign dynasty retired to the city and, in the Ming and Qing, still more built gardens in their retirement. Surrounded by rich agricultural lands 'of fish and rice' and a prosperous silk industry, Suzhou became not only wealthy but also a great centre of art and scholarship. The city provided more successful candidates in the imperial examinations than any other in China. After achieving political appointments and amassing (usually) large fortunes, many of these men retired to Suzhou to build gardens. Ideally situated with plentiful water, pleasant hills beyond their town, a genial climate, the finest garden stones (Taihu rock) nearby and excellent communications

The Zhuo Zheng Yuan in Suzhou, first built between 1506 and 1521, is especially remarkable for the complex arrangement of irregular and interconnecting pools, giving it the dreamy atmosphere of the water villages in the southern region of China known as Chiangnan.

by canal for importing others, Suzhou also offered them a pool of skilled garden craftsmen.

Shi Zi Lin

Though many of Suzhou's gardens were damaged during the Taiping rebellion in the 19th century, some hundred were recorded in the 1950s. A few of the largest have been restored and opened to the public. Of these, Shi Zi Lin is the most famous, though by no means the best. Commissioned by a Buddhist monk, Tian Ru, in memory of his teacher, and built in 1336 during the Yuan dynasty, it originally formed the northernmost section of the Temple of Bodhi Orthodoxy, in the north-west district of the city. This was already sometimes known as the Lion Grove Temple with several levels of meaning hidden behind the name: for example, one interpretation is that the teacher, Zhong Feng, once lived in retreat by the so-called Lion Cliff at Tien Mu mountain; another that over half the garden is given over to an extended false mountain of rocks often thought to resemble lions. The garden's most notable feature is certainly its rockery. According to records, more than ten well-known artists were commissioned to work on its design and one of them, Ni Zhan, one of the greatest painters of the Yuan period, left a scroll of it in his inimitably austere style. Little remains today of the garden he recorded. From a distance, the eye wanders restlessly over the strange rocks and hollows reflected in the slatey gleam of the lake, but close-up the 'mountain' is a labyrinth with grottos and interior caverns. Tiny paths wind up through it to give sudden glimpses, through sharp fissures or from its top, of the

lake, the garden, or other visitors as they cross at different levels. It is an evocation of the Chinese Immortals, strange, flamboyant and removed from ordinary life.

Zhuo Zheng Yuan

The largest of Suzhou's old private gardens, Zhuo Zheng Yuan, was first built between 1506 and 1521 by a Ming Court Examiner, Wang Xian Chen, on his retirement. Its name is variously translated as the humble, foolish, or unsuccessful politician's garden. Wen Cheng Ming, one of the Four Great Painters of the Ming, lived here for a time and left a record of it in two albums of poetry and drawings. Only the middle section of the present garden corresponds to the original site.

More than half the Zhuo Zheng Yuan is taken up by a complex arrangement of irregular and interconnecting pools forming a water labyrinth. Though its buildings are grand and of fine workmanship, it is said to

have the atmosphere of the water villages in the prosperous and lovely area south of the Chiangjiang River (Yangtze). The most important building is the formal Hall of Distant Fragrance, standing back from the south bank of the lake at the centre of this part of the garden. Northwards it looks across water to two mounded green islands, embellished with the Pavilion of Fragrant Snow and Glorious Clouds and a little gazebo called Waiting for the Frost.

In the north-west corner, a peninsula planted with flowering shrubs is encircled by roofed and open walkways which zigzag along the edge of the water. In the north-west, a further series leads to a group of

Wen Cheng Ming, one of the Four Great Painters of the Ming, lived at Zhou Zheng Yuan for a time and the record he left of the garden in two albums of poetry and drawings helped give it celebrity. It is the largest of the old private gardens in Suzhou.

secluded rooms and tiny planted enclosures culminating in a courtyard overlooking a shadowy pool. The south-east section is separated from the water by a hill and an undulating grey wall enclosing courtyards which, with their fine proportions and delicate pebble-patterned floorings, are some of the most appealing in the garden.

To the north, on the easternmost shore of the lake, stands the unusual Bamboo Quiet Resort, a square pavilion with a large circular moon door cut in each wall to frame the view.

All these buildings are arranged according to the principles of 'facing views' and 'borrowing views' so that, as the visitor moves through the garden, the views compose themselves around him, sometimes formally and sometimes in the distance as if by chance. There are two other sections of the garden, of which the western is the most interesting. It was built at the end of the Qing dynasty and imitates the water theme of the Zhuo Zheng garden.

Liu Yuan

The only garden in the north-western suburbs of Suzhou to survive the Taiping rebellion was the Liu Yuan. It was first built by a retired Ming-dynasty official between 1522 and 1566 but subsequent changes included an enlargement in the 1870s. At the heart of the layout is the main pool, which is surrounded by a labyrinth of open corridors and to the east by a complex of linked halls, courtyards and garden rooms. A more open section in the south includes a double Hall of Mandarin Ducks overlooking a small pond and a water-worn Taihu stone, Cloud-capped Peak, said to have been chosen originally for the Song imperial garden Gen Yue. In the northern and western parts of the garden there are rockeries and, on artificial hills in the north, there is an open pavilion with views across the garden's central pond and its surrounding trees. The complexity of the garden, with narrow passageways that twist and turn, undulating corridors with openings that give unexpected views, and ingeniously contrived spatial relations all help to make the garden seem very much larger than it is.

Wang Shi Yuan

No less intricate, and a garden of subtlety and refinement, is the Wang Shi Yuan, among the smallest of the Suzhou gardens that have been restored. There has been a garden on this site in the south-eastern district of the city since the 12th century, when Shi Zhengzhi, a cultivated scholar-official, called it Yu Yin, Fisherman's Retreat, to suggest his love of simple pleasures. Its history is obscure until the late 18th century, when it was rebuilt by Song

The complexity of the Liu Yuan, the Lingering Garden is remarkable, even by the standards of old Suzhou gardens. The architectural labyrinth of covered walkways, halls, courtyards and garden rooms provides a remarkable range of visual and spatial experiences within a small compass.

Although small in scale, the Wang Shi Yuan is one of the most intricate and subtle of Suzhou's old gardens and, having been well restored and preserved, it retains the feeling of a place long and deeply loved.

Zenghuan, a Vice-Director of Imperial Entertainment at the court of Qian Long. It was Song who gave the garden the name Wang Shi that it has today, taking it after his own pen name, meaning Master of the Fishing Nets, a nice allusion to the original garden. After a period of subsequent neglect the garden was rescued by Qu Yuancun, who had it rebuilt by local craftsmen to his own design. Later owners have elaborated a compositon of more than ten tiny enclosed gardens and over a dozen halls and pavilions around the central pool.

The garden can be approached from the street through a simple door in the high white-plastered surrounding walls. The sequence of courtyards acts as a kind of layering, gradually separating the visitor from the world of the city outside. The culmination of this process is the little rock-bordered lake, apparently much larger than it is, with trees and shrubs half hiding many different buildings scattered irregularly around the water's edge. On the opposite bank the elegant Pavilion of the Moon Appearing and the Breeze Arriving lures the visitor on. Whichever choice is made, whether to go left or right around the lake, many unexpected and delightful diversions open up, leading to courtyards, pavilions and halls, each of distinctive character. Many bear names chosen by Qu Yuancun and their literary allusions provide another pleasurable dimension to the garden. The house and its small yards and all the other buildings are strictly rectangular but the way they are fitted together leaves small slivers of space, which are planted with bamboo and set with rocks so that even the smallest room gets light and air.

Huan Xiu Villa

Despite the ruin of most of the buildings of the Huan Xiu Villa, an important part of the garden survives. The history of the site goes back to the 10th century but the name, meaning literally a Villa Surrounded by Elegance, was given to the property by the Wang family who owned it in the mid 19th century. The huge artificial hill of Taihu rock that takes up nearly half the site has long been ranked as one of the best examples of its kind. Its design has been attributed to Ge Yu-liang, considered among the finest of the Qing rock-artists

and active in the late 18th century. His great skill lay in bonding together rocks by interlocking their natural edges like hooks. It is said that the longer his rockworks stand the more stable they become. The main part of the artificial hill at Huan Xiu Villa lies on the eastern side of the garden, its steep cliffs and peaks imitating in form and structure, and in the veins and graining of the rock, those of a natural rocky hill. Beneath the 'mountain' are grottos and chambers that add a sense of strangeness and adventure to the domestic beauties of the garden.

Ou Yuan

A high artificial mountain, this time of yellow rock, is the dominant feature of the eastern part of the garden known as Ou Yuan in the north-eastern district of Suzhou. The name refers to the garden's two sections (*ou* means 'couple'), which lie east and west of the old city residence. Although the eastern part already existed in the early Qing period, the garden's present form dates from the 19th century, when the property came into the hands of a government official, Shen Bingcheng. The artificial mountain in the eastern garden, which hides the approach to the two-storeyed and double-eaved main hall, falls away on the east side to a narrow splash of reflecting water. Winding steps cut into the hill's

The Ou Yuan in the north-east district of Suzhou consists of two parts, lying east and west of an old residence.It acquired its present form in the 19th century. The space is skilfully manipulated to create numerous quiet corners and unexpected views within the intricate layout.

steep face give the visitor the sensation of walking by a 'profound valley', Sui Gu, which is its name. This section includes a gallery pierced by a succession of decorative windows and, along the eastern boundary, a double-storeyed pavilion that once gave views of the canal and city outside the boundary wall. There are many peaceful and hidden corners in this garden, including, in the western section, two courtyards, the first containing an unusual rockery.

Yi Yuan

The most recent of Suzhou's famous gardens is the Yi Yuan, created between 1862 and 1908 by a high-ranking official, Gu Wen Bin. The eastern part of the site had been occupied since the Ming dynasty, but the chief interest of the garden lies in the western part. Here Gu Wen Bin's son, Gu Cheng, with the help of several well-known artists, developed the garden by borrowing themes and motives from older Suzhou gardens. A double covered walkway was probably inspired by one at Cang Lang Ting: the artificial mountain, by the great rockery at Huan Xiu Villa; a rock-bordered lotus pond, by that in the Wang Shi Yuan; and a boat-shaped pavilion, by one called Fragrant Land in the Zhuo Zheng Yuan. In each case the borrowing is subtle, more adaptation than direct copy, the elements linked together with great skill in a comparatively small space.

The gardens of Yangzhou

Another city famed for its culture and charm is Yangzhou, which became a prosperous centre because of its position on the left bank of the Grand Canal at its junction with the Chiangjiang River (Yangtze) and its long association with the salt trade. There were once many fine gardens in the city and along the shores of the Narrow West Lake, Shou Xi Hu. In the early Qing dynasty a number of gardens are believed to have been laid out by Shi Tao, whose real identity as a member of the Ming imperial family was hidden throughout his life. In old age, after years of wandering as a Buddhist monk, he settled in Yangzhou, gaining fame for his skill in piling rocks and for his accomplishments as poet, calligrapher and landscape painter. The original artificial mountain in a surviving Yangzhou garden, the Ge Yuan, it has been claimed, was designed and executed under Shi Tao's direction.

Ge Yuan

At the end of the 18th century Ge Yuan was made on the site of an older garden. It was owned by a salt tycoon, Huang Yingtai, and his byname, Geyuan, was applied to the garden. The Chinese character for *ge* also resembles a twig of three bamboo leaves and this became a symbol of the garden. The hill as it is today constitutes Ge Yuan's best-known feature and is Yangzhou's most unusual contribution to China's gardening tradition. It is a rare example of an artificial mountain composed of various kinds of rock to distinguish different areas of the garden and to symbolize the four seasons. Spring is suggested near the entrance moongate by a juxtaposition of real and false, with needle-like stalactite rocks, known as stone bamboo shoots (*shi sun*) planted among living bamboo groves. In the west,

summer is symbolized by an artificial hill of Taihu rocks overshadowed by the dense foliage of pine trees. A neighbouring pool runs on underneath a rocky overhang, which then widens into a shadowy room lit by water-reflected light. This chamber remains a cool retreat in Yangzhou's heavy summers. In the east a labyrinthine hill of yellow rocks rises sharply to steep peaks. Narrow passageways wind up and through it to tiny courtyards and a central cave room. A gazebo on the crest overlooks the miniature landscape. When this hill turns rosy red at sunset it is thought to look exactly like a painting of autumn mountains. The last of the hills, laid out along a wall of a courtyard facing a large hall in one corner of the garden, uses white-capped rocks to suggest snowy peaks in winter.

He Yuan

Of other gardens in the Yangzhou region the He Yuan, created at the turn of the 19th century, is of special interest for the way a double-storeyed covered walkway divides the garden into two sections of contrasting character, the western section dynamic and vivid, the eastern more peaceful and secluded. By allowing views of its rocks, trees, buildings and lake from above and all around, the covered way also makes the garden seem larger than its real size.

The gardens of Beijing

The old gardens of Beijing have a reputation for being stiffer and more formal than those of the Chiangnan region and the south. Often their pools are edged with cut stone rather than irregular lake-rock and their open-sided galleries often run in straight lines and at right angles instead of in the irregular zigzags familiar from Suzhou.

Ban Mu Yuan

One of the most celebrated of Beijing gardens, does not, however, conform to the generalization. The garden, which is off Huang Mi Hu Tung near the north-east corner of the Forbidden City, was originally built about 1680 by a well-known literary figure, Li Yu, for a government official. Ban Mu means Half Acre, a modest name in keeping with the one Li Yu chose for his own house in Beijing, 'The Garden Small as

a Mustard Seed'. After many changes of ownership Ban Mu Yuan was eventually acquired by a high-ranking Manchu official, Lin Jian Ting, who began to restore the estate in 1840. The intimate record he left of it in his woodcut-illustrated diaries has added to the fame brought to it by its various owners and by the art and rock collections they have gathered there. The garden still contains a rock 'mountain', supposedly composed by Li himself, and there is much that dates from Lin's time. The most interesting feature of the plan is the pavilion shaped like a Greek cross that stands on a rocky isle which divides the Pond of Rippling Jade. To the south a hexagonal pavilion on a rocky mound overlooks the whole garden, with its zigzag covered gallery connecting halls and study rooms to the east and, to the west, the old rockery of yellow stones. The timeless quality of old Beijing gardens is preserved in this example to a remarkable degree.

Since the middle of the last century periods of great turmoil within China have taken a heavy toll of old gardens in Beijing and other parts of the country. The social and cultural context of the masterpieces that have survived has been transformed so dramatically that there is a danger of their complex resonances going unrecognized, and not only by foreigners. As an aid to an appreciation of the spirit in which many were created and of the qualities that gave them distinction in their prime there can be few more appealing guides than the great 18th-century novel *Hong Lou Meng (Dream of the Red Chamber)*, begun by Cao Xueqin and completed by Gao E. Many of the significant events in this long novel are set in the Da Guan Yuan or Grand View Garden, which is vividly and precisely described. Indeed, the garden is so powerfully evoked that its description not only helps bring to life the surviving private gardens of China but it also influenced subsequent garden design. The monumental and luxurious style of the buildings and the freedom and elegance of the garden in a minor Qing palace in Beijing, Gong Wang Fu, support the belief that these may have been the hidden models for the Rong mansion and the Da Guan Yuan of this classic novel.

JAPAN

Although deeply influenced by China, Japan has developed a unique tradition of garden-making, of which imperial, private and temple examples survive. The Shugaku-in Imperial Villa, Kyoto.

In the development of the Japanese garden Chinese culture and Buddhism go hand in hand, but even before Buddhism arrived in the country in the 6th century AD a religion existed that combined a veneration for the natural world and a delight in its beauties. The precise content of early Shinto, the Way of the Gods, has been obscured by subsequent revivals and, especially, by the impact made on it by Buddhism. At its core, however, was a belief in supernatural pow-ers controlling, for example, fertility, health and weather, which could be favourably influenced by the observance of certain rituals. Its first holy places were not temples but remarkable natural features. An island or a striking rock, a waterfall or a cliff, even a splendid tree, all could be objects of worship, each with its own divinity. The attitude to nature that underlies Shinto permeates the whole history of Japanese gardens. Buddhism itself may have fortified this attitude by suggesting that portions of the departed could combine with fragments of others who had reached the same degree of spiritual advancement to constitute, for instance, plants.

THE IMAGE OF PARADISE

Even before the 6th century, when the introduction of Buddhism provided a powerful vehicle for Chinese influence, progressive ideas had entered Japan either directly from China or indirectly via Korea. The establishment of the first permanent capital, Nara, in 710, was, however, part of a major surge in influence from China. Like the even grander new capital, Heian-Kyo (Capital of Peace and Tranquillity), later known as Kyoto (Capital of Capitals), founded in 794 after careful study of Chinese geomancy, was modelled after the Chinese Tang capital, Chang'an. No trace remains of the gardens that formed part of the first capital nor of early examples in the new capital, but the probability is that they followed Chinese models, main features being a large pool and an island.

Gardens of the Heian period

Little remains even from the four centuries of the Heian period that followed the founding of the new capital. It is clear, though, that during this epoch of exceptional refinement in all branches of the arts a garden type emerged that had a lasting influence on the Japanese tradition. In court circles there were many adherents of the Pure Land School of Buddhism that had reached Japan from China. According to this school, for those of complete faith and

A major source of information on garden art and court life in the Heian period is provided by the 11th-century novel The Tale of Genji, *written by the Lady Murasaka Shikibu. The story of the amorous Prince Genji was a major subject for Japanese art in subsequent centuries, particularly among artists of the Tosa school.*

purity of heart the simple repetition of a mystical invocation secures, through the saving grace of Amida Buddha, salvation in his own Paradise, the Pure Land in the West. The vivid descriptions in the Amidist sutras of this Pure Land, in which beautiful pavilions overlooked lotus-filled pools, fused with the imagery of Chinese Tang dynasty imperial palaces and gardens to provide a model for the setting of court mansions.

In the *shinden-zukuri* style, as it is known, a main pavilion (*shinden*) and subsidiary pavilions linked to it by raised and covered passages faced south to a garden consisting largely of a lake of sufficient size to permit boating. A stream wound its way to the lake from the north-east and left the lake towards the west. Each of the pavilions was a separate entity. The area in between, known as *tsubo* (a unit of space), had plants and rocks arranged to suit the taste of the pavilion's occupant. Stepping-stones, which at first were a practical necessity, were later to become a cliché. In front of the main pavilion was a space, covered with white sand, that was used for entertainments; at either side pavilions, known as Fishing Pavilions, extended to the lake. The outer walls of the pavilions had shutters which could be hooked up so that at the right season of the year the occupants could be living virtually in the open air in a way that suited a belief in the idea of harmony with nature.

The supreme example of Heian literature, *The Tale of Genji*, by the Lady

Murasaki Shikibu, written in the first half of the 11th century, shows what an extremely important role the garden played in court life and gives vivid glimpses of garden details that are more telling than the surviving remnants of actual gardens.

In the fictitious palace occupied by the amorous Prince Genji, each of his lady friends had a *tsubo* garden planted to suit her choice. Of his own mansion Lady Murasaki writes:

He effected great improvement in the appearance of the grounds by a judicious handling of knoll and lake, for though such features were already there in abundance, he found it necessary here to cut away a slope, there to dam a stream, that each occupant of the various quarters might look out of her windows upon such a prospect as pleased her best. To the south-east he raised the level of the ground, and on this bank planted a profusion of early flowering trees. At the foot of this slope the lake curved with especial beauty, and in the foreground, just beneath the windows, he planted borders of cinquefoil, of red plum, cherry, wisteria, kerria, rock azalea, and other such plants as are at their best in springtime; for he knew that Murasaki (his favourite) specially loved the spring.

Another invaluable source of information concerning gardens of this period is the *Sakuteiki* ('Treatise on Garden-Making'),

probably the oldest known document dealing with garden construction. It has been attributed to the 11th-century nobleman Tachibana-no Toshitsuna, who, it seems, collected together the secret knowledge of his day on the making of gardens and to it added his own knowledge based on experience. While the document has many details concerning taboos and matters of religious significance – it deals exhaustively with the considerations to be borne in mind in arranging stones – the technical information on the construction of the waterfalls and different kinds of naturalistic scenery is so thorough and excellent that on these points the work became for generations the ultimate guide for Japanese gardeners.

Of the few remnants of this period that survive, it is the country estates that have fared the best, escaping to some extent the vicissitudes of war. One example, Saga-no-in, which dates from about 823, gives some idea of what living in the *shinden-zukuri* style entailed. Its pond, the Osawa-ike, remains nearly intact, with some indication of its islands of the Immortals (a legacy of Chinese imperial gardens) and its waterfall.

Another interesting survival is the Byodo-in at Uji, half-way between Kyoto and Nara. The Phoenix Hall is the sole survivor of a number of sacred buildings erected within the precincts of the monastery, converted in 1052 from a villa belonging to the powerful Fujiwara family by Regent Fujiwara-no Yorimichi (whose son is believed to have written *Sakuteiki*), when he entered the religious life. The new buildings were dedicated to Amida Buddha, and it is clear that what survives is the fragment of something created in the tradition of the Pure Land paradise. The pool in front of the temple is the treasure pond, the temple itself is the treasure hall. Presumably, worshippers entering at the south gate would have crossed one bridge on to the island in the lake and reached the temple by a second, but today there are no bridges. The temple contains a magnificent Buddha of lacquered wood covered in gold leaf, by the sculptor Jocho, which faces towards the pond.

Gardens of the Muromachi period

During the Heian period the supremacy of the emperors became theoretical, real power being exercised by members of the Fujiwara family who, as shoguns or military dictators, ruled in the emperor's name. When the Minamoto family ousted the Fujiwaras from what had become their hereditary role, the Minamoto leader, Yoritomo, took the capital to Kamakura, nearly 500 km (300 miles) north-west of Kyoto. The austere military regime of the Kamakura period, which lasted from 1185 to 1333, brought relative peace and prosperity but did not favour the art of garden-making. The defeat of the Kamakura government (in 1338) and the establishment of the Ashikaga shogunate with Kyoto once again the capital ushered in a new epoch, the Muromachi period, in which the taste of the Chinese Northern Song dynasty (960-1127) prevailed.

In the garden design of the Muromachi period the image of paradise continued as a major theme, but from an early date the influence of Zen Buddhism can be detected. The Zen sect, which originated in China, became firmly established in Japan during the 13th century and appealed particularly

The Phoenix Hall at the Byodo-in, Uji, is a remarkable survival of a 10th-century sacred building, distinctively Chinese in style, dedicated to Amida Buddha. There are the remains of a late Heian paradise garden, with a treasure pond in front of the temple.

to members of the warrior class. Zen Buddhism shows a marked distrust of intellectual dogma and rejects the simple route to salvation offered by devotion to Amida Buddha. The Zen disciple, guided by a qualified master, seeks through his own efforts for 'sudden enlightenment' by performing strenuous meditational exercises designed to deepen his awareness. The rigorous search for essentials and the self-discipline of Zen have left their stamp on every aspect of Japanese art, including garden design. Its full severity is seen in later gardens of contemplation, dry landscapes (*kare-sansui*), composed of raked sand or quartz and rocks, in which trees, bushes and water have been eliminated. However, even before this development Zen influenced the style of gardens.

Saiho-ji

Two gardens designed in the first half of the 14th century by a Zen Buddhist priest, Muso Soseki (also sometimes known as Muso Kokushi), are examples of the transitional phase between the Kamakura and Muromachi periods. Saiho-ji in Kyoto owes its other name, Koke-dera (moss garden), to the many different mosses which cover much of the ground. They have almost become the main attraction though they date only from the 19th century, when the monastery was too poor to maintain the gardens properly.

The original paradise garden extended much further up the slopes of Mount Arashiyama, but the lake at the bottom (the 'golden pond') was always the principal feature. The formal arrangement of pavilions typical of Heian paradise gardens was not followed here, multi-storeyed pavilions being arranged in a loose way along the lake's shore. The central hall on the west side provided the model for the Kinkaku-ji and Ginkaku-ji pavilions. The lake itself, divided in two by islands, is shaped like the Japanese character for 'heart' or 'spirit', as was the case with many gardens of the period. At an upper level there is a dry landscape in front of a small Zen temple. The waterless stream and sophisticated use of flat-topped rocks mark the beginning of a distinctively Japanese style of rock-work.

Tenryu-ji Abbot's Garden

The Zen temple of Tenryu-ji at Saga, Kyoto, was built at Muso Soseki's request by the shogun Ashikaga Takauji on the site of a villa belonging to the ex-emperor Gosaga. The present Abbot's Garden is only a portion of the total layout conceived by Muso Soseki, which included the 'borrowed landscape' (*shakkei*) of Mount Arashiyama. The pond, known as Sogenchi, is now the centre of the garden and its gentle shoreline belongs to the style of the Heian paradise. While the arrangement of the rocks in the garden may be a deliberate allusion to a Chinese imperial park, the stonework is modelled with great subtlety.

Kinkaku-ji

In 1397, the third of the Ashikaga shoguns, Yoshimitsu, built one of Kyoto's most celebrated buildings, the Kinkaku-ji or

Although an interesting example of a 14th-century Zen garden, the Saiho-ji in Kyoto owes much of its fame to the many mosses that became established as a result of neglect in the 19th century. It is also known as the Koke-dera ('moss garden').

The Kinkaku-ji (Golden Pavilion) in Kyoto, built in 1397, has been lavishly restored since it was destroyed by fire in 1950. The design of the garden surrounding it, including the lake dotted with islands and rocks, was influenced by Chinese painting of the Song dynasty.

Golden Pavilion. This residence was constructed on the site of an earlier paradise garden and later transformed into a temple, called Rokuon-ji after the deer-park where Buddha first preached on receiving enlightenment. The opulent building survived through periods of great turmoil only to be burnt down in 1950. It has subsequently been completely restored, even to the gold leaf. The pavilion, which is modelled on that of the Saiho-ji, has three storeys with verandahs, the middle one projecting out over the lake, beyond the other two; each has a different 'borrowed landscape' view. Originally the lake was probably larger, with the pavilion standing in the water – the building is sometimes said to symbolize the palace of the dragons, and a position surrounded by water would be in keeping with this symbolism. The lake, its outline accentuated by rocks and trees, is divided in two by the tortoise island, while near the pavilion the water is dotted with small islands and rocks. The design shows the influence of Chinese painters of the Song dynasty. Largely for this reason, the design is sometimes attributed to the great Japanese art connoisseur and painter Soami, whose own painting was modelled on the style of Southern Song masters. He, however, lived from 1472 to 1523 so that attribution is highly improbable.

Ginkaku-ji

In the second half of the 15th century the last of the Muromachi shoguns, Yoshimasa, set about creating the Ginkaku-ji or Silver Pavilion on the eastern side of Kyoto. The Onin civil war between 1466 and 1476 interrupted work, which was resumed in 1482. After Yoshimasa's death the garden was given over to a temple, known as Jisho-ji. Alterations carried out in the 17th century make it difficult to pick out the elements of the original paradise garden, but the large treasure pond still acts as a mirror for the two-storeyed pavilion. This, like the Golden Pavilion, was modelled on

The pavilion of the Ginkaku-ji, built in the 15th century for the Shogun Yoshimasa was to have had its roof covered in silver foil but this project was never carried out. The treasure pond in front of the pavilion is part of the original paradise garden.

the Saiho-ji pavilion and was to have had its roof covered with silver leaf but the project was never carried out.

The garden is approached by a long narrow walk lined with bamboo fencing and topped by evergreens, a spatial contrast with the openness and biological forms of the main garden. Here there is a raised bed of white quartz raked into ridges – its wave pattern said to imitate a lake in China – and a flat-topped cone nearly 2 m (6ft) high, intended to simulate Mount Fuji. These were for viewing the effects of moonlight, their luminosity standing out against the dark 'borrowed landscape' formed by the wooded slope of Mount Higashiyama just beyond the confines of the garden. Within

the woods is a very small dry landscape garden.

Under Yoshimasa the elaborate aesthetic ritual associated with tea drinking was taking on the form that was to be codified later by tea masters of the 16th century. The Toguda or East-Seeking Pavilion at Gin-kaku-ji was adapted for the tea ceremony and some of its architectural details subsequently became standard features not only of the tea-hut but also of the Japanese home. The *sho-in* style that replaced the *shinden-zukuri* style included a main room or study (*sho-in*), with a built-in desk looking through shutters on to the garden. An alcove (*tokonoma*) was originally used to display a Buddhist statue; later it came to be used for

Zen Buddhism used the garden as an aid to disciplined contemplation. Design at its most severe excluded almost all plant material. The most famous example of a dry landscape (kare-sansui) is at Ryoan-ji in Kyoto. The temple verandah looks on to a rectangle of raked quartz on which lie groups of rocks.

displaying a painting, pot or flower arrangement. The floors, treated as areas for sitting, were covered with matting (*tatami*). Although the main room faced south as before, the garden was designed as a picture to be seen from inside, often with the scale a perspective subtly modified so that a figure in it might destroy the proportions so ingeniously created.

GARDENS OF CONTEMPLATION

The decline in the power of the Ashikaga shogunate after the death of Yoshimitsu in 1409 led to a period of increased political instability that continued until the late 16th century. Widespread warfare destroyed much during the second half of the 15th century and yet this was a period of considerable cultural and intellectual activity. Zen Buddhism flourished and gardens designed to express its contemplative rigour are among the finest achievements of Japanese culture.

Ryoan-ji

The most profound and austere of these gardens is Ryoan-ji in Kyoto, where the whole garden, not just a single feature, has been treated as a dry landscape, without water or trees and shrubs. Work on its early stages, dating from the middle of the 15th century, is thought to have been carried out by Hosokawa Katsumoto. The garden, destroyed by fire in 1488, was restored by the end of the century, perhaps to the design of the painter Soami. Even if this popular attribution is mistaken, the design shows the influence of Chinese Song and Yuan dynasty black and white painting.

The garden consists of a rectangular bed of raked quartz bounded on two sides by the temple verandah and, on the south and west, by walls topped with sloping tiles. Fifteen rocks, set out in groups of five, two, three, two and three, are arranged on the raked floor. The somewhat fanciful name 'Garden of Crossing Tiger-Cubs' represents one of many attempts to explain the significance of an arrangement where an underlying harmony links the perceptive viewer to nature in the abstract.

Daisen-in

Almost as well known as Ryoan-ji is Daisen-in, which lies in Kyoto's temple complex of Daitoku-ji. This garden, completed in about 1513, has also been ascribed to Soami but may have been the work of a Zen Buddhist monk, Kogaku, or even the result of collaboration between the two men. An L-shaped garden runs round two sides of the temple verandah, the two arms separated by a partition that is pierced by a bell-shaped window. In the angle formed by these two arms vertical rocks simulate mountains from which 'flows' a dry stream of quartz

The Daisen-in, part of the large temple complex of Daitoku-ji in Kyoto, contains a fine example of a small private temple garden of the early 16th century. There is debate about the appropriateness of the partition, pierced by a bell-shaped window, that divides the L-shaped design.

Traditional Japanese gardens have made a virtue of the controlled use of a relatively limited repertoire of elements.

Left: The range of flowers grown is small and they are used sparingly. Here irises grow by the water's edge at the Heian Shrine, Kyoto.

Bottom left: The austerity of Zen Buddhism has left its mark on almost all garden design, with the emphasis on evergreens, often trimmed, rocks, moss and raked gravel, as in this corner of the Kyao Zo, Kyoto.

Bottom right: Much thought is given to the placing and construction of wooden and stone bridges, as in the stroll garden of the Kyoto Imperial Palace.

Opposite: The selection of suitable rocks and the arrangement of stepping stones becomes an art of refined abstract patterning, as at the Katsura Imperial Villa, Kyoto.

pebbles. In this current a boat-shaped stone appears to be negotiating a waterfall and other hazards. A larger garden south of the temple consists of a rectangle of raked quartz pebbles, called by some the Ocean of Nothingness. Apart from the quiet pattern created by the raked surface the only incidents in this large rectangle are a single tree and two low conical mounds of quartz.

THE TEA GARDEN

With the return of peace, secured by the authority of a succession of generals (Oda Nobunaga, Toyotomi Hideyoshi and Toku-

gawa Ieyasu), Kyoto was restored and new buildings erected. The Momoyama period, from 1573 to 1603, takes its name from a hill at Fushimi, south of Kyoto, where the second of the great generals, Toyotomi Hideyoshi, built a castle-palace. Because it was later so extensively planted with peach trees the hill became known as Peach Hill (Momoyama), making it an apt allusion for a period characterized by its use of gold and rich colours.

Hideyoshi was personally involved in the expansion and reconstruction of a garden near Fushimi, the Daigo Sambo-in. The extravagant use of rocks (perhaps as many

A covering of snow softens the outlines of the best-known element in the dry landscape belonging to the abbot's residence at the Daisen-in, Kyoto. A stone cargo junk appears to be drifting gently on a river of sand. Tempting though literal interpretations are, they diminish the power of Zen gardens.

as 700) marks a significant stage in the development of Japanese gardens, but perhaps even more important in the Muromachi period was the elaboration of the tea-garden as the setting for the *cha-no-yu*, the Japanese tea ceremony.

The drinking of powdered tea, which is

prepared by whisking it with boiling water, was a practice introduced to Japan from China by Zen monks, who initially used it to help concentration during meditational exercises. An element of ritual was introduced with a communal ceremony of tea-drinking before meditation. The ceremonial drinking of tea was subsequently taken up by the warrior class and, as has been mentioned, by the time of the Ashikaga shogun Yoshimasa, a prescribed ritual was already established for the tea ceremony. Men who in earlier periods would have become monks now became 'tea masters', a refuge from the perils of the times. The art and philosophy of the greatest of these masters, Sen No Rikyu (1522-91), was very influential in developing the *roji* (dewy path) style of garden, so called because of the 'dewy ground' surrounding the tea-hut. In one of the Buddhist sutras, the word symbolizes the tea-garden's retreat from everyday life.

The tea-ceremony room or hut was a very small rustic edifice which combined the functions of the Chinese scholar's study and the mountain retreat. There, in the natural-coloured interior, five friends should be able to meet and drink a ceremonial bowl of tea before discussing philosophy or works of art – business or politics were specifically excluded. There should be an outside waiting-room, where the visitors could discard their cares, and a stone basin to wash away impurities. These requirements brought into Japanese gardens a sobriety far removed from Heian taste.

The tea masters made three new contributions to the design of Japanese gardens: the stepping-stones, the stone lantern and the stone water basin. All derive from the practical requirements of the tea ceremony – the stepping-stones to prevent the garden moss from being worn, the lantern to light the path, since in the Momoyama period the ceremony was often held at night, and the basin to provide water for the ritual washing of hands.

Within the tea garden the ground was covered with moss, ferns and other small plants growing at the base of rocks. Gone were the colourful plants of Heian gardens in favour of broadleaved evergreens – satisfying the requirement that a garden should be beautiful at all seasons and not dependent on the flowering habits of plants. Azaleas were pruned ruthlessly to look like green boulders, until they burst into flower. Camellias were permissible, but not roses, which are a sorry sight when not in flower. Somewhat irrationally tree peonies in raised stone beds were allowed, as were the rather untidy *Platycodon grandiflora*. Even chrysanthemums (the national flower) were reared in pots out of sight and placed strategically in the garden when flowering.

Examples of the tea-garden are to be found all over Japan, often as elements within much larger gardens. They represent one of the most vital strands in the Japanese garden tradition. In fulfilling their principal purpose – to create an atmosphere that induces a serene state of mind (necessary for the full appreciation of the tea ceremony) – they satisfy an expectation that is so often disappointed by larger and more elaborate gardens.

IMPERIAL GARDENS OF THE EDO PERIOD

Katsura Detached Palace

The tea ceremony made a lasting impact on the details even of imperial gardens. The most successful of these from the Edo period (1603 to 1867) is the Katsura Detached Palace, also known as the Katsura Imperial Villa. This was begun in 1620 on the site of an old garden near the Katsurayama River south of Kyoto by Prince Toshihito and completed in about 1658 by his son. The design was probably directed by the prince, whose literary interests inspired allusions throughout the garden to the Heian classic *The Tale of Genji*. Kobori Enshu, the founder of the Enshu school of the tea ceremony and flower arrangement, is also credited with having contributed to the design. No documentary evidence exists to support this, but the touches of artificiality and the use of straight lines in paving and bridges were innovations that characterized his work as it is known from other buildings and gardens.

The garden is completely surrounded by trees and turns in upon itself round the central lake. This is shaped like a flying crane, while one of its islands is shaped like a tortoise; both are symbols of longevity and reflect the prince's Heian tastes. There is a stand for moon-viewing but the intricacies of this garden are not revealed from a single position and can only be enjoyed by walking through its ingeniously complex layout. A clockwise path of 1,760 stepping-stones reveals a succession of new views: a maple mountain; a promontory on the lake shore, said to be a miniature of a much-admired spit of sand at Amanohashidate; a large tea-house (*shokin-tei*) reached by a flat bridge made of a huge monolith. Stepping-stones, each chosen for its individuality, continue towards a bridge leading to the tortoise island. At its highest point a small tea-house (*shoka-tei*) looks out on cherry blossom in spring, brilliant maple leaves in autumn. Also on the island is a small Zen

The stone water basin was one of the contributions made by the tea masters to the design of Japanese gardens. A simple water scoop lies across a basin in the form of a square within a circle at the Ryoan-ji, Kyoto.

At the Katsura Imperial Villa, also known as the Katsura Detached Palace, on the outskirts of Kyoto, innovations include the use of straight lines in paving and bridges. Touches such as these have been attributed to the designer Kobori Enshu but no documentary evidence confirms his involvement in the project.

Above and left: The Katsura Imperial Villa has an exceptionally fine stroll garden, with a succession of views unfolding along a path of 1,760 stepping stones.

temple (*Onrin-do*). An arched bridge made of packed earth leads back to the palace, whose three sections are arranged to give maximum opportunities for moon-viewing.

Sento Gosho

The term 'stroll garden' is sometimes used to describe examples such as the Katsura Detached Palace where the rich detailing is only revealed to the person who enters the garden and follows its sinuous paths. Two other imperial gardens of the 17th century belong to this category. Sento Gosho is the garden of a palace for retired emperors built in 1634 for ex-Emperor Gomitsunoō and designed by Kobori Enshu. Its three sections are in consciously differing styles, *shin*, *gyo* and *so* (finished, intermediary and rough). In the formal *shin* section the palace (since destroyed) looked on to a long narrow lake for boating, its beach covered with individually chosen stones, each sent wrapped in cotton out of respect for the stones. The lake has a tortoise island with rock composition. A packed-earth bridge separates this section from the next two.

Nearby is one of two tea-houses, its small enclosed garden a bare patch of earth crossed by a path of magnificent water-worn stepping-stones. A farm for the education of noble children in the rigours of common life formed part of the estate.

Shugaku-in Imperial Villa

The ex-Emperor Gomitsunoō also began work, in about 1655, on the Shugaku-in Imperial Villa, which lies in the foothills of Mount Hiei, on the northern outskirts of Kyoto. The gardens contain three separate villas, linked by pine avenues and set against a forested background. As well as being a stroll garden, the setting of the upper villa is an outstanding example of the technique of 'borrowed landscape'. Though this technique had been widely used before, it had seldom been the main feature of a garden and it had never been employed on such a scale. From the Rinun-tei pavilion above the large artificial lake all Kyoto can be seen within the encircling bowl of hills. The slopes below the pavilion are thickly planted with clipped evergreens, occasionally interspersed with cryptomerias, that follow the contours down to the lake.

This, once used for boating, is retained by an earth dam, with four tiers of stone walls concealed from outside by three tiers of tall hedges topped with solid clipped shrub-planting and a row of large maples. The garden has two waterfalls, Male and Female, and a tea-house (Kyusui-tei) on an island, which is linked to its neighbour by a 19th-century bridge in Chinese style.

Rikugien Park

From the beginning of the 17th century a new town began to grow up around Edo Castle, the shogun's headquarters, in the eastern part of Japan. Sited for strategic reasons, it had few views apart from that of Mount Fuji. Parks were laid out on the edge of the town, the earliest being Koraku-en. None of them has the sophistication of the gardens of Kyoto, with the possible exception of Rikugien Park, built by Yanagisawa-Yoshimasa between 1695 and 1702. This stroll garden was originally designed to represent 88 picturesque scenes of literary inspiration. (The name Rikugien was derived from the six principles of poetry in the ancient Chinese classics.) As it exists now the garden is the result of a careful restoration made earlier this century by Baron Iwasaki, whose family gave the property to the City of Tokyo in 1938. The garden has a large central pond with small islets and a main island, on which a collection of rare stones is preserved. A high point in the north gives a view over the whole garden.

With the decline of military feudalism, a complex process which perhaps began as early as the late 17th century and continued to the Meiji restoration in 1868, the period of great garden estates on any scale was effectively finished.

The upper garden of the Shugaku-in Imperial Villa, on the outskirts of Kyoto, is one of the finest examples in Japan of shakkei *('borrowed landscape').*

GARDENS IN THE 20TH CENTURY

The garden is a timeless expression of man's relationship with nature, and in one sense all the old definitions apply as to its place in our lives in the 20th century. It is still a place for growing flowers, fruit, vegetables; a place for ornamental display; a place for recreation and relaxation; for retreat and meditation – a personal paradise. However, the social, economic and technological changes that characterize the 20th century and distinguish it from the 19th and previous centuries have had radical implications for gardens and garden making. In practical terms, gardens are smaller, there are many more of them, and they are largely owner-occupied and owner-maintained. We are all dependent upon technology: from piped water and electricity to the lawn-mower and the motor-car. Above all, we are subject to many and disparate cultural influences which affect our ways of seeing, thinking and behaving. Acceptance of progress in technology has inevitably been accompanied by a familiarity with – if not an acceptance of – 'modern' cultural values in art and architecture.

The changes have not occurred uniformly throughout the world; they are reflections of the social and economic state of a nation or region and fluctuate accordingly. In many countries no significant examples of gardens have been created – or at least recorded. In others, such as those of the developing Middle East, where lavish new gardens have been conceived for kings and princes, security forbids publicity. Where change has occurred, publication of the designs has generally been through journals and books aimed at the gardening public or at the professions of architecture and landscape architecture; most commonly in the case of the latter, in connection with particular stylistic trends. This has occurred, for example, in the cases of Burle Marx in Brazil and to a lesser extent, Luis Barragán in Mexico, both of whom have become identified with national styles. Significantly, most of their work is connected with large private gardens and estates unlike that of European designers who are much more dependent upon publicly-sponsored work. Since the Second World War only a few professional garden designers have been able to survive on private commissions alone; the majority depend, as landscape architects, upon the large and lucrative commissions of the public sector. Nevertheless, some countries, such as Denmark, Germany and Britain, have managed to develop their own small garden traditions which have been well publicized.

As at the Monteiro Garden, Petrópolis, the bold designs of the Brazilian Roberto Burle Marx often incorporate 'painting' with different colours of ground-cover plants.

The battle of styles over which William Robinson and the architect Sir Reginald Blomfield had almost come to blows at the end of the 19th century, continued into the 20th century but broadened into a conflict specifically between the architect and the plantsman. This conflict was resolved to some extent by the growth of the new profession of landscape architecture which began in North America with the pioneering work of Olmsted and Downing, who saw the need for a properly planned landscape to resist the pressures of development. Although effective from the 1850s the profession was not formally constituted in the United States until 1899. The British institute followed in 1929, gathering together a group of architects, planners and garden designers. Although the preoccupation of members on both sides of the Atlantic was initially predominantly with style, it is possible in retrospect to detect the beginnings and development of movements or influences of much more lasting significance, the two most important of these being modernism and the return to naturalism.

Naturalism in North America

Interest in nature was evident in the – albeit idealized – landscape parks of 18th-century England, and extolled by writers such as Rousseau in France, and Emerson, Thoreau and Whitman in America. When Olmsted and his partner Calvert Vaux created some of the first park systems in America, including Central Park, New York, it was the English landscape style that they considered most appropriate. The seemingly casual informality, with opportunities for the conservation of natural lakes, forests and farmland, seemed peculiarly fitted to the large open spaces of America. The concept was furthered by Jens Jensen, who emigrated from Denmark in 1884 and became both a private practitioner and Superintendent of Chicago Parks, in which he pioneered the planting of native trees, shrubs and flowers. His work exerted a strong influence on the 'Prairie School' of architects, exemplified by Frank Lloyd Wright, working in the Mid-West during the early part of the century.

Frank Lloyd Wright, like Olmsted, had spent much of his early life on a farm. He derived strength and inspiration from the soil, from natural growth and the use of natural materials. His contribution to garden design derived from his greatest architectural achievement, the creation of a new concept of space in which rooms could overlap and interpenetrate both horizontally and vertically. This provided opportunities for subtle effects of natural lighting and views; by extension, it reduced the barriers between house and garden. However, Wright's most outstanding houses were not created until 1937. In Fallingwater, his house for Edgar J. Kaufmann at Bear Run, Pennsylvania, stream, waterfall, rocks, house and trees are inextricably interwoven. At his own house and studio at Taliesin West, like Fallingwater dating from 1937, forms, materials and colours have been carefully selected to harmonize with the desert and its plants.

The principle was developed and fully exploited by the Viennese-born architect Richard Neutra, who worked with Wright for a short time after his arrival in the United States in 1923. Together with his son Dion he developed a unique style of desert house which extends characteristically over the site, gaining enrichment both from its enclosed garden with native plants and immaculately framed views of the desert landscape. One of the most

The American architect Frank Lloyd Wright did not feel constrained to express a machine aesthetic as did some of his European counterparts. In Fallingwater, Bear Run, Pennsylvania, he created a complex of stream, waterfall, rocks, house and trees in which there is little rigid distinction between indoor and outdoor spaces.

famous, the Kaufmann House or San Jacinto, California (1946), emphasizes the contrast between pure geometry and the natural world and at the same time expresses the essential unity of man with that world.

Jensen's best surviving work dates from the same period. A fine example is the Lincoln Memorial Garden in Springfield, Illinois, which was begun in 1933. There, on farmland bordering Lake Illinois, lanes leading down to the lakeside walk separate a series of meadows, each of which is given over to a single species or association. Planting was carried out over many years, using 'masses of young trees and shrubs planted close together for informal protection as in nature'. Jensen's plan allowed considerable freedom of execution but demanded strict adherence to principle. Today the garden appears deceptively like a natural landscape.

Naturalism in Europe

In 1906 the designer Willy Lange laid out his own garden in Berlin 'according to the laws of nature', in sharp contrast to the developing architectural style of the period. The plan of this garden differs fundamentally from the landscape gardens of the previous century in having no areas of grass and in the reduction of paths to a functional minimum, without representing design elements.

Lange's example was followed by Erwin Barth, who would become one of the most influential designers of public parks and gardens of his day. At one time Garden Director at Charlottenburg, a rapidly growing suburb of Berlin, Barth became, from 1926, Garden Director of the Greater Berlin authority. One of his Charlottenburg squares, the Sachsenplatz, executed in 1921, anticipates the application of ecological and phytosociological principles to garden design that was to become influential in Germany in the 1930s. The site, a disused gravel pit, was to contain examples of typical 'natural plant communities and geological formations' of the locality, laid out according to 'ecological considerations'.

In Holland the teacher and biologist Jaques P. Thijsse was aware of the change that would inevitably come to the Dutch landscape when towns and industry began to expand and believed that the landscape

In the Netherlands the ecological approach to garden design was pioneered by the biologist and teacher Jaques P. Thijsee. The heem *parks and gardens that this work has inspired, such as the Jaques P. Thijsee Park in Amstelveen south of Amsterdam, are carefully managed landscapes including characteristic habitats and plant communities of the surrounding area.*

would be destroyed before people were aware of its beauty and significance. He was also acutely conscious that existing parks and gardens failed to give people an experience of their natural environment. In 1925 the Thijsse Hof opened in Bloemendaal near Haarlem and on a small site Thijsse and his gardener, C. Sipkes, created a natural garden, following the design of the landscape architect Leonard Springer. The garden contains a small woodland, a pond and marsh, a piece of heathland, a dune landscape, and a cereal field with rare arable weeds. It was intended for use by teachers, children and other visitors, a function it still performs.

Early instructive gardens such as the Thijsse Hof led to the development of the so-called *heem* park and garden. The oldest and most beautiful of these in Amstelveen, south of Amsterdam, is called appropriately the Jaques P. Thijsse Park. This *heem* park, started in 1940, takes the form of a series of woodland glades, each one successfully creating a landscape picture. The edge where woody vegetation and water merge is

specially designed to bring together the widest range of habitats and plants. In spite of their naturalness, *heem* parks and gardens require careful maintenance to remove unwanted plants. To overcome this, the phytosociological garden has been developed in which the characteristic habitats and plant communities of the surrounding area are recreated.

Different interpretations of naturalism were pursued in many countries, from the 'borrowed landscape' associations of Frank Lloyd Wright and Richard Neutra to the use of native plants both decoratively and according to ecological principles (not usually compatible in small gardens). In post-war Sweden the Stockholm Parks Department under Holger Blom was significantly influenced by the ideas of William Robinson; an approach particularly appropriate for a land with harsh winters and a short growing season. The principle of 'ecological' planting is being applied increasingly in Australia and New Zealand, Canada and the newly conservation conscious countries of the Third World.

*In England the partnership of Gertrude Jekyll and the architect Sir Edwin Lutyens produced some of the finest country-house gardens of the late 19th and early 20th centuries. At Hestercombe in Somerset the design is based upon the Great Plat (**above**), a sunken parterre bounded by stone walls supporting walks and terraces. In the detailing a wide variety of materials is used with great imagination (**left**).*

English styles and influence

Robinson's idea of the 'wild' garden was enthusiastically taken up by Gertrude Jekyll, who gave it substance in a way that Robinson had failed to do, developing a new language of naturalistic design and gardening on a small scale to equal that of the English landscape style. Her education in arts and crafts and painting enabled her to appreciate the qualities of form, texture and colour of plants, and to organize them in meaningful combinations; her work on colour, particularly, has never been surpassed. She was ideally suited to work with Edwin Lutyens during his early years as a designer of country houses. Together they explored the English vernacular in buildings and cottage gardens which they were able to translate into a new and peculiarly English blend of naturalness and domestic formality thus achieving an effective resolution of the formal-informal conflict. Between 1893 and 1912 they created some 70 gardens for country houses, notably at The Deanery, Sonning, Berkshire and Hestercombe in Somerset. The gardens at Hestercombe are formal in the sense of their strong geometric structure, but arranged informally in line with Arts and Crafts thinking, and the geometry was balanced with the small-scale geometry of plants, each element carefully considered as an essential part of the whole on the principle that 'Every garden scheme should have a backbone, a central idea beautifully phrased. Every wall, path, stone and flower should have its relationship to the central idea.' This was not, as might be supposed, written by an advocate of modernism, but by Lutyens, who hated the Modern Movement when it became established in architecture.

The development of the Arts and Crafts philosophy had, by the beginning of the 20th century, produced a wealth of English country houses and gardens that were considered models of the best modern domestic architecture of their time; so much so that the German government sent the architect Herman Muthesius to London in 1900 specifically to study them. He described the gardens as 'a continuation of the rooms of the house, almost a series of outdoor rooms, each of which is self-contained and performs a separate function.

Thus the garden extends the house into the midst of nature.' (*Das englische Haus 1904/5*). Muthesius' exposure of the great qualities of these houses initiated a comparable movement in Germany which, in turn, influenced the Bauhaus, a generator of the Modern Movement.

The houses of the period and their gardens varied from the comfortable informality of the Arts and Crafts to the grandeur of the Italian style, with their designers sometimes working in both. Designers working in this way included Inigo Thomas, H. A. Tipping, Harold Peto and Oliver Hill, who later contributed to the Modern Movement. Thomas Mawson laid out a complex Italian garden for Lord Leverhulme as well as a cottage garden in the Arts and Crafts style. Sir George Sitwell, the father of Dame Edith, Sir Osbert and Sir Sacheverell Sitwell, spent many years studying Italian gardens, wrote a book about them (*On the Making of Gardens, 1909*), and then spent a fortune making two

gardens in an Arts and Crafts version of the Italian style, at Renishaw in Derbyshire and Montegufoni in Italy.

Among the most satisfying gardens, and still the most popular, are three created not by professional designers, but gradually, by their owners. Great Dixter (Nathaniel Lloyd), Sissinghurst (Vita Sackville-West with her husband Sir Harold Nicolson) and Hidcote (Lawrence Johnston). All owe much to the Arts and Crafts Movement and particularly to the planting theories of Gertrude Jekyll, 'the greatest *artist* in horti- culture and garden-planting that England has produced.' (C. Hussey).

A notable example of English planting in a formal framework in the United States is Dumbarton Oaks, Washington DC, which Beatrix Farrand (Beatrix Jones) designed between 1921 and 1947 with her client Mildred Barnes Bliss; in 1941 the garden as it is now constituted was presented to Harvard University. Dumbarton Oaks is a compartmented garden in the Arts and

*Vita Sackville-West with her husband, Sir Harold Nicolson, belonged to the tradition of passionate amateur gardeners. The garden they created at Sissinghurst Castle in Kent has become one of the best-known English gardens of the 20th century. Although the cottage garden was an important source of inspiration (**above**) the design is not unsophisticated, as can be seen from the tower which dominates the group of old buildings. A series of outdoor 'rooms', linked by strong axes, are planted informally with great artistry. **Left** is a view of the White Garden.*

In the 20th century a respect for regional climate and vegetation, as well as the originality of individual designers, has produced gardens differing markedly in character in different parts of the world.
Right: *The Castlecrag Estate on the shores of Sydney Harbour, Australia, developed in the 1920s, reflects an enthusiasm for the Australian landscape, the houses being built with a minimum of disturbance to the bush.*
Below left: *In Thailand the development of an indigenous style is of relatively recent date. The bold foliage and bright flowers of tropical plants are used imaginatively in the M.R. Kukrit Pramoj Garden, Bangkok, made in about 1980.*
Below right: *The first South African garden to specialize in indigenous plants was the National Botanic Gardens at Kirstenbosch, established in 1913.*
Opposite: *Antonio Gaudi's Parque Güell in Barcelona is one of the rare truly original garden designs of the 20th century.*

The Pebble Garden at Dumbarton Oaks, Washington, DC, is one element in a large and complex design executed between 1921 and 1947 by Beatrix Farrand working closely with her client, Mildred Barnes Bliss. In 1941 the gardens were presented to Harvard University.

Crafts manner, with Italianate detailing and oriental influences. The informal planting is strongly in the tradition of Gertrude Jekyll. Farrand, one of the eleven founder members of the American Society of Landscape Architects (ASLA), later designed several college campuses, and contributed to Dartington Hall in Devon.

In England and elsewhere Gertrude Jekyll's influential books had encouraged the use of a wide range of plant material. In the first half of the century Lawrence Johnston, an American who had made his home in Europe, created two great gardens, one in England, at Hidcote Manor, Gloucestershire, and one near Menton in France, containing rich collections of plants grouped according to colour and form.

Sissinghurst in Kent is similar in style to Hidcote, with a formal layout of small compartments containing detailed planting of exceptional quality. This creation of two highly talented amateurs, Vita Sackville-West and Sir Harold Nicolson, is laid out on the site of a romantic ruin they had bought in 1930 and has come to epitomize the English garden, intimate in scale and rich in plants, its variety given cohesion by subtle colour schemes and the unifying effect of a strong architectural framework.

The eclectic approach

The period of country-house building in Britain coincided with the so-called Country Place era in America (see page 111) when businessmen spent their virtually untaxed fortunes on buying large country houses and laying out gardens to match, usually in a (just) recognizable European style. French and Italian styles were favoured in the main, taste for the latter being influenced by Charles A. Platt's book *Italian Gardens* (1894). In

In the first half of the 20th century an American, Lawrence Johnston, created at Hidcote Manor in Gloucestershire, England, a tightly structured garden planted with a rich diversity of material.

Left and far left: *In France one of the most celebrated examples of a recreated Renaissance garden is Villandry in the Loire Valley. The Jardin Potager consists of nine large squares with vegetables planted in geometric patterns.*

France, too, the building and adornment of country houses and gardens became a fashion (one might also say a pasttime), employing designers such as Ferdinand Duprat, Thomas Mawson, Percy Cane and Russell Page. For the most part they were eclectic in their designs, although occasionally selected for particular skills, as in the case of the elaborate French water-garden at Blenheim by Achille Duchêne, a celebrated restorer of gardens. One of the most celebrated restorations was that made by Dr Joachim Carvallo at Villandry in the Loire Valley between 1906 and 1924. It is a creative restoration based upon a number of Renaissance models and incorporating a unique feature: a large *potager* parterre which depends upon fruit and vegetables for its decorative qualities. For Carvallo the geometry of the garden and its hierarchical arrangement expressed ideas of absolute order, at the same time theological, social and aesthetic, representing the antithesis of the *jardin anglais*, associated with Rousseau and 'the principles of an absurd egalitarianism, contrary to nature and good sense'.

The favourable climate of the French and Italian Rivieras provided ideal conditions for the exotic planting that had been introduced into Europe and North America during the 19th century, and this was to some extent matched by the eclectic approach to garden design.

The reputation of this region as a winter resort, established by the middle of the 19th century, continued to draw an affluent and leisured class so that sumptuous villas and magnificent gardens multiplied all along the coastline. Their makers, who were fond of developing the natural beauties of the sites, freely drew from the antique – Italian Renaissance, Hispano Mooresque, oriental or medieval repertoires – to make up the elements of the decoration; thus there are a large number of pergolas for supporting climbing plants, antique temples, medieval cloisters, and porticoes, as well as sculpture, urns and earthenware jars. The so-called Mediterranean style, 'bringing into play the light of the south, the natural flora of the coast and provençal stone, in an unaffected manner', was the invention of Ferdinand Bac, who, before turning to garden design, had been a painter and man of letters. He designed the garden of the Villa Croisset at Grasse, La Fiorentina at Cap Ferrat and, above all, the gardens of Colombières at Menton. In such a milieu, where modern architecture seemed like an intrusion, patrons of modern art were rare.

The French Riviera offers favourable conditions for the creation of gardens, a fact seized on by French and foreign amateurs in the late 19th and early 20th centuries. The Villa Noailles at Grasse is formal in character but richly planted.

In the 20th century garden designers, professional and amateur, have had to come to terms with working on a reduced scale, particularly in town and suburban gardens.

Left: Some designers find their inspiration directly in the gardens of the past, here a knot garden making a small feature at Barnsley House, Gloucestershire, England.

Below left: In modern Japanese domestic gardens, tiny but even so a luxury in such a heavily populated country, traditional values are evident in the restrained use of materials and textures.

Below right: The English designer John Brookes is best known for designs in which he reveals an assurance in the handling of both geometric and organic elements, as at Clock House, Fontwell, Sussex.

Opposite: The designs of the Dutch landscape architect Mien Ruys combine clarity of concept with richness of detail, particularly in the planting.

The Modern Movement in Europe

The relative austerity of Cubism, with its exclusion of atmosphere and light, even of colour, had little appeal for those who indulged in the sensuous delights of gardens and gardening. The majority of garden designers were unimpressed, seeing in the new philosophy only a rejection of the things they loved, rather than an opportunity for renewal, a totally fresh approach to design, free of unnecessary ornamentation. Not surprisingly, one of the first garden designs of the Modern Movement was presented by an architect, Gabriel Guevrékian, at the Paris exhibition in 1925. This was for a small triangular garden that was wholly modern. Its division into triangular facets on different planes exploited the effects of water and light, opening up unexpected vistas. Guevrékian, like most architects, kept the plants firmly in their place, but relied upon strong colours – an expression of his Armenian origin – which might be associated more with the Orphic Cubism of Delaunay and others experimenting with the emotional impact of pure colour than with the austere intellectual Cubism of Picasso, Braque and Gris.

The critics were scandalized, but Guevrékian received a commission from the Vicomte Charles de Noailles, an art collector, to design a much larger triangular garden for his villa at Hyères in the south of France. This is organized as a series of stepped rectangles, alternately of paving and plants, which lead the eye (and the body) gently upwards in normal perspective, in dramatic contrast to the false perspective created by the strong walls, to converge upon the focal sculpture by Jacques Lipchitz, seen against the 'borrowed landscape' beyond. Colour was again a strong feature of the paving, but the most significant effect was the difference, due to foreshortening, between the view out and the view towards the house, an authentic Cubist effect, which is entirely of the 20th century.

Another garden of the period was commissioned, also by the Vicomte Charles de Noailles, from the garden designers André and Paul Vera at St Germain-en-Laye. The brothers were generally accustomed to working within the French formal tradition, and this garden is apparently based upon the 'British flag' parterre pattern which the French had exported to South America, but the radiating bands of gravel and plants are oddly asymmetrical. The illusion is compounded by a mirror fence which effectively extends the space well beyond the boundary.

These gardens are unusual in using striking visual techiques to solve spatial problems; most solutions were less exciting, providing rather rigidly controlled spaces for plants within strong geometric structures. Initially, Germany and Holland were the most progressive countries; the former on account of the Bauhaus lead in design and the profession of *Gartenarchitekten* accustomed to working with architects, and the latter inspired by the de Stijl Movement.

During the 1920s the formalism of the *Architekturgarten* began to break down in two respects. First, the overall layout remained fundamentally geometric, but, as can be seen at the Schramm Garden, designed by Otto Valentien for Ludwig Spath, it was no longer symmetrical in form. In the second development, inspired particulary by Karl Foerster, the rigidity of symmetrical designs was softened by rich and varied perennial planting. This second tendency was taken further by Hermann Mattern, who, in 1927, went to head the design section of Foerster's nursery near Potsdam.

Foerster encouraged the use of a wide range of plant material, especially the taller perennials, alpines, ferns and grasses. He was not himself a designer but he and his major competitor, Ludwig Spath, influenced a generation of young designers, who still in the 1920s generally learnt their trade working for one of the large horticultural firms.

Mattern, together with Herta Hammerbacher, developed a very sensitive style of garden design which soon moved away from the formality and geometry of the architectural garden to become particularly characterized by the use of subtle ground modelling to define spaces. The Baensch Garden created on a hillside site in Berlin by Mattern, Hammerbacher and Foerster between 1930 and 1935 illustrates how completely they had turned their backs on the formalism of a few years previously. In this case the architect, Hans Scharoun, had difficulty obtaining planning permission for the house from the new Nazi authorities, and the garden was in stark contrast to the officially approved style.

The Modern Movement in Britain

The Lutyens–Jekyll partnership marked the end of an era in private garden design. Lutyens's adoption of a more grandiose classical style coincided with a decline in the partnership. The plentiful supply of cheap labour disappeared with the Second World War, effectively changing the emphasis of garden and landscape design. Although large gardens continued to be created and altered, it is the small garden that is the true expression of the age. As the towns and cities expanded, the suburb with its leafy avenues, privacy, and sense of security, represented for many an ideal way of living. The garden cities of Letchworth and Welwyn, and Hampstead Garden Suburb were models. The garden, like the house, remained a show-piece, but it was an individual show-piece: the creation of its owners. While a few, particularly in the remote country, continued the tradition of the cottage garden, the majority of gardeners in one way or another subscribed to the burgeoning gardening industry. The period also marks a watershed for designers. As the scale of gardens decreased and the market contracted, some moved into the industry in the belief that designing and building was the only effective method; others saw the need for expansion to deal with more pressing problems of public open space.

The first steps towards founding a profession of landscape architecture in Britain were taken in 1927, when a handful of practitioners met at Chelsea Flower Show. A constitution was drawn up and the first meeting held in May 1929 with Thomas Mawson, the garden designer and town planner, as President. The name chosen was the British Institute of Garden Architects. Within months, however, it was changed to the Institute of Landscape Architects, following Olmsted's description.

Garden design, like architecture, was at this period in a state of uncertainty. Unlike the Art Nouveau Movement, which had a dramatic effect upon building and design generally, the international Modern Movement caused little more than a ripple upon

In England Christopher Tunnard was almost alone in interpreting into landscape the modern movement in architecture of the 1930s. Halland in Sussex, where he collaborated with the architect Serge Chermayeff is one of the most outstanding examples.

Sir Geoffrey Jellicoe, who in the 1930s showed great interest in the Modern Movement, has continued as a practising landscape architect into the 1980s, for example, creating a large garden at Sutton Place, England, juxtaposing irrational elements with 'classical values'.

the surface of life in England. The neo-classical and Arts and Crafts influences continued to dominate garden design. Percy Cane and Russell Page, who were pre-eminently garden designers, both worked in an eclectic manner, gaining wide reputations at home and abroad. Cane's claim to fame is rather for his horticultural knowledge and attention to detail, while Page's approach shows a much greater control of space, using hard materials and plants. For some years he was in partnership with (Sir) Geoffrey Jellicoe. Jellicoe was involved in alterations and improvements to a variety of large gardens in England, notably a reinterpretation of James Gibbs' 18th-century design for Ditchley Park, Oxfordshire, and later Sutton Place. He was also responsible for creating a significant modern structure with a roof-garden, incorporating a glass-bottomed pool, for the Cheddar caves (1933), the beginning of his life-long promotion of modern values through his work and writing in association with his wife Susan. While expressing great confidence in their form and structure, few such modern designs did more than tentatively reach out into the landscape. An exception was the house at Halland in Sussex, built in 1938, where the architect Serge Chermayeff and the landscape architect Christopher Tunnard achieved a unique synthesis of architecture and landscape design; intimacy and grandeur, unity, simplicity, and sympathy with the surroundings. Using traditional techniques but forms and details that were uncompromisingly modern, they succeeded in expressing the freedom of a new age, comparable to that seen in the desert houses and gardens of Richard Neutra in the United States. Simultaneously Tunnard was publishing what in effect was his manifesto, *Gardens in the Modern Landscape* (1938). His appreciation of past styles and indictment of those who refused to progress are followed by a statement of faith in the new architecture. Supported by his

colleague Frank Clark he proposed a new landscape based upon function and utility, asymmetrical when appropriate, allowing sunlight and views, screened or framed with opportunities for activities and relaxation, avoidance of axial planning and monumental construction, and the use of contrasts: hard and soft, light and dark, rough and smooth, and colour. But he was able to show disappointingly few built examples. In 1939 he emigrated to teach in

the United States, spending many years at Yale.

It was to be another decade before a 'modern' approach to landscape and garden design began to develop, when landscape architects were appointed as consultants to the New Towns. Modern design became identified with post-war hopes for a better Britain, providing unprecedented opportunities for designers at all scales, from planning to the design of public gardens.

In the 20th century the intimate relationship between sculpture and garden is still very much alive.

Right: *In England the private garden of the architect Frederick Gibberd at Harlow in Essex was designed as a series of carefully controlled vistas linking a sequence of spaces, peopled with sculptures and* objets trouvés *along the side of a small river valley.*

Below left: *At another English garden, that at Dartington Hall in Devon, a Henry Moore figure of a reclining woman looks out over a view where much of the planting is in a natural style.*

Below right: *A highly individual approach to the treatment of a fence is the barrier sculpted out of redwood by the American landscape architect Garrett Eckbo in his own garden at Berkeley, California.*

Left: *The Louisiana Museum in Denmark, created in a 19th-century house and garden sited on the sound facing Sweden, is one of the earliest outdoor art museums of this century. Some of the sculptures are in the open while others occupy a variety of enclosures, each of different character, linked by carefully detailed paths. The whole is a successful amalgam of landscape, architecture, painting and sculpture.*

Below: *The juxtaposition of sculpture and water is a recurrent feature of European gardens. One of the most original English gardens of the second half of the 20th century is that designed by Sir Geoffrey Jellicoe at Sutton Place, Surrey. It includes a formal space dominated by a large relief sculpture in white marble by Ben Nicholson.*

In the 20th century architects and designers have been able to explore the potential of the roof garden as a result of developments in the technology of water-proofing materials coupled with wide-span steel and concrete structures. Le Corbusier advocated roof-gardens as the second of his five points towards a new architecture, believing that for a city they meant 'the winning back of the whole of its developed area'.
Right: *As well as working on large-scale projects, the American landscape architect Daniel Kiley has designed a number of gardens, notably the roof and terrace gardens for the Oakland Museum.*
Below: *The development of roof-gardens in Britain has been characteristically slow. Mountbatten House in Basingstoke was designed in 1979 for IBM by Arup Associates.*

Modernism in the United States

The leading figures in the search for a new landscape style in the United States were Thomas Church and a group of three students: James Rose, Daniel Urban Kiley and Garrett Eckbo who rebelled against the Beaux Arts style which they were taught at Harvard University's Graduate School of Design.

Church, the pioneer of what later came to be known as the 'California Style', had already rejected in theory the Beaux Arts tradition by the time he went into practice in San Francisco in 1930. During the 1930s most of his work consisted of small gardens in the San Francisco area. Faced with the challenge of small irregular plots and steep hillside sites, his response – asymmetrical plans, raised planting beds, seat walls, bridges, paving and broad timber decks – established an entirely new vocabulary of

garden design. He was the first garden designer to come to terms with the needs of modern life and respond to them positively, especially to the increasing use of garden space by families living in smaller houses and the requirement for low-maintenance gardens. He made a place in the landscape for the motor car, and realized that as the modern house evolved with walls of glass the garden had to become a functional extension of the house, an outdoor living-room.

In the 1930s he experimented with angular forms that gave the illusion of greater size. For example in the Sullivan Garden in San Francisco, dating from 1937, the longer arm of an L-shaped path extends two-thirds along the diagonal of a rectangular site. On a second visit to Europe in 1937 he met the Finnish architect and designer Alvar Aalto, whose architecture and glasswork inspired

him to adopt more relaxed, informal and organic garden plans with curvilinear forms. The best-known example of his work in this vein is El Novillero, the garden he designed for Mr and Mrs Dewey Donnell at Sonoma, California. This was created between 1947 and 1948 with the assistance of, among others, the young Lawrence Halprin.

The garden, which is situated on a hill in the rocky terrain of the Californian live oak woodland with views over the salt-marshes of San Pablo Bay, comprises a swimming pool with guest-house, summer-house, and bar, surrounded by concrete paving and redwood decking. The elegant and apparently simple design was a response to the needs of the client and to the nature of the site. Its essential features – the meandering channels of the salt-marsh, the rocky hillside and the oakwoods – are echoed by the strong curvilinear forms of the pool and the sculptured island; the rocks and trees are emphasized by the paving and decking which they penetrate. The V-shaped pool is placed in such a way that it cuts across the pattern of concrete and redwood squares. Line plays against line, form against form, but the whole composition has its own unique identity and at the same time belongs essentially to the site.

Although Church undertook public commissions during the war years and after, the small residential garden remained his dominant concern until the end of his career. In his writing as well as in his practice he affirmed his view of the garden as a work of art, a composition in form and space but one which must emerge from the needs of the client and the nature of the site.

The rebellion of Eckbo, Kiley and Rose against the Beaux Arts design traditions offered at Harvard contributed to a radical change in professional design philosophies but did not lead to a uniform approach to the problems of garden design. A central point for Eckbo, as landscape architect and city planner, is the concept that gardens are for people, and for each individual in particular.

According to Thomas Church, the pioneer of what came to be known as the 'Californian style', the design of a garden must take into account the needs of the client and the nature of the site. Church's practice concentrated on small residential gardens such as this at Carmel, California.

*The early
preoccupation of the
American landscape
architect Daniel Kiley
with form rather than
function gave way to
the belief that the form
results from dealing
with the functional
aspects of a design. The
indoor garden for the
Ford Foundation in
New York City is one
of the relatively few
small-scale
commissions he has
undertaken.*

roof and terrace gardens for the Oakland Museum and an indoor garden for the Ford Foundation in New York City.

Lawrence Halprin, who set up his own practice in San Francisco four years after working as Church's assistant at El Novillero, has been a powerful influence on contemporary landscape architecture. Although his early work involved the re-interpretation of the Californian garden in contemporary terms, the designing of housing schemes and shopping malls led him to develop a broad concern for the value of urban space. He has constantly advocated the city – as opposed to the Arcadian suburban community of the kind Olmsted created in Riverside, Chicago – as a valid means of living and has urged its rehabilitation and continuance. He pioneered the restoration and re-use of old structures and thus the preservation of the character and fabric of the city, as successfully shown at Ghiradelli Square, San Francisco (1962).

The McIntyre Garden in Bay Area, California which dates from 1960, was the first major work of Lawrence Halprin, who has become one of the most influential figures in American landscape architecture.

Rose's search for a new style was strongly influenced by the work of contemporary constructivist and abstractionist artists and by his exposure to oriental life-styles and philosophies, particularly Zen Buddhism, during the Second World War. His work, which was primarily residential, displays a strong sense of spatial structure, with landscape and architecture skilfully merged into each other, an appreciation of the intrinsic qualities of garden materials and an understanding of evolving 20th-century life-styles. His gardens, such as Rose Residence, Ridgewood, New Jersey, dating from 1954, acknowledge the changing character and temporary nature of their components and celebrate the effects of light, shadow, texture, sound and space.

Kiley's early work was dominated by a

preoccupation with form rather than function in the solution of design problems, but was later tempered by the belief that form is achieved as a by-product of the several functional solutions to a problem. His great strength lay in his ability to make a rapid assessment of the functional relationships of buildings on a large site in order to establish a clear spatial hierarchy and appropriate scale. The geometry and layout of his schemes were frequently reminiscent of the formal qualities of 17th-century French gardens (which he much admired) and reflected his opinion that the man-made landscape should be an obvious contrast to the world of nature. Although much of his work is on a large scale associated with public and commercial buildings, it includes a number of gardens, notably the

He has been highly successful as a propagandist and has shown a remarkable talent for drawing together and inspiring teams of gifted designers to produce work of such high calibre as the Lovejoy Plaza in Portland, Oregon, dating from 1961.

Tropical landscapes

The intensity and scale of post-war developments in the industrialized countries have left little room for individuality or for naturalism, the latter becoming focused more upon national and, recently, international Green movements. However, both qualities have found significant expression in the developing world, and particularly in the work of Roberto Burle Marx and Luis Barragán.

Burle Marx is unique in developing a reputation equally for his skills as a painter and designer and, in the garden, for his handling of architectural elements and for his use of native plants, many of which he had to collect himself. When he was 19 years' old his family spent 18 months in Berlin, where he studied painting and the native flora of Brazil in the Dahlem Botanic Garden. He returned to Brazil with two ambitions: to paint and to create a style of gardening using native plants. His first public commission in Brazil was to redesign the municipal gardens at Recife and this was followed, in the late 1930s, with commissions to design the garden and two roof terraces for the new Ministry of Education (inspired by Le Corbusier) and the Resurgeros Insurance

building in Rio. These designs bore the hallmark of what became identified as the Burle Marx Brazilian style, with native plants arranged as sculptural groups within the free-flowing pattern of ground cover, pools and paths. This 'painting' with different colours of ground-cover plants was developed in a number of much larger gardens and parks during the next decades, notably the Monteiro Garden, Petrópolis, Rio de Janeiro, in 1948 and the Cavanelas

The designs of the Brazilian Roberto Burle Marx strive for a unity of art and nature. At the Megalheaes Garden near Rio de Janeiro he has achieved a smooth transition from man-made forms to the natural landscape by linking the planting to natural vegetation.

and the Kronforth Gardens in the 1950s. In creating a style of landscape design which is at once essentially Brazilian and wholly of the 20th century, Burle Marx managed to combine the two great driving forces of his life, a love of art and a love of plants.

The architect Luis Barragán became the spiritual leader of three generations of Mexican Minimalists. From 1940 he designed a number of gardens, experimenting with the juxtapositioning of stone retaining walls and horizontal planes; with water in pools, channels and artificial waterfalls. Important influences were the gardens of Islam, the naïve painter Jesus Reyes, the German-born sculptor Mathias Goeritz and the 'architecture of the poor': the indigenous buildings of the Mediterranean and the Mexican pueblos. From these he developed his highly personal idiom, contrasting pure forms which were sometimes broken down into almost abstract planes, with the wilder forms of nature. Memories of his native Guadalajara – the brightly coloured houses, the elevated wooden aqueducts which carried water to the pueblos, the life and colour of the market-place and, above all, the horse – are ever-present in his work. Many of his designs are actually for horses: ranches in which trees, coloured walls and water are combined to form a kind of theatre in which they can be displayed. The water element in one of his most distinguished designs, that of the Plaza del Bebedero de los Caballos (1958–62) in Las Arboledas, Mexico City, is in fact a horse-trough. Using the simplest of materials – water, a single species of tree and walls (one white to provide a backcloth for tree shadows, one blue to suggest distance) – he achieved a majesty worthy of his Islamic masters.

In El Pedregal (the rocky place) (1945–50), the site of an extinct volcano, he attempted to create a residential development in which all the houses and gardens would be in harmony with the fantastic lava land-forms and the existing vegetation. 'My house is my refuge', he wrote, 'an emotional piece of architecture', and 'the garden a magic place for the enjoyment of meditation and companionship ... the garden is the soul of the house'.

The two great driving forces of Roberto Burle Marx's life, a love of art and a love of plants, have been most fully expressed in his garden designs, including those for his own garden at Sitio San Antonio da Bica, Campo Grande, Brazil.

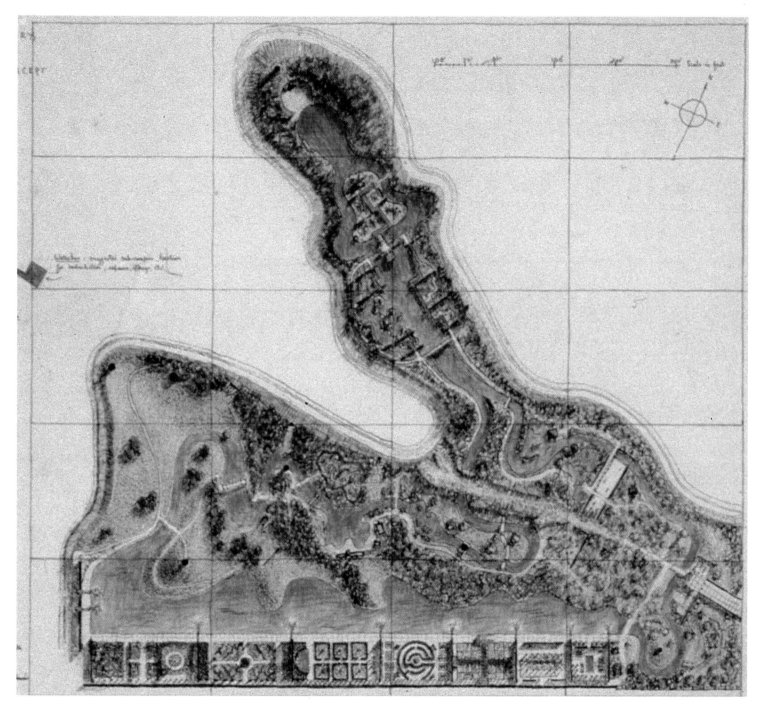

Epilogue

After the Second World War the 'modern' approach to garden design was a vital strand in the greatly expanded profession of landscape architecture. In Britain the profession provided opportunities for designers to work on all scales. Germany, which had employed landscape architects for the autobahn system in the 1930s, energetically developed the tradition of local garden shows into international as well as regional garden shows (*Gartenschauen*) that were instrumental in reconstructing the parks and gardens of her new societies of the welfare states. Impressive, too, is the quality of innumerable shattered cities. In the Netherlands landscape architects who had long been engaged in creating new landscapes from the sea were also now faced with urban reconstruction; and in Scandinavia they played an important part in the development of the private gardens, the creation of amateurs as well as professionals, often in size no more than suburban plots, where, within the limits imposed by site and finance, great originality is shown in the handling of space around domestic buildings.

When they are completed, the Moody Gardens planned for Galveston Island off the southeast coast of Texas will present a unique perspective on the history of gardens as conceived by the English landscape architect Sir Geoffrey Jellicoe. The plan is the culmination of a distinguished career in which Sir Geoffrey has thought long and deeply about man's relation to landscape. The components are 'essences' of historic gardens and landscapes rather than copies of particular examples and the overall design includes elements aimed to play upon the subconscious.

GLOSSARY

Allée A walk of sand, gravel or turf bordered by trees or clipped hedges. In the French formal garden the *allées* constitute the framework and are its most important feature.

Allée en berceau A short fragrant walk protected from the sun by climbing plants.

Amphitheatre A rounded auditorium embraced in the landscape or a garden feature that may be architectural or formed of terraces of turf approximating in form to the semicircular auditorium of antiquity. In late 17th-century French gardens the term was applied to symmetrically arranged shallow terraces of grass. See Claremont, page 68.

Arboretum A living collection of trees grown to illustrate the diversity of species and forms.

Arbour A wooden framework such as a bower or pergola over which plants are trained. See also Herbarium.

Arcade A tall hedgerow clipped into the form of a row of arches supported on smooth tree-trunks.

Automata Hydraulic devices, allied to trick fountains and *giochi d'acqua*, that are intended to astonish or amuse. They are often accompanied by acoustic devices or contrivances simulating the motion of animals. See Villa d'Este, page 25.

Avenue A wide way bordered on each side by a row of trees.

Azulejo A decorated tile made from sand, water and a little glaze baked in ovens or left to harden in the sun. The practice of making them was introduced to the Iberian peninsula by the Moors and it became a characteristic feature. See Fronteira, page 104.

Bassin A tank or reservoir, in gardens an ornamental pond or small lake.

Bed Any area of a garden well demarcated from its surroundings and devoted to the cultivation of a particular group of plants.

Bedding or change-bedding The practice of planting beds with different subjects at different times of the year, by removal and replanting.

Belt In 18th-century English landscape, either a planting of trees round the perimeter of an estate, with or without a walk or drive; or the perimeter walk or drive itself.

Belvedere A look-out or turret usually sited in a commanding position, either as a separate building or as part of a villa.

Berceau A vault-shaped trellis, on which creepers, vines, roses or other climbing plants are trained.

Bian In Chinese gardens a calligraphic board, rectangular, wooden and usually lacquered, hung horizontally under the eaves of a building or on an interior wall and carrying the name of the structure or a phrase in praise of the owner or the view.

Borrowed view See Jie jing; Shakkei.

Bosco In Italian gardens a grove, generally of evergreen ilex, providing a contrast to the rational geometry of the garden as a whole.

Bosquet An ornamental grove, thicket or shrubbery pierced by walks arranged in geometric or sinuous patterns, sometimes, as at Versailles, with an elaborate set-piece at the centre. See Bosquet des Rocailles, page 52.

Buffet d'eau An ornamental architectural feature placed against a wall or in a niche, with water flowing over it into bowls, basins or troughs.

Burladores The Spanish equivalent of *giochi d'acqua*.

Cabinet de verdure A small garden enclosure within a *bosquet* or surrounded by clipped hedges.

Calligraphic board See Bian.

Carpet bedding The practice of making patterned beds using dwarf or creeping foliage plants that can be trained into a uniform surface.

Cascade A dramatic fall of water which can take one of several forms, including that of a water-staircase. See Villa Garzoni, page 32, and La Reggia, page 34.

Casino An ornamental lodge, pavilion or small house, often but not invariably in the grounds of a larger house, particularly associated with Italian gardens of the 16th to 18th centuries.

Chabutra In Mogul gardens a large stone dais for sitting which is placed to catch refreshing breezes and to afford a view over the surrounding garden.

Chadar In Persian and Mogul gardens a form of water-chute with a patterned surface causing the water to catch the light and make a pleasant sound.

Chahar bagh In the Persian tradition literally 'fourfold garden', that is a garden divided into four equal parts by intersecting water channels.

Charmille A tall hedge clipped to give a smooth wall-like surface.

Chini-kanas Rows of small niches or pigeonholes set in the wall at the back of some Mogul cascades where at night lamps could be set to shine through the water.

Chinoiserie Literally 'in the Chinese taste', applied to a style of decoration or design imitating real or imagined Chinese motifs. See Biddulph Grange, page 79.

Claire-voie or Claire-voyée Any kind of open-work fence, at the further end of an *allée*, which does not completely block the view.

Cottage orné A small, usually asymmetrically designed building containing elaborate rustic elements, used as a feature in a park, or as a lodge or for housing and generally associated with the picturesque style in England.

Cour d'honneur The principal courtyard of a château, where visitors are received.

Deer-park In England parks, generally created in the late Middle Ages and surrounded by a ditch and huge earth bank, topped by a pale (the symbol for a park in early maps), where deer were kept under licence from the Crown. In the 18th century a number were transformed into landscaped parks; for example, Blenheim, Chatsworth and Mount Edgcumbe.

Di xue In Chinese gardens a decorative doorway in either a boundary or an interior wall, the opening of circular shape, hence the name moon door. More fanciful outlines were also commonly used. See Ji Chang Yuan, page 142.

Dry landscape See Kare-sansui.

Dui jing In Chinese gardens the facing view or end vista to which the eye is led by paths, turnings, successive doorways, window openings, etc.

Entrelacs Designs of interlacing bands as in a knot garden.

Espalier A line of fruit-trees whose branches are pruned and trained into formal patterns against a wall or fence so as to make the most of sunshine, warmth and protection; the wall against which such fruit-trees are trained can also be called an espalier.

Estrade The form of clipped shrub or small tree which appeared in the Burgundian style of gardening in the 15th century with branches trained to grow out horizontally, often upon metal wheel-shaped frames, or clipped to form successive level tiers surrounding the trunk.

Etang A pond in gardens; a piece of ornamental water of natural origin.

Etoile An intersection of straight walks in a forest.

Exedra In Greek and Roman architecture an open building, generally independent of the main structure, furnished with seats; in 18th-century English gardens semicircular architectural forms alluding to antique models.

Eye-catcher A feature, often seen in silhouette, placed on a distant eminence as part of the overall landscape design, but not necessarily on the owner's property.

Fabrique In French gardens all constructions erected for an ornamental or picturesque end.

Facing view See Dui jing.

Fang In Chinese landscape architecture a boat-like pavilion, often of stone, although the superstructure may be stone or timber, generally built in water.

Feng shui An ancient Chinese art, of which the nearest Western equivalent is geomancy, based on the principle that currents of 'vital spirit' or 'cosmic breath' (*ch'i*) run through the earth according to its topography, influencing the fortunes of individuals and their descendants, depending on how they place their houses and – most importantly – their graves, in relation to the winds (*feng*), waters (*shui*), hills (*kan*) and valleys (*yu*) of the landscape in which they live.

Ferme ornée A farm made for enjoyment with paths laid alongside hedgerows which are made ornamental with mixed shrubs and herbaceous plants. See Rousham, page 71.

Folly A garden structure characterized by a certain excess in terms of eccentricity, cost or conspicuous inutility.

Gardenesque A term first proposed by J. C. Loudon to describe a style of planting design in which each individual plant is allowed to develop its natural character as fully as possible. The term was later used to describe a style of garden layout characterized by rampant eclecticism and lack of artistic unity.

Gartenschau In Germany garden shows combining exhibitions for professional and commercial interests with the creation of public pleasure-grounds.

Gazebo A structure from which one may 'gaze out' over a garden.

Gazon coupé Literally 'cut turf'; grass with shapes cut out of turf and filled with coloured earths or gravels.

Ge A type of Chinese garden pavilion of two or more storeys, usually with a double-hipped roof. Its windows, often surrounded by balconies with balustraded seats inset between them, open fully on all four sides.

Giardino segreto Literally, 'secret garden', a feature found in most Italian gardens, at its simplest a small enclosed garden-room but also an impressive composition in its own right. See Villa Farnese, page 27.

Giochi d'acqua Literally 'water games', a term applied to devices by which the onlooker can be showered with water, and to water-powered automata. See Villa Mondragone, page 31.

Gloriet In Spanish the word *glorieta*, the literal translation of the Arabic *al-'aziz* (glorious) came, to mean any summer-house, bower or arbour, the open space at the centre of a garden where such a pavilion might be placed; and hence a circus where walks or avenues meet.

The dry landscape (kare-sansui) of Zen Buddhist gardens has been developed as a feature in many Japanese gardens.

Gloriette A feature constructed on the crown of a hill to form a focal point to the landscape. See Schönbrunn, page 94.

Goose-foot See *Patte d'oie*.

Grille A railing, fence or gate of vertical iron rods, often elaborately wrought. A *grille d'eau* is a series of vertical jets resembling a *grille*.

Grotto A natural covered opening in the earth or an artificial recess imitating a natural grotto or in the form of an architectural nymphaeum.

Grove A group of trees, usually of a single species, either growing naturally or planted in formation. It is probably the oldest of all garden features.

Ha-ha A dry ditch with a raised retaining wall, used to conceal the boundaries of an estate or landscape.

Hameau A hamlet; in gardens a mock group of rustic buildings designed to allow the aristocracy to experience the every-day life of ordinary people.

park or garden designed on ecological principles including natural habitats and their plant communities. See Amstelveen, page 165.

Herbaceous border A border planted with herbaceous perennials, usually set against a wall.

Herbarium In medieval Latin the normal word for a small garden, such as a physic garden of medicinal herbs or an ornamental flower garden, and for a lawn, normally the main feature of such small gardens. Later the word changed its meaning to an arbour and was confused with the Latin *arbor*, a tree. In English the word appears as herber. The modern meaning of herbarium is a room or building which contains a classified collection of preserved plants.

Herm A representation of a head of Hermes rising from a pedestal, used in classical times to mark boundaries. In gardens the word is used to signify any head on a pedestal base, which is either rectangular or tapers towards the lower end.

Hortus conclusus Literally an enclosed garden, a secret garden within a garden.

Hortus medicus See Physic garden.

Huang shi Literally yellow rock, a kind of limestone rock commonly used in making artificial hills in Chinese gardens.

Ice-house A structure for storing ice, often built into the side of a hill and typically with a shaft or well made of brick or stone.

Imp-garden, imp-garth, imp-yard Old equivalents for the term nursery garden.

Italian garden In the 19th century a garden in an Italian style, of which the French and Dutch styles were considered mere variants. In the second half of the century any garden with a formal arrangement of flowerbeds, with or without an architectural terrace, might be described as Italian.

Japanese garden A garden in the West the design of which is inspired by or imitates the style of traditional gardens in Japan.

Jardin anglais, jardin à l'anglaise A French expression used to signify the opposite of the formal style as developed by Le Nôtre.

Jardin anglo-chinois A term used in France to describe informal gardens in the English manner, assumed to have been inspired by Chinese models. See Désert de Retz, page 59.

Jie jing Literally 'borrowing views'; in China buildings, trees or natural scenes outside either a garden or courtyard within a garden adopted into the composition to become part of the view.

Kare-sansui Dry landscape, the name given to Buddhist gardens of contemplation composed of raked sand or quartz and rocks. See Ryoan-ji, page 154 and page 185.

Kiosk See Ottoman kiosk.

Klein garten Literally 'small garden', in Ger-

many a piece of land leased from the State and used as a garden by a family which does not have a garden attached to its home.

Knot garden Originally part of a garden planted in the form of a knot, a figure of continuous interlacing bands. Later it became a general term for the quarters of a square flower garden intersected by walks at right angles, and today it is loosely used to mean a flowerbed of intricate design or laid-out flowerbed.

Labyrinth See Maze, labyrinth.

Laiterie A dairy; in gardens a fanciful building used mainly for amusement.

Lang In Chinese gardens a covered but open-sided walkway. See He Yuan, page 148, and illustration at top right on page 133.

Luan shi pu di In Chinese gardens flooring for courtyards and pathways patterned with designs made of pebbles, broken porcelain pieces, bricks and tiles set on edge. See illustration at bottom left on page 133.

Maze, labyrinth In garden design a confusing arrangement of paths formed, for example, by a pattern of turf on gravel or by hedged walkways.

Mei ren kao In Chinese gardens a balustrade combined with a seat.

Mirador A belvedere on a Spanish house giving views of the surroundings.

Moon door See Di xue.

Mosaïculture A composite form of carpet and flower bedding.

Mount A garden feature, probably functional in origin, forming walled terraces creating micro-climates according to the direction faced. The term is also used for the raised walk at the end of a garden that was a standard feature in Tudor times.

Nappe A sheet of smooth water, either falling in a cascade or spreading in an ornamental basin.

Niche A recess generally in a wall or façade and often containing sculpture or fountains. The term is applied to domestic arbours with seats as well as to examples of monumental architecture.

Nymphaeum A shrine or grotto dedicated to the nymphs and composed of fountains either imitating or alluding to the form of a natural grotto.

Obelisk A pillar, generally of stone, with a square or rectangular cross section, the sides tapering towards the top, which terminates in a pyramid shape.

Orangery In northern Europe a heated structure for conserving orange trees and other tender plants through the winter. In Germany it also served as a venue for concerts and theatrical entertainments.

Ottoman kiosk In Turkish gardens an enclosed, partially enclosed or open-sided pavilion gener-

ally standing close to water and often containing an inner fountain or pool.

Palissade A row of trees or shrubs forming a hedge clipped into a green wall (generally reaching to the ground), for bordering *allées*, concealing walls or facing terraces.

Palm house A type of glasshouse popular in the 19th century that was designed to accommodate palms.

Paradeisos In ancient Persia a great park-like estate with large enclosures filled with wild animals.

Parterre A flower garden, particularly in the area adjoining a house, laid out in a regular ornamental way, which developed recognized types and styles.
Parterres de broderies (embroidered parterres) have flowing plant-like designs made of box against a background of coloured earth, sometimes with bands of turf. See Vaux-le-Vicomte, pages 52–3.
Parterres à l'anglaise (in the English manner) have designs of cut turf and are either of plain grass often with a statue in the centre, known in England as plats, or they have cut-out designs known as *gazon coupé*. See Cliveden, page 80.
Parterres de pièces coupés (cutwork parterres) have flowerbeds as the individual pieces of the design.

Patte d'oie In woods, forests, parks or towns the place where three or more straight allées or streets meet at rather acute angles, which suggests the shape of the foot of a goose. See Fredensborg Castle, page 101.

Peng jing (Chinese bonsai) In Chinese gardening miniaturized plants cultivated either on their own or arranged in shallow containers with stones, water and, sometimes, miniature buildings and figures as landscape (*shansui*) *peng jing*. Some are compositions of stones alone. See bottom right illustration on page 133.

Percée A cutting through a wood in order to establish an *allée*, create a vista or open a view.

Pergola A structure of upright and cross members to support climbing plants.

Physic garden A garden devoted to the cultivation of plants of real or supposed medicinal value.

Picturesque A term applied to landscapes made in the manner of pictures. See Mount Edgcumbe, page 77.

Pinetum An arboretum composed mainly of evergreen conifers.

Plat In England an area of level grass of regular outline that is generally plain but may have a central ornament.

Pleasance An enclosed medieval park used for hunting but improved for aesthetic and recreational purposes.

Pratum In classical Latin a meadow; later often

used in the special sense of grassland planted with trees and used for public walks and recreation. The medieval diminutives *pratella* and *pratellum* might merely denote a lawn in a pleasure-ground.

Préau A small field (now obsolete in this sense); the space or quadrangle encompassed by the four walks of a cloister, or any small square enclosed orchard or garden.

Quincunx Literally an arrangement by fives, applied to trees arranged one at each corner of a square, with one in the centre.

Qu qiao In Chinese gardens a type of flat stone zigzag bridge.

Rond-point A half-circle facing the main entrance of an estate; in parks or woods a large circular clearing where a number of *allées* meet and in towns a circular area upon which avenues converge.

Rotunda, rotundo A small building, circular in plan, usually in the form of a dome supported by a circle of columns. In English garden history the term tends to be applied to buildings that are classical in style with no structure within, although it is also used for some with a colonnade and a room inside and sometimes for round temples with a straight portico.

Salle de verdure A central space within a *bosquet*.

Saut de loup A deep ditch or trench dug at the further end of an *allée* to prevent trespassing without interfering with the view.

Secret garden See Giardino segreto.

Shakkei The Japanese word for 'borrowed landscape', used in describing gardens where external views form an intergral part of the design. See Shugaku-in Imperial Villa, page 161.

Shell-work The placing of shells in patterns to form either ceilings or a grotto effect. See Rosendael, page 41.

Shi feng Rocks placed in courtyards, along streams or at other places in Chinese gardens as centre pieces of interest or elements in a view. See Ji Chang Yuan, page 142.

Shi sun A stalactite (literally a 'bamboo-shoot rock'). In many Chinese gardens groups are set into the ground among other rocks and trees.

Spring The medieval English word commonly used for a plantation or nursery of young trees, or for a coppice.

Stroll garden A type of Japanese garden in which, as the visitor strolls round, different aspects of the garden are gradually revealed. See Katsura Detached Villa, page 160.

Subtropical bedding The use of plants with large, variegated, brightly-coloured or otherwise ornamental leaves, planted in informal groups in which the picturesque effect of the individual plants was more important than the pattern of the bed.

Tai In Chinese garden design an observation platform or terrace, often on a hill or by a pond, especially used for admiring the garden by moonlight.

Taihu rock Rock from Lake Tai (Taihu) near Suzhou, Jiangsu province, highly prized for making artificial 'mountains' in Chinese gardens.

Tang See Ting.

Tapis vert Literally 'green cloth', a stretch of grass cut in a regular (usually rectangular) shape and a prominent feature of French 17th-century gardens.

Tempietto Literally a small temple and as garden architecture usually derived from the Tempietto next to the church of S. Pietro in Montorio, Rome, designed by Bramante.

Temple A garden building inspired by classical models, especially the Temple of Vesta, near Rome, much used in English landscape gardens of the 18th century and in gardens influenced by the English style.

Term A statue or bust like those of the god Terminus, representing the upper part of the body.

Ting A hall, often the main and also the loftiest structure in a Chinese garden. It is distinguished from a *tang*, also a hall, by its timbers, which are circular in cross-section instead of square.

Ting In Chinese gardens a pavilion for respose and viewing consisting of a a roof supported by free-standing pillars without windows or walls.

Tomb garden A distinctive type of Mogul garden, uniting the idea of the Persian paradise garden and the Tartar tradition of garden tombs. See Taj Mahal, page 126.

Tonnelle A tunnel-shaped trellis or a series of arches over which climbing plants are trained; a bower or arbour so made.

Topia Literally the elements typical of a place. In classical antiquity paintings on the walls of porticoes representing the sea, rivers, springs, rustic retreats, mountains, shepherds and flocks. The practice of painting *topia* was revived in the Renaissance.

Topiaria opera A term used by the ancient Roman encyclopaedist Pliny the elder to indicate kinds of landscape or ornamental garden, and in the singular form (*opus topiarium*) to describe the whole art of ornamental gardening.

Topiarius The Roman term for a landscape or ornamental gardener.

Topiary The art of shaping trees and shrubs by clipping and training. See Levens Hall, page 78.

Treillage Trellis work for supporting climbing plants.

Trompe-l'oeil A deceptive device, usually a painting on a wall at the further end of a short *allée*, that prolongs its perspective and makes it look much longer than it actually is.

Turfed seat A raised seat or bench covered in turf, a feature of many enclosed medieval gardens. See illustration on page 18.

Turkish tent An exotic pavilion, ostensibly decorated in the manner of a Turkish tent, brought into the landscape garden in the second half of the 18th century. See Drottningholm, page 99.

Vertugadin Literally a semicircular pad worn by women round the hips to puff out the skirt; in gardens a curved grass bank, or amphitheatre narrowing at both ends.

Viretum In classical Latin turf, greensward; during the Middle Ages (often spelt *virectum*) the word acquired the meaning of a pleasure-ground for recreation, confused with both *virgultum* and *viridarium*.

Virgultum From the Latin *virgula*, a twig or sapling, and with the primary meaning of a copse or shrubbery. In the Middle Ages it meant a plantation of young trees, tree-nursery or coppice, although it was sometimes used as a synonym for *viretum* and *viridarium*.

Viridarium In classical Latin used for a plantation of trees and for a pleasure-garden. In the Middle Ages it became the usual term for the larger garden or planted grounds. Since pleasure-grounds were commonly planted with fruit-trees, although for beauty rather than crops, *viridarium* was often Englished as orchard.

Vista A closely framed view such as an avenue, a sequence of openings or a forest glade.

Wilderness, wildness In late 17th- and 18th-century European gardens a wooded feature, in effect a version of the *bosquet*, with paths, usually winding, running through it. See Ham House, page 64.

Wild garden A garden that is managed in such a way as to encourage the growth of wild plants in a natural manner.

Xie In Chinese gardens a type of spacious garden pavilion that has open sides, with pivoting windows and doors, characteristically built beside lakes or streams to afford the enjoyment of water.

Xuan In Chinese gardens a small building or covered corridor with low walls between its supporting pillars, used for leisure and sited to make use of the better views of a pond or hill.

Yun qiang A wall, usually plastered and white- or occasionally colour-washed, which surrounds a Chinese garden or separates its interior spaces. Its undulating top suggests floating clouds, hence its name (literally 'cloud wall'). It may also look like a flying dragon and is also called a dragon wall.

Zenana Part of a house or garden in Mogul India reserved for women (particularly those of high caste) and in which they were secluded.

Index

ACKNOWLEDGEMENTS

The publishers wish to thank the following agencies and individuals for supplying illustrations for use in this project:

AGE Fotostock 102, 118top, 169; Heather Angel 72t, 74t&b, 109, 131, 133tl&br, 144t, 145, 147, 154, 156t, 159, 166t; Arcaid/Richard Bryant 164; Artothek/Frankfurt Stadelsch Kunstinst 17; Ashmolean Museum 62; John Bethell 65b, 67, 69, 71, 73, 87, 95, 125, 126, 170b; Bridgeman Art Library/Art Museum of Ateneum, Helsinki 49/Château de Versailles 56, Lauros Giraudon 43; British Library 150; Chatsworth/Devonshire Collections 70; Country Life Publications 175t; Bernard Cox 95, 125, 126; Eric Crichton 82; Documentation Photographique de le Réunion des Musées Nationaux/Musées Versailles 54; ET Archive 26, 65t/Biblioteque Nationale 129, 177t; Explorer/Louis Salou 47, 171b&tr; French Picture Library 53; Garden Art Press, *The Landscape of Civilization* by Geoffrey Jellicoe 183; Garden Picture Library/Clive Boursnell 172t, 175bl/Brian Carter 172br/Henk Dijkman 39, 40, 86, 41t/Derek Fell 107b, 108, 110t, 168br, 176br, 179/Marijke Heuff 185/Alan Mitchell 172br/John Neubauer 110b, 170t/Pacific Press, Takeyi Twamiya 149, 151, 153t, 155, 156bl, 157, 158, 160, 161/Alex Ramsay title page, 25, 32, 33t/Gary Rogers 122, 167br/Lorna Rose 166b, 168t/Wolfram Stehling 90t/Ron Sutherland 173/Nigel Temple 72b/Ulrich Tim 89/George Waters 111b, 163, 181, 182; Dennis Gilbert 178b; Giraudon/Chantilly Musée Condé 15/Château de Versailles 55; Sonia Halliday 136; Lawrence Halprin 180b; Robert Harding 91b, 92, 94, 98, 103, 127, 146t, 156br; Jerry Harpur 105, 106, 111t; Haupt Collection/Universität Bibliothek Hanover 84; Peter Hayden 27b, 41b, 42, 96, 97, 99t&b, 100, 116b, 133tr, 142, 144b, 146b; India Office & Records Library 123, 124; David Joyce 152b; A F Kersting 176t, 177b; Maggie Keswick 138; Kunsthistorisches Museum, Vienna 83; Lamontagne 28b, 36t, 104t&b, 107t, 118b, 133bl, 134, 143; Maurice Lee 168bl; Leiden University Library 37; S&O Mathews 167t; John Medhurst 50b, 116t, 117; Tony Mott 22, 23t&b, 27t, 29t, 31, 33b, 34t&b, 45b, 59b, 93; National Gallery 38; National Trust half title page, 66, 76, 80; Oakland Museum/Joe Samberg 178t; Octopus Picture Library Museum 113; Österreichische Nationalbibliothek 18; Oxford University Press/Biblioteque Nationale 48, 50t/60b; Private Collection 44, 57, 59t, 63, 75, 90b, 91t; Hugh Palmer 19; Scala/Roma Museo delle Terme 7/Museo di Firenze Com'era 21, 24/30/Museo Reale Belle Arti 35; Piet Schreuders 165; Ronald Sheridan 10; Sotheby's 61/Drummond Castle 81; Spectrum 101; Ezra Stoller/Esto 180t; Sydney Moss Gallery 130; Wim Swaam/Victoria & Albert Museum 114; Nigel Temple 45t, 52, 68, 78; Christopher Thacker 29b, 36b, 58b, 60, 77, 79, 85, 152, 176bl; Judy Todd 121, 135, 139; Victoria & Albert Museum 20, 64, 120; Weidenfeld & Nicolson/R. Cesar 46, 51, 171t/V&A 58t/British Museum 141; Werner Forman Archive 13.